Beginning
Shakespeare

MANCHESTER
1824

Manchester University Press

Beginnings
Series editors: Peter Barry and Helen Carr

'**Beginnings**' is a series of books designed to give practical help to students beginning to tackle recent developments in English, Literary Studies and Cultural Studies. The books in the series

- demonstrate and encourage a questioning engagement with the new;
- give essential information about the context and history of each topic covered;
- show how to develop a practice which is up-to-date and informed by theory.

Each book focuses uncompromisingly upon the needs of its readers, who have the right to expect lucidity and clarity to be the distinctive feature of a book which includes the word 'beginning' in its title.

Each aims to lay a firm foundation of well understood initial principles as a basis for further study and is committed to explaining new aspects of the discipline without over-simplification, but in a manner appropriate to the needs of beginners.

Each book, finally, aims to be both an introduction and a contribution to the topic area it discusses.

Also in the series

Beginning theory (second edition)
Peter Barry

Beginning ethnic American literatures
Helena Grice, Candida Hepworth,
Maria Lauret and Martin Padget

Beginning postcolonialism
John McLeod

Beginning postmodernism
Tim Woods

Beginning
Shakespeare

Lisa Hopkins

Manchester University Press

Manchester and New York

distributed exclusively in the USA by Palgrave

Published by Manchester University Press
Oxford Road, Manchester M13 9NR, UK
and Room 400, 175 Fifth Avenue, New York, NY 10010, USA
www.manchesteruniversitypress.co.uk

Distributed exclusively in the USA by
Palgrave, 175 Fifth Avenue, New York,
NY 10010, USA

Distributed exclusively in Canada by
UBC Press, University of British Columbia, 2029 West Mall,
Vancouver, BC, Canada V6T 1Z2

British Library Cataloguing-in-Publication Data
A catalogue record for this book is available from the British Library

Library of Congress Cataloging-in-Publication Data applied for

ISBN 0 7190 6422 8 *hardback*
EAN   987 0 7190 6422 7
ISBN 0 7190 6423 6 *paperback*
EAN   978 0 7190 6423 4

First published 2005

14 13 12 11 09 08 07 06 05   10 9 8 7 6 5 4 3 2 1

Typeset in Ehrhardt
by Northern Phototypesetting Co Ltd, Bolton

Printed in Great Britain
by Bell & Bain Ltd, Glasgow

For Ian Baker
il miglior fabbro

Contents

Acknowledgements

This book grew out of a suggestion by Steve Earnshaw, and has been encouraged from the outset by Matthew Frost and Peter Barry, who also gave the first draft an immensely thorough and helpful first reading. Thanks too to James Cummings for mathematical help, to Jeremy Lopez for permission to quote from the *Shakespeare Bulletin* reviewer guidelines, and to the anonymous reader of the manuscript. Ian Baker, Matthew Steggle, Chris Hoplins, Mike Davis, Ben Spiller, Rhonda White and Rosie Butcher have all read substantial parts of the book, and in some cases the whole manuscript, and I am immensely indebted to their many helpful suggestions. All remaining error and infelicities are, of course, my own.

Introduction

> I dreamt last night that Shakespeare's Ghost
> Sat for a civil service post.
> The English paper for that year
> Had several questions on King Lear,
> Which Shakespeare answered very badly
> Because he hadn't read his Bradley.

In 1926, this poem from *Punch* registered an only half-joking response to the growing prominence and cultural authority of academic criticism of Shakespeare. Four years after the publication of T. S. Eliot's *The Waste Land* had made 'difficult' literature fashionable, the *Punch* satirist is here poking fun at the absurdity of the fact that Shakespeare's plays and poems were, then as now, being discussed and analysed in ways of which Shakespeare himself could have had no conception. (As we shall see in Chapter 1, 'Bradley' was the leading early character critic A. C. Bradley, whose book *Shakespearean Tragedy* was published in 1904.)

As I write this seventy-six years after the *Punch* satirist's lament, the number of possible critical approaches to Shakespeare has proliferated even more bewilderingly. Moreover, one of the biggest problems for students studying Shakespeare is that almost nobody ever does begin him. The name 'Shakespeare' comes loaded with cultural baggage and preconceptions. Allusions to his plays, particularly *Romeo and Juliet* and *Hamlet*, are staples of even the most popular cultural forms (my son knew about *Hamlet* when he was four, because it was mentioned on the children's TV programme *Scooby Doo*), and almost all English Studies undergraduates will have had previous, and quite possibly unhappy, experience of studying him. Even where they are not deterred by this, they commonly express the fear that 'everything has already been said' and that therefore it is quite impossible that their own approaches could ever be original. In this book, I aim to break down such fears and preconceptions and to offer you both a map of the range of current critical practices and a sense of the possibilities for your own, since I will be including inter-active exercises at the end of sections: these are intended to stimulate you to think through the issues for yourself and to see what princi-ples and protocols you think appropriate for your own critical prac-tice. I will be following these with comments of my own (except at the ends of chapters where I will simply be raising broader issues for you to continue to think about as you work through the book), but it is important to stress that what I say is not 'the right answer', but merely one possible response; indeed it is one of the main points of this book that there *is* no right or single answer where Shakespeare is concerned. I hope to show that the nature of literary theory is such that it always allows for new inflections and permutations in ways which do indeed allow you to continue to say new things even about an author as much discussed as Shakespeare. Equally, any theoretical perspective, while it may illuminate one particular aspect of the text, almost automatically entails a blind spot to another aspect. In this sense, any approach can be seen to have both strengths and weak-nesses; it is up to you to decide what you consider really important and what you think it is legitimate to overlook or leave to one side.

The first chapter, 'Critical histories', begins with an overview of the history of Shakespeare criticism up until the watershed year of 1985, when the publication of *Political Shakespeare*, a ground-breaking collection of essays, changed the face of all subsequent Shakespeare criticism. In this and in all the chapters, I seek not only to explain what previous ideas have been but also to make you aware of their accompanying cultural and ideological baggage, in order to encourage a grasp of the wider implications of theoretical stances. Theories do not come from nowhere, but arise from particular historical circumstances and from particular ways of viewing the world, and it is important to have a grasp of what these are.

The second chapter, 'Psychoanalysis', goes back in time again to trace the impact which psychoanalytic theories have had on Shakespeare criticism since their inception at the beginning of the twentieth century. It begins by returning briefly to Bradleyan character-based approaches to Shakespeare and then considers how these were later developed and nuanced in the light of Freudian and other theories. It looks at the theories of Freud himself, of Jung, and of Lacan, and then considers whether the most recent psychoanalytic criticism of Shakespeare has in fact succeeded in countering the traditional reproach levelled against psychoanalysis, which is that it is blind both to history and to non-traditional sexualities and gender identities, since it has historically assumed that everyone is (or at any rate should be) heterosexual, and has also generally postulated that men's and women's mental make-up is fundamentally different.

The third and fourth chapters look at two approaches which are often treated together, firstly New Historicism and secondly Cultural Materialism. I argue that it is in fact important to distinguish between them. Inevitably, much of the discussion of New Historicism focuses on the work of its founding father Stephen Greenblatt, but I also examine three essays by Louis Montrose and work by Leonard Tennenhouse and Karen Newman, whose analysis of *The Taming of the Shrew* may go some way towards countering the accusation often made not only that New Historicism is politically defeatist in the way that it suggests that power will always triumph over the forces which are attempting to bring about change, but also that it ignores gender issues. Equally inevitably, the discussion of Cultural Materialism emphasises the importance of *Political Shakespeare* in changing the landscape of Shakespeare studies, but also looks at the influential work of Terence Hawkes in his *Meaning by Shakespeare*.

The fifth chapter, 'New factualisms', focuses on three separate but interrelated areas. Firstly, it looks at the current flurry of concentration on unearthing new features of Shakespeare's own biography, particularly in connection with his possible Catholicism. Secondly, it briefly surveys the proposed expansion or redefinition of the Shakespearean canon by means of computer testing, particularly in the wake of the furore over Donald Foster's ascription of 'A Funeral Elegy for Master William Peter' to Shakespeare, and Foster's subsequent recantation. Finally, I turn to the areas of editing and textual studies. These actually represent some of the oldest forms of Shakespeare scholarship, but, whereas they used to be thought of as rather sterile and antiquated, there has recently been a strong renewal of interest in them. In this chapter, I consider why textual scholarship and the theory and practice of editing are currently at the heart of some of the most vigorous debate in Shakespeare studies.

The sixth chapter, 'Gender studies and queer theory', examines the use of gender and sexuality as key subjects of analytical enquiry. Such approaches have come an astonishingly long way since the relatively unsophisticated analyses of *The Woman's Part* in 1980, and are often very attractive to students, seeming to offer them a personal foothold on the text. But the work of the French historian Michel Foucault suggests that previous societies' understandings of sexuality and gender are precisely *not* rooted in our own experiences but require some historicisation of concepts of gender, and these in themselves are subject to change. In this chapter, I look at the work of a number of critics to illustrate something of the divergence of the readings that can be produced.

Chapter 7, 'Postcolonial criticism', focuses extensively on *The Tempest*, which has, for obvious reasons, traditionally been the most popular play for postcolonial critics, but also considers *Othello* as a way of opening up one of the key questions of postcolonial approaches to Shakespeare, which is the degree to which the texts themselves are or have been complicit in colonialism, and the extent to which colonialism can profitably be treated alongside postcolonialism. Finally, the last chapter, 'Shakespeare in performance', looks at the growth in performance studies and analysis, both of films and of live theatre performances.

Each chapter concludes with further details of the books and articles in which the work of the various critics it discusses can be found, so that you can follow them up on your own if you wish to, and with some pointers to related reading which will allow you to explore the particular approach further. I hope that the way in which each chapter analyses the strengths and weaknesses of the perspective on which it focuses will allow you a clear critical purchase on the respective approaches and enable you to make informed choices between them, and thus to see ways of continuing to make meanings out of Shakespeare which are both theoretically informed and new. Each chapter, by addressing what is primarily at stake in these various theoretical approaches and by mapping the territory, should allow you to negotiate it for yourself.

1
Critical histories

The watershed date in Shakespearean criticism in the twentieth century is generally agreed to be 1985, when Jonathan Dollimore and Alan Sinfield published their groundbreaking collection of essays *Political Shakespeare*. This book inaugurated Cultural Materialism, the approach which, it is probably fair to say, is still dominant in British university teaching early in the twenty-first century, and I shall be discussing it at greater length in Chapter 4. But what was there before?

1598–1741: a bumpy ride

We are now so steeped in the idea of Shakespeare as the greatest playwright who ever lived that it sometimes comes as a surprise to realise that people did not always think so. However, Shakespeare's critical reputation has undergone significant fluctuations. Initially, his talent was recognised, but not regarded as anything overwhelming. There was praise from the early literary commentator Francis Meres, who in his 1598 commonplace book *Palladis Tamia* (*The Treasury of Wit*) declared that 'As *Plautus* and *Seneca* are accounted the best for Comedy and Tragedy among the Latines: so *Shakespeare* among ye English is the most excellent in both kinds for the stage' (certain words are in italics because they are proper names, and to put them in italics was the practice of the time) and referred too to 'his *Venus and Adonis*, his *Lucrece*, his sugred Sonnets among his private friends'. However, Shakespeare's fellow playwright Greene called him 'an upstart Crow, beautified with our feathers, that with his *Tygers hart wrapt in a Players hyde* [a parody of a line in *Henry VI, Part Three*], supposes he is as well able to bombast out a blank verse as the best of you: and beeing an absolute *Johannes fac totum* ['John do-it-all', or Jack-of all-trades], is in his owne conceit the onely Shake-scene in a countrey'. Greene, who was himself enormously proud of the fact that he held degrees from both Oxford and Cambridge and counted himself amongst the so-called 'University Wits', despised the less well educated Shakespeare, who had never been to university and whom Ben Jonson famously described as having 'small Latin and less Greek' (although that was of course in comparison to Jonson's own near-fluency in both languages; even after attending only a grammar school, Shakespeare will certainly have had considerable acquaintance with both classical languages). Greene was probably also motivated by envy, since his own career (and health – he died soon after) was failing just as Shakespeare's star was beginning to rise.

Even twenty years later when Shakespeare's star was defininitively in the ascendant, though, the Jacobean dramatist John Webster, in his preface to *The White Devil*, also ranked Shakespeare notably low in the ranks of the distinguished contemporaries whom he praised for various features of their style:

> For mine own part I have ever truly cherished my good opinion of other men's worthy labours, especially of that full and heightened style of Master Chapman; the laboured and understanding works of Master Jonson; the no less worthy composures of the both worthily excellent Master Beaumont, and Master Fletcher; and lastly (without wrong last to be named) the right happy and copious industry of Master Shakespeare, Master Dekker, and Master Heywood.

George Chapman was famous principally for heroic tragedies based on events in French history; Francis Beaumont and John Fletcher collaborated on plays distinguished primarily by frequent and surprising plot twists; and Ben Jonson's most prominent works were satirical comedies driven by a moralising impulse. These, it seems, are what Webster principally values, while Shakespeare is bundled together with Thomas Dekker and Thomas Heywood, both playwrights famous mainly for versatile and frequent collaboration, generally on plays designed to appeal more to the groundlings

(theatregoers who couldn't afford to pay for seats and were prover-
bially uninterested in subtlety) than to the learned. (Heywood himself boasted that he had been at least partly responsible for no fewer
than 220 plays, very few of which now survive: 'copious' indeed!)
Finally, Ben Jonson himself, arguably Shakespeare's greatest contemporary, deplored Shakespeare's departures from the classical
unities of time, place and action, codified in the ancient Greek
philosopher Aristotle's *Poetics*, which stipulate that a play should
have only one setting and one plot, and that all the events should
take place within twenty-four hours – all conditions which Shakespeare's romances, in particular, spectacularly violate, so it is no
surprise that Jonson called one of them, *Pericles*, a 'mouldy tale'
(Jonson, 'Ode to Himself').

Jonson, though, did write a poem entitled 'To the memory of my
beloved, the author Mr. William Shakespeare' for the publication in
1623 of the First Folio of Shakespeare's works, which was the first
collected edition of Shakespeare's works, and the first time that
many of them had appeared in print at all. Indeed the very fact that
there *was* a First Folio testifies to the fact that both Shakespeare and
his works must have been held in esteem by his colleagues, since it
was two of his fellow actors who compiled it. As far as we can tell,
plays – unlike poetry – seem to have been thought of as things of the
moment, rather than lasting literature; certainly we know from the
additions which continued to be made to Marlowe's *Doctor Faustus*
after his death that even this, which most critics would now consider
one of the greatest plays of the age, was not thought to be in any way
sacrosanct. It is true that Jonson had taken the trouble to publish his
own plays in a handsome Folio volume, but it is also true that he had
been much mocked for doing so. That Shakespeare's colleagues
John Heminges and Henry Condell, fellow members of the King's
Men (the acting company for which Shakeseare wrote), should
think it worthwhile to assemble all the works of Shakespeare which
they could find, as late as seven years after his death, implies that
they had a very high opinion of the plays' continued appeal. Moreover, Shakespeare retained sufficient popularity for there to be a
Second Folio in 1632, a Third in 1663–64, and a Fourth in 1685.

It is clear that Heminges and Condell were not alone in their high
opinion of the plays' continued appeal, for Shakespeare's influence

continued to be felt in plays written for a considerable time after his death. John Ford's *'Tis Pity She's a Whore*, published in 1633 (though we do not know when it was first acted), depends for much of its effect on the fact that it is a deliberate and shocking rewriting of *Romeo and Juliet* (the lovers in Ford's play are brother and sister). Two of Ford's later plays, *Love's Sacrifice* and *The Lady's Trial*, are equally obviously influenced by *Othello*, and his chronicle history *Perkin Warbeck*, written in 1633, delicately revisits the long-abandoned genre of the Shakespearean history play. Even after the start of the Civil War between Royalist and Parliamentarian forces from 1642 to 1649, when the theatres had been closed and acting was forbidden, two Royalist sisters in a besieged house in Nottinghamshire, Lady Jane Cavendish and Lady Elizabeth Brackley, wrote a play called *The Concealed Fancies* in which one of the female characters, captured and brought in front of the Parliamentarians, keeps up her spirits by pretending to be Cleopatra, and declares 'I would have performed his gallant tragedy and so have made myself glorious for time to come' (III.iv.18). That 'he' is Shakespeare, and that it is specifically Shakespeare's Cleopatra whom she has in mind, is made clear by the many other Shakespearean echoes in the play; later, the Cavendish sisters' stepmother, Margaret Cavendish, Duchess of Newcastle, was to ask of Shakespeare 'who could Describe *Cleopatra* Better than he hath done, and many other Females of his own Creating?' (Margaret Cavendish, *CCXI Sociable Letters*).

For John Ford and for the Cavendish sisters, Shakespeare clearly functioned as an important reference point. He was obviously already possessed of what the French theorist Pierre Bourdieu has termed 'cultural capital' – making allusion to him and quoting from his works was like a badge which one could use to boost one's own literary status. It is also clear that both Ford and the Cavendish sisters are using him not only to align themselves generally with a literary tradition but also to make specific points or suggestions. In the case of *'Tis Pity She's a Whore*, Ford is able to accentuate the shock and novelty of his own play by the contrast with something older. The contrast would work even better if, despite what some modern critics have suggested about the behaviour of Romeo and Juliet contravening what was considered proper at the time, the audience were to think of Shakespeare's lovers as behaving naturally and understandably, whereas Ford's behave in a way generally considered abnormal and indeed abhorrent. Similarly, for the Cavendish sisters, Shakespeare is clearly associated with the Royalist cause rather than with its Parliamentarian opponents. Thus, though neither Ford nor the Cavendish sisters would recognise the term, they are all, in their own ways, not just alluding to Shakespeare but also in fact theorising the plays to which they refer, and doing so in ways which are clearly related to their own positions and concerns – something which, as I shall be reiterating throughout this book, is always important in theoretical responses, which do not arise from a vacuum but from particular situations and pressures.

It may well seem ironic that, although the Cavendish sisters seem to think of Shakespeare as almost an icon of the Royalist cause, he actually fell from favour after the Restoration of King Charles II in 1660. In part this was because society's taste in plays changed in general around that time; it is a critical truism that there were far fewer tragedies written during the Restoration than there were before the closing of the theatres, and that these did not find as much favour with the audiences as comedies did. (Indeed, Thomas Otway, author of perhaps the period's most famous tragedy, *Venice Preserv'd*, fell on such hard times that he was reduced to begging in the street, and choked to death on a penny roll given him by a passer-by.) Histories had also fallen out of favour, perhaps because the memories of recent history, in the shape of the Civil War, were so painful.

Of course it is true that Shakespeare wrote comedies too, but these were not to the taste of the age either. Perhaps there is some truth in the old idea that tragedy is a form which can be afforded only by stable, self-confident societies, and it is also important to remember that the Civil War had broken the entire continuity of the theatrical tradition, so that the only actors still surviving from before the closure of the theatres would have been young boys at the time when they last acted, and thus used to playing women's or minor parts rather than tragic heroes, something which seems to be reflected in the shorter speeches and more equal distribution of parts found in Restoration plays. Shakespearean tragedy, with its concentration on the heroic individual, did not fit this model, and Shakespearen comedy was also not well suited to the very different performance practices of the Restoration stage. As we shall see in Chapter 6, much of the power and humour of Shakespearean comedy comes from the way in which it plays with gender and explores the possibilities of having boy actors playing girls who disguise themselves as boys; but the Restoration stage used real actresses, and much of the tension and effect was lost. The diarist Samuel Pepys often reports finding Shakespearean comedies silly, calling *A Midsummer Night's Dream* 'the most insipid ridiculous play that ever I saw in my life', and though William Wycherley's comedy *The Country Wife*, with its heroine disguised as a boy and its fake parson, obviously recalls *As You Like It*, it equally obviously recasts it into an entirely different mode and mood, as though the Shakespearean model will no longer work unless radically revised. Indeed where Shakespeare's plays did survive on the stage, they frequently found themselves subject to drastic rewriting, often in ways which reflected the period's sense of itself as more urbane and sophisticated than pre war England had been. Thus *Antony and Cleopatra* was reworked by John Dryden as the much more sentimental *All for Love*, and *King Lear* was given a happy ending (in which Cordelia not only survives but marries Edgar) by Nahum Tate, and not much later *Othello* was openly laughed at by Thomas Rymer and condemned as 'a caution to all Maidens of Quality how, without their Parents consent, they run away with *Blackamoors*' and 'a warning to all good Wives that they look well to their Linnen'.

STOP and THINK

• The Civil War pitted Royalists, who broadly speaking believed in traditional values and forms of authority, against a broad church of people, loosely classified as 'Parliamentarians', who challenged the power of the king and tended to believe that true religion was incompatible with wordliness and triviality. (Under the heading of 'triviality' they included theatres, as well as many folk customs such as maypoles; as the parodic history of Britain *1066 And All That* famously put it, the Parliamentarians were 'right but repulsive' and the Cavaliers were 'wrong but romantic'.) Do you think the Cavendish sisters were justified in seeing Shakespeare as more in tune with the sympathies and

values of the Royalists than with those of the Parliamentarians?
* Does their use of him tell us anything about Shakespeare, or only about them?

It is an interesting sidelight that all the traditions which have come down to us about Shakespeare's career as an *actor* agree that he was particularly good at playing kings, and Shakespeare has often been read as being on the side of kings, the aristocracy and the established order (see, for instance, the work of E. M. W. Tillyard, discussed later in this chapter). In one way, Shakespeare's sympathies would certainly have been with the Cavaliers rather than with the Roundheads: although he also wrote poetry, Shakespeare was above all a man of the theatre, and the Parliamentarians closed down the theatres. Nevertheless, I do not think that this means that Shakespeare would necessarily have disagreed with everything they stood for. Like a number of serious and conscientious thinkers at the time, he would probably have found his sympathies genuinely divided, recognising the need for reform but apprehensive about whether general chaos would follow. It is certainly the case that many of the most influential recent Shakespearean critics have offered radical readings of Shakespeare rather than conservative ones, and he was also much valued by the passionately Parliamentarian John Milton. However, if different people see such dramatically different Shakespeares, maybe it is because Shakespeare is genuinely open to so many interpretative possibilities that any individual interpretation tells us as much about the interpreter as it does about the thing interpreted. This would become even clearer as Shakespeare's reputation began to recover more generally in the century that followed.

1741–1904: enter Shakespear

Shakespeare did begin to find admirers again in the eighteenth century; as the poet Alexander Pope wrote about the erection of the monument to him in Westminster Abbey in 1741, for which Pope himself had been largely responsible, 'After an hundred and thirty years' nap, / Enter Shakespear, with a loud clap'. Shakespeare was still regarded as by no means infallible, though. Pope himself prepared an edition of Shakespeare's plays, but felt free to downplay or

even delete lines he particularly disliked. Others too were very ready
to pit their own judgement against Shakespeare's. The eighteenth-
century man of letters Dr Samuel Johnson famously took issue
with the ending of *King Lear* in a long comment (by 'the Spectator'
Johnson means the journal of that name):

> *Shakespeare* has suffered the virtue of *Cordelia* to perish in a just
> cause, contrary to the natural ideas of justice, to the hope of the reader,
> and, what is yet more strange, to the faith of chronicles. Yet this con-
> duct is justified by the Spectator, who blames *Tate* for giving *Cordelia*
> success and happiness in his alteration, and declares, that, in his opin-
> ion, *the tragedy has lost half its beauty* . . . A play in which the wicked
> prosper, and the virtuous miscarry, may doubtless be good, because it
> is a just representation of the common events of human life: but since
> all reasonable beings naturally love justice, I cannot easily be per-
> suaded, that the observation of justice makes a play worse; or, that if
> other excellencies are equal, the audience will not always rise better
> pleased from the final triumph of persecuted virtue.

There are several noteworthy assumptions here. Living as he did in
a world which the scientific discoveries of Sir Isaac Newton had presented as rational and ordered, Dr Johnson thinks that plays should
be true to life and indeed to facts – the culmination of his list of
strange things about Cordelia's death is that Shakespeare has
diverged from the 'historical' accounts he used as sources, though
Johnson has to concede that such things as Cordelia's death do
happen. Johnson also, though, believes that people (whom he imagines as very much all the same in their attributes and opinions) 'naturally love justice', and will therefore prefer a happy ending. For
later critics such as Jan Kott, Shakespeare's failure to supply this
was precisely what made *King Lear* great, since it acknowledged the
cruel realities of the world. Dr Johnson, though, belonged to an age
of optimism and reason, in which Pope could write 'Whatever is, is
right'. For Dr Johnson, therefore, though Shakespeare was a great
playwright, *King Lear* is a failure.

STOP and THINK

- From what you have gleaned of the views and assumptions of
  Pope and Dr Johnson, can you see anything in Shakespeare

which might particularly have appealed to them and to their age? Does he, for instance, extol the virtues of reason, or offer a generally comic and optimistic vision?

For both Pope and Dr Johnson, Nature was an extremely important concept – we have just seen Dr Johnson declaring that 'all reasonable beings naturally love justice'. They believed that literature should provide accurate representations of what was natural, and particularly of human nature – as Pope wrote in his *An Essay on Man*, 'The proper study of Mankind is Man'. In this respect, critics of the age agreed, Shakespeare excelled, producing, as Dr Johnson put it, 'just representations of general nature'. Shakespeare was seen as the writer who had rescued English literature from the excesses and 'barbarity' (a favourite term of the age) of earlier, more artificial plays such as *The Spanish Tragedy*, in which the characters are prone to making immensely long and highly patterned speeches even at times of great distress, and where there is more emphasis on rhetorical effects than on psychological plausibility. The degree to which Shakespeare could be seen as natural would become even more important as, in the years that followed, his status grew by leaps and bounds.

Enshrinement

As the eighteenth century drew on, interest in Shakespeare grew dramatically. It was then that scholarly work on Shakespeare really began, ranging from the editions and commentaries on editing produced by Pope, Johnson, Nicholas Rowe and Lewis Theobald to the work of the indefatigable Edmond Malone, who did much to clarify Shakespeare's biography and the chronology of his works as well as producing an edition of them. Appreciation of his plays was also much more evident. Falstaff in particular took on a life of his own, most notably in Maurice Morgann's *On the Dramatic Character of Sir John Falstaff* (1777). The culmination of the growing wave of 'bardolatry' (though the term itself was not coined until 1901, by George Bernard Shaw) was David Garrick's 1769 'Jubilee', a kind of grand fair at Stratford with a Shakespeare theme (although it was in the end almost entirely spoilt by rain). As in the earlier views of Pope and Johnson, Shakespeare was seen above all as an epitome of naturalness, which was a key value of Romantic poetry, as when the Romantic poet John Keats remarked on 'How much more Shakespeare delights in dwelling upon the romantic and wildly natural than upon the monumental'. For Keats, this applied not only to Shakespeare the poet but also to Shakespeare the man, for he praised two things above all: firstly Shakespeare's intensity, and secondly 'the "Negative Capability" of his character, which Keats glossed as the state "when a man is capable of being in uncertainties, mysteries, doubts, without any irritable reaching after fact and reason"'. It is also implicit in Keats's approach to Shakespeare that he assumes that he himself, implicitly because of his own positioning as a Romantic poet, is better placed to appreciate Shakespeare than others have been: his own heavily annotated copy reveals numerous instances of his 'humorous impatience and scorn of Dr. Johnson's measured and matter of fact criticism of the plays'. Keats's rebukes often take the form of a quotation from Shakespeare, including one which begins 'Such tricks hath *weak* imagination' (Keats's emphasis, and intended as a comment on Johnson) (Caroline Spurgeon, *Keats's Shakespeare*, pp. 29–30).

Another Romantic poet, Samuel Taylor Coleridge, shared Keats's assumption that poets were best placed to appreciate Shakespeare, though for very different reasons. Coleridge objected to the idea that Shakespeare was somehow a wild untutored genius, a child solely of nature who, as Milton so famously put it, 'warbles his native wood-notes wild':

> It is my earnest desire – my passionate endeavour – to enforce at various times and by various arguments and instances the close and reciprocal connection of just taste with pure morality. Without that acquaintance with the heart of man, or that docility and childlike gladness to be made acquainted with it, which those only can have, who dare look at their own hearts – and that with a steadiness which religion only has the power of reconciling with sincere humility; without this, and the modesty produced by it, I am deeply convinced that no man, however wide his erudition, however patient his antiquarian researches, can possibly understand, or be worthy of understanding, the writings of Shakespeare. (*Lectures and Notes on Shakespeare and Other Dramatists*, p. 49)

Coleridge amplified the point further in the course of an attack on the French philosopher Voltaire, who, like Ben Jonson before him, had condemned Shakespeare for failing to abide by the 'rules' (most notably the classical unities):

> Make out your amplest catalogue of all the human faculties, as reason or the moral law, the will, the feeling of the coincidence of the two . . . called the conscience, the understanding, or prudence, wit, fancy, imagination, judgment, and then of the objects on which these are to be employed, as the beauties, the terrors, and the seeming caprices of nature, the capabilities, that is, the actual and the ideal, of the human mind, conceived as an individual or as a social being, as in innocence or in guilt, in a play-paradise or in a war-field of temptation; and then compare with Shakespeare under each of these heads all or any of the writers in prose and verse that have ever lived! Who, that is competent to judge, doubts the result? And ask your own hearts, ask your own commonsense to conceive the possibility of this man being – I say not, the drunken savage of that wretched sciolist [someone with a smattering of information in many fields but no real grasp of any], whom Frenchmen, to their shame, have honoured before their elder and better worthies – but that anomalous, the wild, the irregular, genius of our daily criticism! What! are we to have miracles in sport? – Or, I speak reverently, does God choose idiots by whom to convey divine truths to man? (pp. 54–5)

There are several things worthy of note here: Shakespeare exemplifies not only nature, but what is apparently higher still, *English* nature, which God himself has sanctified – and by the time of the final sentence there seems to be no discernible difference between Shakespeare and the Bible, since both are seen as infallible sources of God's truth.

STOP and THINK

- Do you think Shakespeare is a particularly 'English' writer? Does he, for instance, present characters who are English as better or more interesting than others? Do you believe there is such a thing as a typical Englishman, and if so is Shakespeare one? Do his plays inspire patriotic feeling? And what about his representations of Scotland, Ireland and Wales?

It is said by those who are competent to judge that Shakespeare translates badly into French, well into German, and superbly into

Russian. (It has also famously been claimed that you haven't really read Shakespeare at all if you haven't read him in the original Klingon!) Some of the ways in which Shakespeare has been associated with Englishness will be explored in Chapter 7, 'Postcolonial criticism', but he has also flourished overseas, proving particularly popular in Germany, and there are now Shakespeare Associations in many countries and continents, not least America. Shakespeare's adaptability in this respect seems to be another instance of that openness to interpretation which Keats implied by 'Negative Capability' and Coleridge by his term 'myriad-minded Shakespeare'. Certainly it was as a universal rather than simply a national dramatist that Shakespeare was understood by the man who was soon to emerge as his most systematic critic yet, A. C. Bradley.

A. C. Bradley and character study

Coleridge's view that Shakespeare was primarily a student of human nature, forcefully though it was expressed, was clearly the opinion of a poet, and was, moreover, uttered before the study of literature had attained the status of a university discipline, although Coleridge himself did deliver a course of lectures on Shakespeare, thus clearly acknowledging Shakespeare as a worthy object of systematic study of the type that we would now call literary criticism. The first critic of Shakespeare to have a really major and long-lasting impact, however, was Andrew Charles Bradley (1851–1935), always known as A. C. Bradley. Bradley's lectures on *Hamlet*, *Othello*, *King Lear* and *Macbeth*, which were eventually collected in book form as *Shakespearean Tragedy* in 1904, proved hugely influential. Bradley's approach was entirely character-based, and although this was by no means entirely novel, as Morgann's 1777 work on the character of Falstaff had shown, Bradley was exceptionally thoroughgoing. Treating the characters of the plays as though they were completely real people, he seized, often ingeniously and perceptively, on even the tiniest clues in the text to offer a wide-ranging account of their personalities. Here he is, for instance, on Gertrude in *Hamlet*:

> The Queen was not a bad-hearted woman, not at all the woman to think little of murder. But she had a soft animal nature, and was very dull and very shallow. She loved to be happy, like a sheep in the sun;

and, to do her justice, it pleased her to see others happy, like more
sheep in the sun. She never saw that drunkenness is disgusting till
Hamlet told her so; and, though she knew that he considered her marriage 'o'er-hasty' (II. ii. 57), she was untroubled by any shame at the
feelings which had led her to it. It was pleasant to sit upon her throne
and see smiling faces round her, and foolish and unkind in Hamlet to
persist in grieving for his father instead of marrying Ophelia and
making everything comfortable. She was fond of Ophelia and genuinely attached to her son (though willing to see her lover exclude him
from the throne); and, no doubt, she considered equality of rank a
mere trifle compared with the claims of love. The belief at the bottom
of her heart was that the world is a place constructed simply that
people may be happy in it in a good-humoured sensual fashion.
(Bradley, *Shakespearean Tragedy*, p. 135)

This sounds more like a novelist than a literary critic, and indeed
reminds me very much of the descriptions of Lady Bertram in Jane
Austen's *Mansfield Park*. Or maybe the more appropriate comparison is with Sherlock Holmes, piecing together the clues he can glean
from a visitor's appearance to astonish Watson with a complete
account of the stranger's character and recent history.

Like Holmes, too, Bradley is principally concerned with his own
'character-building' narrative; he pays little attention here to the
main events in Gertrude's life, for instance. Another critic might see
the things which happen to us as shaping and perhaps even determining forces in making us what we are, but as far as Bradley is concerned character is about nature, not nurture: Gertrude 'had a soft
animal nature, and it was very dull and very shallow'. Moreover, she
seems to belong to a recognisable *type*, because Bradley is prepared
to go beyond what the play actually tells us about her to guess at
what the other features of her character must be: 'no doubt, she considered equality of rank a mere trifle compared with the claims of
love'. Bradley's readiness to deduce this implies a view of human
character as not only formed by nature rather than by nurture or
culture but also as falling into fixed, predictable categories, which
have not changed since Shakespeare's day.

Ironically, for all Bradley's privileging of nature over culture,
there was a cultural reason which made it important to him to think
this. In a tribute to Bradley in *The Times*, the 1960s Shakespeare
scholar Peter Alexander wrote:

Even in Bradley's own day there were dissenting voices; but the very ambiguity in Bradley's position extended his appeal. He regarded the tragic characters as embodiments of the qualities that will always command the respect and admiration of man, yet at the same time he seemed to find a formula that justified the scheme of things and absolved the cosmos from the charges that Huxley and others were bringing against it. In addition to the careful, learned and sympathetic analysis he gave to every author he discussed, there was the additional attraction, for those generations that were disturbed by the implications of biblical and scientific criticism, of finding in Bradley what seemed, in [the poet Matthew] Arnold's words, a stay in an age of religious doubts and questionings.

The intellectual context to which Alexander draws attention here, especially the reference to the noted scientist Thomas Henry Huxley, does indeed seem to me to be crucial in understanding both Bradley and his impact, and that intellectual context is the theory of evolution. In 1859, Charles Darwin (whose disciple Huxley was) set Victorian England in an uproar with the publication of his *On the Origin of Species by Means of Natural Selection*, which implied, though it never quite dared say, that humans had not been divinely created but had evolved just as Darwin openly declared that other species had. In the backlash against Darwin's ideas Shakespeare, like Milton, proved a culturally potent weapon, and *Hamlet* in particular became a staple referent for writers contesting the idea of evolution, since it seemed to speak so powerfully of a fixed human nature which certainly had not changed in the three hundred years since Shakespeare wrote and was surely not going to do so in the future. Bradley's analysis of a character such as Gertrude as a recognisable 'type' can be seen as firmly in line with this idea that Shakespeare could serve as proof of a stable and unchanging human nature.

Bradley did not always see characters solely in terms of inherent nature and character type; there were other variables too. Another effect of the prominence of the evolution debate is that Bradley's criticism is subtly but significantly conditioned by the strongly developed ideas about fixed racial identities and inherent relationships between physical and mental characteristics to which Darwinian theory gave rise, so that for Bradley, although Othello is by no means a barbarian, he is what he is because 'He has watched with a poet's eye the Arabian trees drooping their med'cinable gum, and the Indian throwing away his chance-found pearl ... So he comes before us, dark and grand, with a light upon him from the sun where he was born' (p. 153). There is a suggestive and rather sinister-seeming contrast here with Bradley's account of Gertrude: she is a type of woman, and there are presumably various other types; but Othello is a black man, a product of the sun where he was born, and that seems to be that. Women may have natures, but black men, it seems, simply have race.

At the same time, though, Bradley's faith in science and the classificatory mechanisms it supplied did not preclude a nostalgia for the divine which drove him to focus not only on the characters of the tragedies but also on the 'mystery of tragedy' as a whole, which he saw as having a virtually sacramental effect. For Bradley, it was an essential part of the effect of Shakespearean tragedy that the fate of the protagonist had a far-reaching impact, and this was so primarily because the protagonist was socially important:

> The pangs of despised love and the anguish of remorse, we say, are the same in a peasant and a prince; but, not to insist that they cannot be so when the prince is really a prince, the story of the prince, the triumvir, or the general, has a greatness and dignity of its own. His fate affects the welfare of a whole nation or empire; and when he falls suddenly from the height of earthly greatness to the dust, his fall produces a sense of contrast, of the powerlessness of man, and of the omnipotence – perhaps the caprice – of Fortune or Fate, which no tale of private life can possibly rival. (p. 5)

Bradley might have been affected by Darwin, but he clearly shows here that he is utterly at odds with that other influential nineteenth-century thinker, Karl Marx. It is a central tenet of his approach that some people matter more than others. (Remember that one of the elements in his critical analysis of Gertrude was his view that 'no doubt, she considered equality of rank a mere trifle compared with the claims of love' – a view which, it is clearly implied, is extremely silly.) Bradley also offered a welcome reassurance to those troubled by the darker implication of Darwinism – that there was no God or any other supernatural force – in his insistence that 'Shakespeare also introduces the supernatural into some of his tragedies; he introduces ghosts, and witches who have supernatural knowledge. This supernatural element certainly cannot in most cases, if in any, be explained away as an illusion in the mind of one of the characters' (p. 8). We have, then, Shakespeare's authority for it that we are more than just a random conglomeration of atoms in a godless universe. Indeed implicit in Bradley's whole approach to Shakespeare is the assumption that Shakespeare's techniques of characterisation and plotting, especially in the creation of comparisons and contrasts, are in essential respects the same as those of the great nineteenth-century novelists – and in their cases there is always an implicit invitation to consider whether the patternings thus created imitate and/or imply the workings of a divine providence.

STOP and THINK

• Are Shakespeare's characters recognisably the same kind of people as we are today? Are they, for instance, motivated by the same kinds of fears, concerns, and emotions as we might be? A particularly interesting case might be Othello: do we understand why he becomes jealous? Or is concern about cuckoldry, so widespread in the early modern period, not so much of a live issue now?

I suppose we would not still be interested in Shakespeare at all if his characters all seemed unrecognisably strange and alien to us. After all, Harold Bloom has famously claimed in *Shakespeare and the Invention of the Human* (1998) that Shakespeare invented humanity as we understand it, and he would surely never have been able to make such an assertion if it were not at least partly true that we can recognise Shakespeare's characters as being like ourselves. But there are also ways in which they are *not* like us. At the end of *The Merchant of Venice*, a supposedly benevolent character demands that Shylock renounce his Jewish faith; Shakespeare may conceivably have thought it was doing someone a favour to convert them by force to Christianity, but I hope that is not a view widely shared now. More generally, there is scarcely a husband in a Shakespearean play who does not at some point express concern about the fidelity of his wife, and, as we shall see in Chapter 2, the sexual fidelity of a female partner is also a major concern of the speaker of Shakespeare's sonnets. This looks like evidence of a widespread paranoia which I do not think is nearly so common now. (The pervasive concern with cuckoldry in early modern England is generally read in terms of anxiety about inheritance customs and property laws, and the danger of a man leaving his wealth to a child who was not genetically his own.) And I will be suggesting in Chapter 6 that views about sexuality, and indeed sexuality itself, may also have been very differently imagined and experienced in the late sixteenth and early seventeenth centuries. In the years that more immediately followed Bradley, however, the whole idea of character as a primary analytic in Shakespearean criticism began to come under fire, as other ways of thinking about Shakespearean texts rose to prominence.

The 1930s: images and patterns

The next major phase of Shakespearean criticism certainly did not entirely disregard the Bradleyan notion of character, but it intoduced alongside it a new emphasis on the study of language and formal properties. Particularly important were Wilson Knight's *The Wheel of Fire* (first published in 1930) and Caroline Spurgeon's *Shakespeare's Imagery and What It Tells Us* (1935). Spurgeon's primary interest, as her title makes plain, was in Shakespeare's images. She had little interest in the formal features of drama, writing early in the book that 'I believe it to be profoundly true that the real revelation of the writer's personality, temperament and quality of mind is to be found in his works, whether he be dramatist or novelist, describing other people's thoughts or putting down his own directly' (p. 4). So far from the medium being the message, as Marshall McLuhan would later influentially propose, it is here relegated to being a matter of virtually no importance. And Spurgeon's disregard for form will soon become even more striking. We might have imagined that the phrase 'whether he be dramatist or novelist' was intended to imply that though Shakespeare *was* a dramatist, he might just as well have been a novelist. However, the whole idea of a dramatist soon proves to be in fact a complete irrelevance, because Shakespeare, it seems, is no more a dramatist than he is a novelist. In Spurgeon's eyes, he is a poet:

> In the case of a poet, I suggest it is chiefly through his images that he,
> to some extent unconsciously, 'gives himself away'. He may be, and in

> Shakespeare's case is, almost entirely objective in his dramatic char-
> acters and their views and opinions, yet, like the man who under stress
> of emotion will show no sign of it in eye or face, but will reveal it in
> some muscular tension, the poet unwittingly lays bare his own inner-
> most likes and dislikes, observations and interests, associations of
> thought, attitudes of mind and beliefs, in and through the images, the
> verbal pictures he draws to illuminate something quite different in the
> speech and thought of his characters. (p. 4)

Shakespeare, then, is a poet rather than a playwright – and poets
give their mind away in their language.

This takes us back to the fact that Spurgeon's title also signals
that her concern is not just with Shakespeare's imagery but with
what it tells us. Her detailed study of Shakespeare's metaphors and
similes was in fact just the handmaid to this principal concern, 'what
it tells us' – and this, she proposed, was actually, as the first half of
the book is so portentously named, 'The Revelation of the Man'.
Thus the first two hundred pages of *Shakespeare's Imagery and
What It Tells Us* culminate in the chapter which closes the first part
of the volume, and which is dramatically entitled 'Shakespeare the
Man'. There she proceeds to offer us nine pages of description of
Shakespeare's character, appearance and habits. Since the length of
this chapter makes it impossible to quote in full, I summarise her
chief findings below:

- He was 'a compactly well-built man, probably on the slight side,
  extraordinarily well-coordinated . . . probably fair-skinned and of
  a fresh colour . . . All his senses were abnormally acute'. (p. 202)
- 'He was healthy in body as in mind, clean and fastidious in his
  habits, very sensitive to dirt and evil smells'. (p. 203)
- He 'wouldn't be debauched'. (p. 203)
- He was 'an almost incredibly sensitive and amazingly observant
  man'. (p. 203)
- 'he is a countryman through and through'. (p. 204)
- He was a good rider, disliked house dogs and spaniels, was an
  expert archer, and was very fond of bowls. (p. 204)
- He was a good carpenter. (p. 205)
- The cornerstones of his character were 'sensitiveness, balance,
  courage, humour and wholesomeness'. (p. 206)

Shakespeare, in short, is a paragon. Indeed, if we hadn't already guessed it from the rather unexpected reference to his carpentry, Spurgeon finally spells out the person he most reminds her of: 'He is indeed himself in many ways in character what one can only describe as Christ-like; that is, gentle, kindly, honest, brave and true, with deep understanding and quick sympathy for all living things' (except, presumably, house dogs and spaniels) (p. 207). He also happens to fit exactly into the image of what was thought at the time that Spurgeon was writing to be typically English. Indeed the description of him as characterised primarily by 'sensitiveness, balance, courage, humour and wholesomeness' reminds me of nothing so much as Bilbo Baggins in J. R. R. Tolkien's *The Hobbit*, and this is by no means such a ludicrous comparison as it might seem, since both Spurgeon and Tolkien were writing in the early to mid 1930s, when events such as the Japanese invasion of Manchuria and the rise to power of Hitler and Mussolini meant that it was already beginning to be apparent that Britain might once again be drawn into global conflict, and the pressures of the international scene were causing ideas about national identity to come to the fore.

For Spurgeon, then, 'character' remains just as important as it was for Bradley, but there are two crucial differences. In the first place, she has lost faith in the Bradleyan way of accessing character through minute examination of speeches and behaviour, and thinks she has found a better key in examination of image patterns (an idea which may owe something to Freud's theories of the ways in which the unconscious manifests itself). In the second, it is Shakespeare's own character that she is interested in, rather than Hamlet's or Othello's or Lear's or Macbeth's, and the reason for this seems to be that she can find in Shakespeare so compelling a role model for English people and icon of Englishness.

Like Caroline Spurgeon, G. Wilson Knight wrote of Shakespeare primarily as 'a philosophic poet rather than a man of the stage', because, he declared, 'my experience as actor, producer and playgoer leaves me uncompromising in my assertion that the literary analysis of great drama in terms of theatrical technique accomplishes singularly little' (*The Wheel of Fire*, p. vi). In other ways, though, Wilson Knight adopted a different approach. Though he denied in the prefatory note to the second edition that he had ever

been 'concerned to repudiate the work of A. C. Bradley', his very
tribute to Bradley registered the difference between them: 'Though
Bradley certainly on occasion pushed "character" analysis to an
unnecessary extreme, yet he it was who first subjected the atmospheric, what I have called the "spatial", qualities of the Shakespear-
ian play to a considered, if rudimentary, comment' (p. v). For
Wilson Knight, then, what mattered were these 'spatial' qualities,
and in the second edition of *The Wheel of Fire* he resorted to a rather
surprising analogy to explain what he meant by that:

> A recent account by Mr. Lance L. Whyte of modern developments in
> physics, which appeared in *The Listener* of July 17th, 1947, can help us
> here. Mr. Whyte explains how the belief in rigid 'particles' with
> predictable motions has been replaced by concepts of 'form, pattern
> and symmetry'; and not by these as static categories only but rather
> by something which he calls the 'transformation of patterns'. For 'par-
> ticles' put 'characters' and we have a clear Shakespearean analogy.
> Even the dates, roughly, fit: 'From about 1870 to 1910' these 'particles'
> were thought to hold the key 'to all the secrets of nature'; but since then
> the conception has been found inadequate. Rigidly distinct and
> unchanging atoms have become 'patterns' occupying certainly a
> 'measurable region of space' but yet themselves, as patterns, dynamic,
> self-transforming. (p. vii)

In the most famous chapters in the book, 'The *Othello* music' and
'*King Lear* and the comedy of the grotesque', Wilson Knight
launches straight into the resulting approach.

In the case of *Othello*, he opens his analysis with the declaration
that 'In *Othello* we are faced with the vividly particular rather than
the vague and universal. The play as a whole has a distinct formal
beauty: within it we are ever confronted with beautiful and solid
forms', and he proposes in particular that 'in first analysing Othello's
poetry, we shall lay the basis for an understanding of the play's
symbolism' (p. 97). In the case of *King Lear*, he begins by proposing
the bold comparison that '*King Lear* is roughly analogous to Tchehov
[i.e. Chekhov] where *Macbeth* is analogous to Dostoievsky' (p. 160).
This decision to concentrate so entirely on form at the expense of any
sense of history or context is reverted to in the closing passage of
the chapter, where Wilson Knight is musing on Lear's grief over the
dead Cordelia, and Cordelia's pity of her mad father:

> What do we touch in these passages? Sometimes we know that all
> human pain holds beauty, that no tear falls but it dews some flower we
> cannot see. Perhaps humour, too, is inwoven in the universal pain, and
> the enigmatic silence holds not only an unutterable sympathy, but also
> the ripples of an impossible laughter whose flight is not for the wing
> of human understanding; and perhaps it is that that casts its darting
> shadow of the grotesque across the furrowed pages of *King Lear*.
> (p. 176)

Initially, Wilson Knight's insistence that even the most tragic events
of *King Lear* tremble on the brink of a grotesque comedy might have
seemed a potential threat to the dignity and *gravitas* of the play; but
in fact we need only to glimpse the extent of the pattern to see that
we are in fact part of a grand cosmos in which all ill and suffering is
counterbalanced by good. We are indeed right back in the Popean
territory of 'whatever is, is right'. If we could only see the whole of
the pattern, we would know that everything was all right; as it is,
Shakespeare has allowed us at least to guess at that.

STOP and THINK

- Is it true that the Shakespeare plays you know place emphasis
  on symmetry and patterning? Can you think of any examples?

King Lear is an obvious instance: the events of the sub-plot mirror
those of the main plot in such a way that we are left in no doubt
that we are invited to compare them. Lear's good and bad daughters are paralleled by Gloucester's good and bad sons; Lear's fig-
urative blindness is echoed in Gloucester's literal blindness, and so
on. It is by no means clear, though, that comparing them will produce a reading which supports the idea of a benevolent deity or a
divinely ordered world; rather, as we will see later in this chapter
in the discussion of Jan Kott, it all looks like the savagely ironic and
fruitless repetition of events characteristic of the Theatre of the
Absurd (most famously exemplified in Samuel Beckett's *Waiting
for Godot*, where, as the critic Vivian Mercer put it, 'Nothing happens, twice'). Another possible example of patterning comes in
Shakespeare's history plays, where we seem to be invited to see
an orderly progression from chaos to the peace and order of Tudor
rule: here, as we shall see, critics have disagreed over whether the

presence of a pattern implies divine providence or not. For one critic, however, there could be no doubt: as far as E. M. W. Tillyard was concerned, Shakespeare was above all the poet of order and pattern, and not only in an imagistic but in a political sense.

Tillyard and The 'Elizabethan world picture'

For the enormously influential E. M. W. Tillyard, pattern was again a crucial part of Shakespearean meaning, but pattern of a different sort: he saw a Shakespeare who showed us a world which worked well because it was hierarchically structured, and who, above all, presented English history as a triumphal march towards a divinely appointed destiny. In his now infamous *The Elizabethan World Picture* (1943), Tillyard declared that Shakespeare subscribed to a number of views which he took so much for granted that he rarely thought of articulating them. Prominent among these is the idea of 'the great chain of being', which Tillyard defined as

> the world-order hinted at by Shakespeare in Ulysses' speech when he calls 'degree' the 'ladder to all high designs' and named by Pope in the *Essay on Man*, 'the vast chain of being'. It is the subject of a long and important book by Arthur Lovejoy. This metaphor served to express the unimaginable plenitude of God's creation, its unfaltering order, and its ultimate unity. The chain stretched from the foot of God's throne to the meanest of inanimate objects. Every speck of creation was a link in the chain. (p. 23)

The speech to which Tillyard is referring occurs in *Troilus and Cressida*. In it, Ulysses declares that the reason the Greeks are failing to conquer Troy is that they have ignored 'degree', i.e. rank:

> Troy, yet upon his basis, had been down,
> And the great Hector's sword had lack'd a master,
> But for these instances:
> The specialty of rule hath been neglected;
> And look how many Grecian tents do stand
> Hollow upon this plain, so many hollow factions.
> When that the general is not like the hive,
> To whom the foragers shall all repair,
> What honey is expected? Degree being vizarded,

(vizarded: masked)

Th'unworthiest shows as fairly in the mask.
The heavens themselves, the planets, and this centre,
Observe degree, priority, and place,
Insisture, course, proportion, season, form,

(insisture: fixed position)

Office, and custom, in all line of order;
And therefore is the glorious planet Sol
In noble eminence enthron'd and spher'd
Amidst the other, whose med'cinable eye
Corrects the ill aspects of planets evil,
And posts, like the commandment of a king,
Sans check, to good and bad. But when the planets
In evil mixture to disorder wander,
What plagues and what portents, what mutiny,
What raging of the sea, shaking of earth,
Commotion in the winds! Frights, changes, horrors,
Divert and crack, rend and deracinate,
The unity and married calm of states
Quite from their fixture! O, when degree is shak'd,
Which is the ladder of all high designs,
The enterprise is sick! How could communities,
Degrees in schools, and brotherhoods in cities,
Peaceful commerce from dividable shores,
The primogenity and due of birth,
Prerogative of age, crowns, sceptres, laurels,
But by degree, stand in authentic place?
Take but degree away, untune that string,
And hark what discord follows! Each thing melts
In mere oppugnancy: the bounded waters

(oppugnancy: act of opposing)

Should lift their bosoms higher than the shores,
And make a sop of all this solid globe;
Strength should be lord of imbecility,
And the rude son should strike his father dead;
Force should be right; or, rather, right and wrong –
Between whose endless jar justice resides –
Should lose their names, and so should justice too.
Then everything includes itself in power,
Power into will, will into appetite;
And appetite, an universal wolf,
So doubly seconded with will and power,
Must make perforce an universal prey,

And last eat up himself. Great Agamemnon,
This chaos, when degree is suffocate,
Follows the choking.
And this neglection of degree it is
That by a pace goes backward, with a purpose
It hath to climb. The general's disdain'd
By him one step below, he by the next,
That next by him beneath; so ever step,
Exampl'd by the first pace that is sick
Of his superior, grows to an envious fever
Of pale and bloodless emulation.
And 'tis this fever that keeps Troy on foot,
Not her own sinews. To end a tale of length,
Troy in our weakness stands, not in her strength.

This speech has, unsurprisingly, been much quoted by those who want to make conservative meanings of Shakespeare. But Tillyard's is hardly the only possible reading of it. The speaker is Ulysses, a clever and cunning Greek who is aiming to manipulate the foolish general Agamemnon and the rest of the Greeks, who in this play are a pretty unimpressive lot. It is a fundamental part of Tillyard's method to disregard the speaker of any particular passage he chooses to cite, since his whole point is that *everyone* believes these things; but if you read *Troilus and Cressida* you will soon see that there are better reasons for the devious Ulysses to *say* these things than there are for him to *believe* them. And even if Ulysses does believe them, it does not follow that Shakespeare did so too.

Even in his own day, there was a reaction against Tillyard. In his 1951 lecture 'Ambivalence and the Dialectic of the Histories' (later printed as part of *Angel with Horns: Fifteen Lectures on Shakespeare*, published in 1961 after the author had been killed in a climbing accident), A. P. Rossiter challenged Tillyard head on. Arguing that it was important to read *Henry V* less as a paean to patriotism, which was how Tillyard interpreted it, than as part of the long, intricately patterned cycle of history plays, Rossiter pointed out that

The closing chorus of Henry V refers back to the Henry VI series, the loss of France – 'which oft our stage hath shown'. Thus the sequel to *Henry V*, in the complete pattern, is 'Hung be the Heavens with black' and the Roses series, where 'civil dissension' carries forward the curse

> of royal murder, uncertain or divided right, brother against brother,
> for the sixty years to Bosworth Field. (p. 43)

Thus the play demonstrated what Rossiter termed the principle of 'retributive reaction', which might be loosely glossed as 'what goes around, comes around'. And, he adds, 'when I say "retributive reaction" I mean just that; for whether it is "justice" or not, God knows . . . (Professor Butterfield would have it that *he* knows too, and that it *is* all the Will of God. To me, it is obscure, ironic, *and* – as far as Shakespeare shows me the scheme of things – seemingly endless.)' (*Angel with Horns*, p. 43). Professor (Herbert) Butterfield was Vice-Chancellor of the University of Cambridge and a historian famous primarily for his 1931 book *The Whig Interpretation of History*, *Christianity, Diplomacy and War* and *Christianity and History* (the Whig interpretation of history being essentially one which sees individual events as divinely ordained, and as working to form a pattern in which the world is constantly improving – in some ways rather like the optimistic viewpoint of comedy as opposed to the pessimistic one of tragedy). Rossiter clearly sees no such triumphalism or clarity of pattern in Shakespeare's work.

It soon becomes clear, however, that Butterfield is not Rossiter's only target:

> This pattern of 'obscure tragedy' runs, for me, far deeper than any feelings *I* can derive from knowing the 'philosophic' system which modern scholarship has extracted from the plays (and other Elizabethan sources *undique coemptis* [brought together from all over the place]). I must briefly outline it, *(a)* because it is indubitably 'there' as a pattern of thought, and *(b)* because it offers simplifications which are in danger of diminishing the true complexity of Shakespearian History – and in the best plays. Remember, then, that I am *not* arguing anything *away*: a pattern is *there*, and it is like Edward Halle's. [Halle, along with Raphael Holinshed, was one of the two chroniclers to whom Shakespeare turned for his source material in the history plays.] But Halle's theory of history is naïve, and though the Elizabethan reader found it as satisfying as the Chronicles of Israel and Judah (with similar formulae on how King So-and-so did that which was evil in the sight of the Lord and followed after the ways of Jeroboam the son of Nebat who made Israel to sin), yet I cannot find it in my reading of Shakespeare to suppose that his mind was quite as naïve as all that. There is more in the dark glass than the moral history of

the Lancastrian House of Jeroboam and the happy ending in the dawn
of Tudarchy. (p. 44)

Urbanely dismissing the further reaches of minor literature into
which Tillyard sometimes strayed in support of material for his
thesis, Rossiter appeals instead to a more general reader, who has
little time for pontificating scholarship and does not take the Bible
seriously, but is distinguished above all by a sophisticated appreciation of irony – both Rossiter's own irony and also that which he finds
in a Shakespeare whom he characterises as in fact very similar to
himself and his readers. For Rossiter, indeed, this likeness means
that Shakespeare is in fact less a man of his own time than a contemporary, since even if we cheerfully grant that everyone else in
Elizabethan England was naive, credulous, and believed in biblical
stories and providential patterns, Shakespeare obviously had little
patience with them. In that sense, to situate Shakespeare in the context of the supposed ideas of his own time, as Tillyard attempted to
do, was actually to misunderstand him; it is only we sophisticated
moderns who can really make sense of him.

STOP and THINK

• Could it be true, do you think, that we are better placed than
  Shakespeare's own contemporaries were to understand the
  meanings of his plays?

Halle and Holinshed both wrote their histories with one eye firmly
directed to pleasing the ruling House of Tudor, of which Elizabeth
I, who was on the throne for much of Shakespeare's life, was the
most famous member. Sometimes Shakespeare is visibly doing
that too, as in *Richard III* where he bends over backwards to paint
Elizabeth's grandfather, Henry VII, as an angel, and the man
whose throne Henry took, Richard III, as a devil. When Shakespeare did not toe the Tudor line quite so carefully, he risked serious trouble, as over a production of a play about Richard II
(probably but not certainly Shakespeare's), which Shakespeare's
company staged at the request of the Earl of Essex the day before
the Earl attempted to lead a rebellion against the Queen (because
the play contained a scene in which a reigning monarch was

deposed, Essex seems to have thought that it would encourage rebellious thoughts). Shakespeare and his company were lucky to avoid punishment over the incident; not long before, the author of a book about Richard II had had his ears cut off. It is, therefore, the case that if Shakespeare had wanted to put anti-Tudor messages into his plays, he would have had to conceal them so carefully that they might well have escaped detection for hundreds of years. Of course, the fact that this *might* have been so does not, of itself, prove that that it *is* so. As we shall see in Chapter 3 and Chapter 4, debate still rages over whether Shakespeare's history plays, and indeed his other plays, were subversive or conservative in intent and effect. For the Polish critic and theoretician of theatre Jan Kott, however, there was no doubt that it was indeed to the modern age that Shakespeare spoke most clearly.

Jan Kott: Shakespeare our contemporary

In his influential book *Shakespeare Our Contemporary* (1965), which inaugurated the next dominant phase in Shakespearean criticism, Jan Kott certainly assumed that Shakespeare spoke more clearly to our age than to his own. For Kott and those who followed him, what mattered most about Shakespeare was not what he had to say about the past, but the ways in which we could think about him in the present and use him to shed light on it. Kott was heavily influenced by the Theatre of the Absurd. This, as Martin Esslin has shown, was itself the product of the collective response to the horrors of the Second World War, and it saw Shakespeare as an important forerunner of its own aesthetic and practices (Esslin, *Theatre of the Absurd*, p. 333). Essentially, the Theatre of the Absurd showed a world in which events had so destabilised the idea of a fixed human nature that not only could Shakespeare the man no longer be considered as knowable, but all humans were to be understood as potentially capable of limitless depravity.

In what was to become the most influential chapter of his book, '"King Lear," or Endgame', Kott began by abruptly severing the play from its historical moorings and considering it instead under the 'timeless' rubrics of art:

> The attitude of modern criticism to *King Lear* is ambiguous and
> somehow embarrassed. Doubtless *King Lear* is still recognized as a
> masterpiece, beside which even *Macbeth* and *Hamlet* seem tame and
> pedestrian. *King Lear* is compared to Bach's *Mass in B Minor*, to
> Beethoven's *Fifth* and *Ninth* Symphonies, to Wagner's *Parsifal*,
> Michelangelo's *Last Judgement*, or Dante's *Purgatory* and *Inferno*. But
> at the same time *King Lear* gives one the impression of a high moun-
> tain that everyone admires, yet no one particularly wishes to climb. It
> is as if the play had lost its power to excite on the stage and in reading;
> as if it were out of place in our time, or, at any rate, had no place in the
> modern theatre. But the question is: what is modern theatre? (*Shake-
> speare our Contemporary*, p. 100)

For Kott, it is specifics not only of cultural context but even of form
which are immaterial, since *King Lear* is compared with music and
even with mountains. What matters is purely its emotional effect on
an audience, specifically on a modern audience, since that, after all,
is the only audience we are likely to find in a theatre now. It is, consequently, to a brief history of staging styles that Kott now turns, to
discuss why *Lear* has not moved audiences in the past – 'When real-
istically treated, Lear and Gloster were too ridiculous to appear
tragic heroes' – and also to explain why this matters, which is, it
seems, because Shakespeare is not just a playwright of the past but
an index and perhaps even a contributing factor to the health of all
modern theatre: 'When Shakespeare is dull and dead on the stage, it
means that not only the theatre but also plays written in that particular period are dead' (p. 103). Finally, Kott offers a way of recuperating *Lear* in the modern theatre. Going even further than Wilson
Knight, he suggests that the proper mode of the play is, quite
simply, pantomime, particularly in the Dover Cliff scene:

> It is easy to imagine this scene. The text itself provides stage directions.
> Edgar is supporting Gloster; he lifts his feet high pretending to
> walk uphill. Gloster, too, lifts his feet, as if expecting the ground to rise,
> but underneath his foot there is only air. This entire scene is written
> for a very definite type of theatre, namely pantomime. (pp. 112–13)

Of course, only a modern audience familiar with pantomime as a
genre could receive the scene in this way, but to Kott that is immaterial: 'we are not concerned here with an historical reconstruction
of the Elizabethan stage. It is the presence and importance of the

mime that is significant' (p. 114), and it is significant because of its effect on the audience: 'The stage must be empty. On it a suicide, or rather its symbol, has been performed' (p. 115). This is, as Kott himself is the first to point out, Shakespeare as Beckett, with *King Lear* as the great forerunner of *Waiting for Godot*.

Kott's emphasis on the *effect* of Shakespeare, and above all on his effect in the theatre, led to a shift in two directions. The first is towards ambiguity: everything is susceptible of at least two meanings, and it is for the audience to choose one. In turn, this makes audience response paramount, and thus allows for a thoroughgoing appropriation of the playwright into the audience's own culture, so that Kott can present a Shakespeare who is in in fact the first Absurd dramatist, and whose tragedies mirror the horrors of Auschwitz. Partly because of this emphasis on the experiences of the audience, Kott's book was a significant influence on Shakespeare in performance, particularly on the ideas of the influential director Peter Brook, and ultimately proved the catalyst which led to the development of studies of Shakespearean performance as a discipline in its own right (something which I will be looking at more closely in Chapter 8).

In this chapter, then, I have tried to trace the broad outline of how Shakespeare grew from one Elizabethan dramatist amongst many to the literary giant we know today, to indicate some of the principal criteria that have been used in evaluating and considering him, and to suggest some of the issues that the use of those criteria might raise. In the chapters that follow, I will go on to look at more specific approaches to reading Shakespeare's plays and poems, starting with psychoanalysis.

STOP and THINK

• Many of the changes in approaches to Shakespeare which we have examined in this chapter have been triggered by events in the outside world. Is there any kind of event or development that you could reasonably expect to see in your own lifetime which might lead to a new approach to Shakespeare?

Further reading

Works discussed in this chapter

Bloom, Harold. *Shakespeare and the Invention of the Human* (New York: Pine-head Books, 1998).

Bradley, A. C. *Shakespearean Tragedy* [1904] (Basingstoke: Macmillan, 1974).

Coleridge, S. T. *Lectures and Notes on Shakespeare and Other Dramatists* [1836] (Oxford: Oxford University Press, 1931).

Kott, Jan. *Shakespeare Our Contemporary*, translated by Boleslaw Taborski (London: Methuen, 1965).

Rossiter, A. P. *Angel with Horns: Fifteen Lectures on Shakespeare*, edited by Graham Storey [1961] (Harlow: Longman, 1989).

Spurgeon, Caroline F. E. *Keats's Shakespeare: A Descriptive Study* (Oxford: The Clarendon Press, 1928).

——. *Shakespeare's Imagery and What It Tells Us* [1935] (Cambridge: Cambridge University Press, 1968).

Tillyard, E. M. W. *The Elizabethan World Picture* [1943] (London: Penguin, 1990).

Wilson Knight, G. *The Wheel of Fire*, 2nd edition (London: Methuen, 1949).

Other works which explore issues touched on in this chapter

Esslin, Martin. *The Theatre of the Absurd* (Harmondsworth: Penguin, 1965). The classic account of the Theatre of the Absurd, with which Shakespeare was sometimes compared in the 1960s.

Greenblatt, Stephen. *Renaissance Self-Fashioning: From More to Shakespeare* (Chicago: University of Chicago Press, 1980). A vigorous account of why Tillyard was wrong.

Hopkins, Lisa. *Giants of the Past: Popular Fictions and the Idea of Evolution* (Lewisburg: Bucknell University Press, 2004). Looks at the way Milton and Shakespeare were used in both evolutionary and counter-evolutionary discourses.

Marsden, Jean I. 'Improving Shakespeare: From the Restoration to Garrick', in *Shakespeare on Stage*, edited by Stanley Wells and Sarah Stanton (Cambridge: Cambridge University Press, 2002), pp. 21–36. A lively account of the sorts of changes and adaptations made to Shakespeare's plays on the Restoration and early eighteenth-century stage.

Ouditt, Sharon. 'Explaining Woman's Frailty: Feminist Readings of Gertrude', in *Hamlet: Theory in Practice*, edited by Peter J. Smith and Nigel Wood (Buckingham: Open University Press, 1996), pp. 83–107. Offers some interesting models of non-Bradleyan ways of reading Gertrude.

Vickers, Brian, ed. *Shakespeare: The Critical Heritage* (London: Routledge & Kegan Paul, 1974). This traces the trajectory of the rising appreciation of Shakespeare.

2
Psychoanalysis

Although, as I shall discuss later in the chapter, there have been many modifications to its ideas since its inception, psychoanalysis will remain for ever associated with the name of its founder, Sigmund Freud (1856–1939). Freud was a Viennese doctor and psychologist who became increasingly convinced that the roots of his patients' disorders lay in the workings of their unconscious mind, which could be accessed most readily through analysis of their dreams. He was particularly interested in infantile sexuality and in repression, and arguably his most famous hypothesis, the Oedipus complex, postulated that neurosis in much later life could be traced back to imperfect resolution of what he saw as the universal boyhood drama of having to come to terms with the fact that one could not, as one would have liked, kill one's father and marry one's mother. (This was later extended by Jung to include a female version of the idea, the Electra complex.)

To some extent, psychoanalysis has an obvious kinship with literature, since in both it is necessary to assume that things are unlikely to be what they seem. When you interpret literary texts, you are presumably accustomed to looking for symbols (for instance, when Macbeth imagines that he sees a dagger hovering in the air in front of him, it is fairly obvious that this represents in his mind the murder he is about to commit). Psychoanalysis similarly seeks to probe beneath the surface to the hidden meaning below. Perhaps Freud's most important assumption was that human behaviour is obliquely influenced by buried trauma (which is invariably of a sexual nature). The aim of 'the talking cure', as psychoanalysis is often called, is to uncover that hidden trauma and, by revealing it, allow the patient to confront it and come to terms with it. Similarly, the psychoanalytic critic probes beneath the surface of the text, seeking the hidden motivation of either the author or the characters or both. The psychoanalytic critic, like the psychoanalyst, must assume that the truth will have been disguised – if it had not been, it could never have slipped past the defences which the conscious mind has erected to keep it buried – and so she or he may have to exercise considerable ingenuity in interpreting the surface of the text before they can uncover what lies beneath. To this extent, a psychoanalytic critic's analysis of a literary text may well resemble a psychoanalyst's account of a dream.

Freud himself was much interested in Shakespeare, and this is undoubtedly one of the reasons why there has been an unusually close relationship between psychoanalysis and Shakespeare. In the words of Philip Armstrong,

> Shakespeare has been *in psychoanalysis* for as long as psychoanalysis itself has been around, and in two senses: that is, Shakespeare has been both subject *to* psychoanalysis and a constitutive presence *in* psychoanalysis at least since Freud's inaugural formulation of the Oedipus complex, which depended . . . upon *Hamlet* as much as on the Sophocles play that gave the theory its name. (*Shakespeare in Psychoanalysis*, p. 5)

This has led to a very considerable number of psychoanalytically based interpretations of Shakespeare, which appears to confirm the ease with which the two can co-exist. When we further take into account the idea that critics' own experiences may explain their critical approaches, psychoanalysis may initially seem to function as the master key to understanding the patterns of Shakespearean criticism. It may, also, be attractive to students because it holds out the promise of allowing us to extrapolate from our own experiences, postulating as it does that what lie at the heart of Shakespeare's plays are universal human experiences.

Not everyone has been convinced, however, and it is indeed this very claim of universalism to which many critics have taken exception. New Historicists, who are, as I shall discuss in the next chapter, heavily influenced by the French historian Michel Foucault's insistence that the structures of desire should be historicised, have been particularly vociferous in this respect. Stephen Greenblatt, for instance, wrote in an influential essay that although 'the universalist claims of psychoanalysis are unruffled by the indifference of the past to its categories', there are nevertheless important historical differences conditioning the construction of the self and that therefore 'the historical mode of selfhood that psychoanalysis has tried to universalize into the very form of the human condition' is a pernicious misrepresentation (Greenblatt, 'Psychoanalysis and Renaissance Culture', p. 136). Greenblatt contends, and many others have concurred with him, that the idea of individual identity is in many ways an essentially modern one; in the early modern period, he suggests, the self was conceived of much more as part of a material and social network, with property a particularly important consideration.

The other principal objection which is often made to psychoanalysis is that it assumes that the sexual make-up and gender orientation of all humans is (or ought to be) the same, which, as many critics have pointed out, is simply not so. Thus Philip Armstrong writes of the 1980 volume *Representing Shakespeare: New Psychoanalytic Essays* that 'the anachronism and universalism of psychoanalytic reading is very evident: the modern Western nuclear family is taken as the norm, and masculinity as the model for self-identity, ... without regard for historical differences, non-hetero sexualities, or non-Oedipal relationships' (*Shakespeare in Psychoanalysis*, p. 168). Armstrong also contends that 'Lacan cannot help but repeat that consignment of "the feminine" to a realm outside of the Symbolic [i.e. the realm in which meaning is made, in which one thing coherently represents another], from which position the attainment of any kind of voice, agency or power would seem to be problematic, to say the least' (p. 93).

One might well take note, too, of the slipperiness which allows psychoanalytic criticism to place particular weight on features which are actually not particularly prominent in the text, on the grounds that their absence is significant and hence evidence of repression. Thus for Janet Adelman the conclusive proof that Hamlet's problem is the remarriage of his mother comes specifically from the fact that, he doesn't talk about it: she refers to 'his mother's remarriage, that "this" he cannot specify for fourteen lines' (*Suffocating Mothers*, p. 17). And there is also the small difficulty of the fact that although psychoanalytic readings of Shakespeare are so popular, Freud himself, the father of psychoanalysis, would not have approved of them: as Nigel Wheale notes, 'Freud himself characterized the appropriation of psychoanalytic ideas by untrained amateurs as "wild psychoanalysis", and disapproved of what he took to be the misapplication of his science' ('"Vnfolde your selfe"', p. 110). Even if we overlook this objection and press on, we are still faced with a final problem: is it the author or his characters who are to be psychoanalysed? If the former, the work of historical recovery must still be attempted; and, even if it is the latter, is it possible to psychoanalyse the characters without in some measure also psychoanalysing the author?

Freud and his early followers

Early psychoanalytic approaches were to some extent the logical development of the character-based criticism of A. C. Bradley; as Philip Armstrong points out, 'Bradley focuses on precisely the "problem" that will provide Freud with his entry into Shakespeare: why, after his encounter with the Ghost, does Hamlet delay his revenge against Claudius for so long?' (*Shakespeare in Psychoanalysis*, pp. 115–16). In his famous *Hamlet and Oedipus*, published as a book in 1949 with a preface noting that the essay was first written 'forty years ago as an exposition of a footnote in Freud's "Traumdeutung" [*The Interpretation of Dreams*]' (p. 9), Freud's disciple Ernest Jones opined in his section on the acting of the play that 'Gertrude is generally too much the dignified queen. She may be shallow, but sensuality is her outstanding characteristic and that is seldom brought out' (*Hamlet and Oedipus*, p. 159). This comes very close indeed to Bradley's celebrated comment on Gertrude, discussed in Chapter 1, that 'she had a soft animal nature, and was very dull and very shallow. She loved to be happy, like a sheep in the sun; and, to do her justice, it pleased her to see others happy, like more sheep in the sun'.

However, early psychoanalytic criticism parted company with Bradley in one very significant respect. While Bradley analysed all the characters he discussed as quite separate beings, psychoanalytic criticism is conditioned by the view that all human characters are at base the same, for this is something which is an inevitable aspect of the universalising closed system postulated by psychoanalysis. Thus Jones, for instance, claims that

> It is now becoming more and more widely recognized that much of mankind lives in an intermediate and unhappy state charged with what Dover Wilson well calls 'that sense of frustration, futility and human inadequacy which is the burden of the whole symphony' and of which Hamlet is the supreme example in literature. This intermediate plight, in the toils of which perhaps the greater part of mankind struggles and suffers, is given the name of psychoneurosis, and long ago the genius of Shakespeare depicted it for us with faultless insight. (pp. 68–9)

We may find it worrying to see human difference swept aside like this, but paradoxically the alternative approach is even more alarming: Philip Armstrong shows how psychoanalysis in South Africa was used to underwrite racialising assumptions (*Shakespeare in Psychoanalysis*, p. 97), and Freud himself postulated very different developmental trajectories for the two genders. Our stark choice, it seems, is either to see all humanity as the same or to see it as fundamentally and irrevocably divided along the lines of race or gender. Many critics, myself included, would feel that these are very unappetising alternatives.

As is also suggested by Jones's view that Shakespeare's achievement in *Hamlet* was essentially the diagnosis of the general unhappiness of humankind, psychoanalysis – or at least Freudian psychoanalysis – does not confine its attention to the character of fictional creations, but also often attempts to analyse that of the author too. Indeed Freudian psychoanalysis has, if necessary, even been prepared to revisit its view of the author to fit what it thought it had gleaned from his works: Freud in his later years espoused the lunatic-fringe view that the works of Shakespeare were in fact written by Edward de Vere, Earl of Oxford, and Armstrong suggests this might be because 'the proffered biography of Edward de Vere fits more closely with the Freudian Hamlet than do the scanty details from the life of the Stratford candidate' (*Shakespeare in Psychoanalysis*, p. 25). (It is true that de Vere had an exciting life, but it is also true that he died in 1604, roughly half-way through the writing career of William Shakespeare.) In fact Jones explains at the outset of his account of *Hamlet* that it is absolutely necessary to analyse the personality of the author: 'It has been found that with poetic creations . . . critical procedure cannot halt at the work of art itself: to isolate this from its creator is to impose artificial limits on our understanding of it' (p. 11). Therefore, Jones goes on, 'all serious critics know that the appreciation of a work and an understanding of its intention are only heightened when it is related to some knowledge of its author's characteristics and to the stages in his artistic development' (p. 12). Consequently he opines of Shakespeare that 'There is good reason to think that a highly significant change in his personality took place when he was about thirty-six years old' (p. 104). For Jones the change in question was the sexual infidelity described in the sonnets, which appear to tell the story of how a middle-aged male lover is doubly betrayed by both his mistress and his best friend, a beautiful young man:

> Two loves I have, of comfort and despair,
> Which, like two spirits, do suggest me still:
> The better angel is a man right fair,
> The worser spirit a woman coloured ill.
> To win me soon to hell my female evil
> Tempteth my better angel from my side,
> And would corrupt my saint to be a devil,
> Wooing his purity with her foul pride;
> And whether that my angel be turned fiend
> Suspect I may, yet not directly tell;
> But being both from me both to each friend,
> I guess one angel in another's hell.
> Yet this shall I ne'er know, but live in doubt,
> Till my bad angel fire my good one out.

'To fire someone out' means to give them venereal disease, a major scourge in the sixteenth century, and 'hell' is a slang term for the vagina, so Shakespeare's – or perhaps more properly the speaker's – mind is dwelling on some very unpleasant areas here. The speaker of the poem appears to be saying that he loves two people – a young man and a woman 'coloured ill', who is often referred to as the Dark Lady of the sonnets. The speaker believes that these two have betrayed him by making love together, but reflects bitterly that he can never be sure of this until he sees the signs of venereal disease in the young man, when he will then know that he has been infected by the Dark Lady. Jones thought that the fallout from this apparent *ménage-à-trois* was compounded by the death of Shakespeare's father, 'which is usually the turning-point in the mental life of a man' (p. 109).

On the basis of this reconstruction of the play's author, Jones therefore expounded his famous theory that Hamlet was unable to kill his uncle because he was suffering from an unresolved Oedipus complex, and that Shakespeare himself could not fully realise this because he was suffering from it too. Actually, Jones presents this as something rather more than a theory: he declares that 'This conclusion, that Hamlet at heart does not want to carry out the task, seems so obvious that it is hard to see how any open-minded reader of the play could avoid making it' (p. 45), and a footnote marker at the end of this sentence directs the reader that 'Anyone who doubts this conclusion is recommended to read Loening's convincing chapter (XII), "Hamlet's Verhalten gegen seine Aufgabe"'. Since few of us will wish to do this (and many of us will not even know what the title means), we shall, it seems, have to take Jones's word for it. Moreover, the alleged knowledge is presented to us as something that we must possess if we are to consider ourselves enlightened, since Jones expressly says,

> Only since Freud's work ... have we learned that corresponding elements commonly operate in the infant's mind before the damping down that evolution into childhood brings; and, further, that the conflicts then aroused, though remaining repressed in the unconscious, may profoundly affect adult life. This theme I had to introduce into my essay somewhat circumspectly forty years ago, when such knowledge was confined to a minute group, and even so it met with much hard abuse. To-day in a more enlightened age I may count on its impact being far less startling. (p. 10)

Jones's phraseology here implies that to agree with him is part and parcel of being 'enlightened'. New Historicism, however, objects that psychoanalysis regards too many things as universal and overlooks the role of change. One might wonder, too, whether it is a valid critical practice to deduce a 'Shakespeare the author' from the sonnets and then read the plays in the light of the author: I would argue that we need to be careful to distinguish between the speaker of Shakespeare's sonnets and the poet himself, because I do not think we can be confident that they are the same person. It is my experience that students today, at least when they first come to university, tend to want a poem to be an authentic and sincere expression of a poet's feelings, and tend to value it highly if they believe that it is. But originality and authenticity were not nearly so highly valued in the Renaissance. Shakespeare might well have considered it a more challenging and estimable task to create a convincing poetic persona than to express his own feelings.

As well as the obvious implications of Jones's theory, there are also some corollaries worth noting. In the first place, Jones perforce sees poetic inspiration as definitively coming from the unconscious rather than any 'quasi-divine' source, and he cites the Biblical episode of the Flight into Egypt as a representative of myths of persecution by the father-figure (p. 123), rather than as being the true revelation of a sacred scripture, which many of Shakespeare's contemporaries would certainly have taken it to be. In the second place, Jones explicitly disallows formalist considerations. This is clear when he writes dismissively that 'Then there is what might flippantly be called the box-office view that the culminating point of a tragedy, especially when this takes the form of a murder, usually comes at the end, so that to make a play long enough to satisfy the audience it has to be dragged out to a presentable length' (p. 23). This disregard of form is a relatively common feature of psychoanalytic criticism: Nigel Wheale cites Brian Vickers's dismissal of Ruth Nevo's psychoanalytic reading of *Pericles* on the grounds that she finds incoherences in the play only because she treats a non-realist form as if it were realist. Wheale himself sees clearly the necessity for considering form, but he also goes straight on to say that

> in defence of literary criticism based in psychoanalytic thought, we can argue that for our own period Shakespeare's *Tragedy of Hamlet, Prince of Denmark* (whatever it was for previous audiences and readers) is first and foremost a tragedy about tortured minds – the traumas experienced by Hamlet, Ophelia and Gertrude, perhaps even Claudius – so we must make a serious attempt to test the adequacy of contemporary psychoanalytic accounts of the play. ('"Vnfolde your selfe"', pp. 111–12)

For Wheale, then, a 'presentist' viewpoint is more important than a historicising one, and for him, as for so many other psychoanalytic critics, it is *Hamlet* which is the ultimate test-case.

STOP and THINK

- Do you agree that *Hamlet* invites a psychoanalytic reading?
- Do you think that any or all of the other Shakespeare plays you know can also be profitably read from a psychoanalytic angle?
- Does it follow that, for psychoanalysis to be a useful method, all literary works must be susceptible to it, or is it acceptable to find *Hamlet* especially well suited to it?

As intelligent readers have always noted, there does seem to be something odd about Hamlet, something almost pathological in his delay. Whether intelligent *viewers* have always thought the same, though, is a different question, and a very interesting one. Does one notice Hamlet's delay in the theatre? It is probably only really possible to answer this question if you have been to see *Hamlet* without ever having read it and without knowing that he is commonly thought to delay. If we do accept that Hamlet delays, then Freudian psychoanalysis might well be able to suggest a convincing reason why, although it would be one that would probably involve relegating to the background many other aspects of the play, such as its close chronological and thematic relationship to the accession of James VI and I and interest in the differences between Protestantism and Catholicism, and disregarding the conditions of its production and reception. However, not all forms of psychoanalysis put as much emphasis on the individual as Freudian psychoanalysis does. Starting with the work of C. G. Jung, later psychoanalytic critics have broadened their enquiry further and further beyond the mind of the individual.

C. G. Jung and the theory of 'types' and 'archetypes'

The Swiss analytical psychologist Carl Gustav Jung (1875–1961) was fundamentally concerned with describing and analysing what he saw as the human condition. He divided people into psychological 'types' (most notably the extravert and the introvert). His most controversial belief was that humans have not only an individual but also a collective unconscious, which is configured by 'archetypes', i.e. beings – animals, humans or sometimes objects – which have a universal symbolic meaning. This has clear affiliations with anthropological thought of the period, and indeed Jung was heavily influenced by Sir James Frazer's *The Golden Bough* (1922), which was a comparative study of religions and mythologies. This gives Jung's work at times an almost mystical feel, and his emphasis is less on changing people – which many Freudian psychoanalysts believe that they are able to do by means of the 'talking cure' – than on describing and classifying them.

It is perhaps for this reason that, whereas Freudian critics have been drawn primarily to *Hamlet*, and to 'solving' his problem, Jungian ones have tended to focus more on *Othello* and on *King Lear*. H. R. Coursen, for instance, argues that *King Lear* exemplifies Jung's views on old age, which Coursen quotes as follows:

> Our life is like the course of the sun. In the morning it gains continually in strength until it reaches the zenith-height of high noon. Then comes the *enantiodromia* [the move to the reversal]: the steady forward movement no longer denotes an increase, but a decrease, in strength ... The afternoon of life is just as full of meaning as the morning; only, its meaning and purpose are different. Man has two aims: the first is the natural aim, the begetting of children and the business of protecting the brood; to this belongs the acquisition of money and social position. When this aim has been reached, a new phase begins: the cultural aim. For the attainment of the former we have the help of nature and, on top of that, education; for the attainment of the latter, little or nothing helps. ('"Age Is Unnecessary"', p. 75)

For Coursen, *King Lear* is essentially a demonstration of the workings of this second phase of human life. Moreover, King Lear has a particularly difficult time of it because his 'problem is exacerbated by his being what Jung calls the "extraverted thinking type"'. As Coursen goes on to explain,

> the extraverted thinker, Jung suggests, 'elevates reality, or an objectively oriented intellectual formula, into the ruling principle not only for himself but for his whole environment.' To his introverted daughter, Cordelia, Lear says, 'Mend your speech a little, / Lest it may mar your fortune' ... The extravert can see only the external goal – in this case the 'more opulent' one third of Britain ... that Lear has promised Cordelia – and cannot understand someone with a different orientation, someone unwilling or unable to make the external adjustment necessary to achieve the objective. Jung's description of the expectations of the extraverted thinker fits Lear and the dynamics of the opening scene only too well. (p. 76)

Thus Shakespeare, in Coursen's account, seems hardly to have created the character of King Lear at all; he has merely transcribed
from life the 'extraverted thinking type' as he presumably saw it
manifested in people he met.

Throughout the play, Coursen sees Lear as following a trajectory
clearly identified by Jung:

> As external objects and people – whom he treats as objects – fail
> to validate his worth, the extraverted thinker is forced to question
> the identity he has known only as it has been reflected back to him:
> 'Who is it that can tell me who I am?' Lear demands . . . The Fool
> replies, 'Lear's shadow' . . . The 'shadow', in Jungian terms, is that
> personality formed of all that the individual has repressed from
> conscious orientation. In Lear's case it would seem to comprise what
> we attribute to the right side of the brain: dreams and the irrational,
> the feminine, or 'Yin,' earth and intuition, and the gestaltian abilities
> that Cordelia possesses but that the thinking type neglects in favor of
> piecemeal analysis. (p. 77)

There is a nice irony here: Lear's fault, it seems, is to analyse 'piece-
meal' rather than in a gestaltian way (i.e. a way that is focused on the
whole experience, the bigger picture); Coursen, consequently, will
pursue his own analysis to the bitter end. Thus he disregards entirely
the question of what meanings the word 'shadow' might have had for
the Fool in favour of glossing it as something which Shakespeare
himself could have had no conception of, 'the right side of the brain',
the 'Yin' (the principle of femininity and submission as opposed to
the 'Yang', which represents masculinity and dominance).

Indeed, because he considers that what Jung has diagnosed is a
universal pattern, Coursen systematically ignores historical variables and specifics. He says, for instance, that 'Both Richard II and
Lear create a kind of jungle in Albion and encourage social Darwinism in their subjects' (p. 76). 'Social Darwinism' was a term of which
Shakespeare could never have heard, and it is highly questionable
whether he could have had any conception of the idea either, since it
is so clearly a product of Charles Darwin's *On the Origin of Species*
(1859) and of the development by Darwin's disciple Herbert
Spencer of the concept of 'survival of the fittest'. But then Coursen
is not concerned about what Shakespeare could or could not have
thought, because for him the author is effectively negligible: the play

expresses a universal human truth, and the author is merely a con-
duit of that truth. It is thus a remarkable fact about Coursen's essay
on *King Lear* that he never mentions the name of Shakespeare at all,
though he does use the adjective 'Shakespearean' twice, when he
says that 'One of the greatest economies of Shakespearean drama is
that as the king is so is his kingdom' and that 'the segment of the
play that culminates in the reconciliation scene between Lear and
Cordelia (IV.vii) can be termed the most profound comedy in the
Shakespearean canon' (p. 84). It is clear in both these instances,
however, that the word 'Shakespearean' is functioning merely as a
convenient categorisation; Coursen, unlike most Freudian critics,
feels no interest in the psychology of the author at all, presumably
because Jungian theory holds so firmly that there is no such thing as
an individual psychology.

Instead, Coursen writes that 'Jung's psychological types help us
understand not merely the phenomenology of individual characters,
but also the dynamics of interaction between characters . . . We can
safely infer that the dynamics of interaction between Lear and
Cordelia in scene one, as Lear has set it up, are likely to result in dis-
astrous misunderstanding' (p. 80). This account of the production of
the work leaves no room for any agency of the dramatist at all: Lear
sets up the scene, and Jung provides the trajectory it must thereafter
follow. *King Lear* is, it seems, a transcription from life rather than a
play at all – and so, moreover, are most of Shakespeare's other plays,
since Coursen believes that 'Jung's analysis of authority speaks
accurately to *King Lear* (and to both Henriads, *Hamlet*, *Measure for
Measure*, *Antony and Cleopatra*, *The Tempest*, and, for that matter, to
Antigone, *The Malcontent*, Giraudoux's *Electra*, *The Wizard of Oz*,
etc)' (p. 87). Perhaps the oddest instance of this attitude is Coursen's
claim that 'Cordelia's plight demonstrates what Jung calls "one of
the greatest errors of our civilization, that is, the superstitious belief
in verbal statements"' (p. 82). A psychoanalyst might perhaps think
that belief in verbal statements is a grievous error, but is there any
sense in which a playwright could agree?

As well as *King Lear*, *Othello* also has been found to be particularly
sympathetic to Jungian analysis. Thus Terrell L. Tebbetts declares
of it that

The play is self-consciously theatrical. At the same time, the play is all
the more psychological. In other words, it compels readers and viewers not because it is a textbook of theatrical conventions and post-
modern theory, using them in its structure and in its action alike, nor
because it is a convincing casebook on sexual repressions. It compels
them precisely because it gives psychological depth to the theatre, the
fiction that sometimes seems to dominate human lives, suggesting the
psychological source, the power, and some of the ends of the pageants
human beings create for themselves and others. ('A Jungian Reading
of Othello's Fictive Self', p. 106)

For Tebbetts, the greatness of *Othello* resides in its 'Awareness of the
pageants that human beings create to keep themselves and others in
false gaze', which, he says, 'is, in fact, a marker of the balanced
psyche that Jung describes. In an unbalanced psyche, the conscious
ego denies anima/animus and shadow, keeping them unconscious
and insisting that the ego alone is the entire Self' (p. 106). When this
happens, 'The ego responds by projecting dimly perceived
anima/animus and shadow onto others ("It is not I who is like this;
it is they")' (p. 107) (for Jung, the anima is the personification within
a male psyche of all female traits, while the animus represents the
male element within the female psyche), and we can see this in
Othello because 'Only a repressive ego denying shadow can claim as
Othello does before the Senate that "My parts, my title, and my perfect soul / Shall manifest me rightly"'; 'Othello thinks his soul is
perfect because he prefers to know nothing about it. That "nothing"
will come to haunt him' (p. 107). To understand this, Tebbetts suggests, will provide the master-key to full comprehension of *Othello*,
reconciling previous critical differences: 'Much of criticism's con-
tradiction over the character of Othello stems from readers'
wrestling with the pageants Othello's repressive ego creates to keep
Othello himself and others in false gaze. The A. C. Bradley/F. R.
Leavis debate over Othello's nobility/savagery is a prime example'
(p. 107) – but this debate, over whether Othello is a noble man
tricked or a man whose innate savagery emerges once the veneer of
civilisation has been stripped away, can be resolved because it
hinges, it seems, on a false dichotomy: 'a Jungian reading supports
alike the Leavis party's denigration of Othello's character and the
Bradley party's admiration of it, explaining in psychological terms a

basis for both, [and] it also explains Othello's suicide in terms of tragic self-discovery rather than mere loss' (p. 110). (F. R. Leavis was an extremely influential twentieth-century Cambridge academic who wrote on the relationship between literature and life.)

Like Coursen, Tebbetts, too, is indifferent to historically specific categories. He says of Iago's 'let me know, / And knowing what I am, I know what she shall be' that 'Iago is encouraging Jungian projection', and of his 'I am not what I am': 'he gives the words distinctly Jungian implications, for the repetition of the "I am," the one cancelling the other, suggests the battle between the repressive ego and full Self in the unbalanced, unindividuated psyche' (p. 109). Jung thus provides not only a complete model for understanding the play but also a transhistorical guide to life, of which *Othello*, like *Lear*, proves to be essentially a transcription.

Although *Othello* and *King Lear* have attracted more attention, *Hamlet* has not been entirely ignored by Jungian critics. In particular, H. R. Coursen has written on that play too. He begins his analysis by declaring provocatively that

> All *Hamlet* criticism must be 'psychological criticism,' even when it claims to be anything but. The play is uniquely framed to elicit from its auditors a subjective response. No matter how 'objective' a critic may be, he must, in dealing with *Hamlet*, answer the question with which the play opens: 'Who's there?' (I.i.1). Any claim to critical objectivity signals an inevitable surrender to unperceived subjectivity. The critic invariably stands and unfolds himself even as he believes that he is illuminating that universe of shadows that is Hamlet character and *Hamlet* play. (*The Compensatory Psyche*, p. 63)

Since Coursen believes so entirely in the inevitability of a subjective response, it is hardly surprising to find that he is relentlessly 'presentist' in his approach to this play also, remarking on Dr Johnson's comments on the play that, because he was dead by then,

> Johnson could have read neither Thomas Erskine's defense of James Hadfield (26 June, 1800) – perhaps the first defense by reason of insanity – nor Darrow's defense of Loeb and Leopold, both of which Shakespeare anticipates in Hamlet's apology to Laertes. Hamlet, of course, is his own attorney. Later experience seems suddenly to illuminate what Shakespeare already knew. (p. 64)

'[W]hat Shakespeare already knew' turns out to be also what Jung would later know, that people fall into types. For Coursen, 'Hamlet represents introverted thinking and Gertrude extraverted feeling', so 'we have a way of understanding the relationship between son and mother tha[t] can incorporate psychoanalytic theory without having to define a specific "reason" for the mystery of Hamlet's character'; indeed 'the oedipal problem may itself be symptomatic of a deeper disturbance within Hamlet's psyche, that is, his inability to contact his "feminine soul," or anima'. For Coursen, it is this which is the key to Hamlet's behaviour: 'The man alienated from the positive energy of his anima will "forget himself," that is, fall victim to the "I don't know what came over me" syndrome, as Hamlet does when he discovers that the woman he loved "once" (III.i.116) is dead' (p. 84).

For Coursen, then, it is not specifically Gertrude who is the source of Hamlet's trouble, and indeed the concentration on the Oedipus complex is something of a red herring, inviting us to read as personal and individual what is in fact general and indeed potentially universal (this is of course a suggestion we might have expected to find, given the Jungian emphasis on the role and importance of the collective unconscious; indeed one could see this as a Jungian's deliberate rebuff to Freud). Hamlet thus is not a man in love with his mother but, like Othello in Tebbetts's analysis, a man who has failed to take account of all the constituent parts of his own psyche. The implication further seems to be that reading criticism of this nature is, at least potentially, therapeutic, since we are having borne in upon us what Hamlet needed to know.

STOP and THINK

- Do you see Hamlet's problem as an individual or a general one? That is, is his dilemma conditioned by historical circumstances, or could it occur in the same form now?

The first of these questions raises an absolutely fundamental issue about Shakespeare's play: is it the story just of one man, or of his whole culture? Surely the most satisfying tragedies (and indeed perhaps the most satisfying plays generally) are essentially both at once: Arthur Miller's 1949 play *Death of a Salesman*, for instance, announces itself as being about a salesman, but is generally read as being about the American Dream – that is, as about a whole society at a specific historical moment. *Hamlet* seems to me to be working in a similar way: as Hamlet himself says, 'The time is out of joint'. I think, therefore, that a psychoanalytic perspective which is blind to wider historical and political considerations will always have serious limitations. But as we shall see, not all psychoanalytic theories do disregard such considerations. In the work of Jacques Lacan, it is not just the mind of the individual but the role of the individual within society which is at the forefront.

Jacques Lacan and the theory of the subject

The French psychoanalyst Jacques Lacan (1901–81) practised in Paris and began to develop his own distinctive version of psychoanalysis from the 1950s onwards. Lacan presented himself as a rediscoverer of Freud, and his Shakespeare criticism can be seen as part of that project – Philip Armstrong comments that because of Lacan's desire for professional pre-eminence it was crucial for him 'to stand in the place of Freud by rereading the texts through which psychoanalysis was first articulated: especially *Oedipus Rex* and *Hamlet*' (*Shakespeare in Psychoanalysis*, p. 63) – but Lacan also proposed three major modifications to Freudian theory.

The first of Lacan's modifications to classic Freudian thought was to see the human being as situated in and constituted by social pressures: as Nigel Wheale puts it, 'Lacan's major revision of Freud attacked any notion of a coherent and unitary structure in the ego. The individual is redescribed as a "subject", which is a space "subjected to" the pulsions of the dominating orders under which it labours' ('"Vnfolde your selfe"', p. 115). This is potentially a very useful political concept, but Lacan is not in fact very interested in this: Wheale objects, for instance, that 'Lacan's psychoanalytic perspective does not allow him to recognize the political dimension which is present in the question of the succession to the throne of Denmark' (p. 127). Thus for Lacan 'the "something rotten" with which poor Hamlet is confronted is most closely connected with the position of the subject with regard to the phallus [that is, the imagined power of the father]' (Lacan, 'Desire and the Interpretation of Desire in *Hamlet*', p. 49), but if he had completed the quotation he would have been forced to acknowledge firstly that this remark is not only not made by Hamlet, he is not even there when it is spoken – it is Marcellus's comment on events after Hamlet has run after the Ghost – and secondly that the text expressly links the 'something rotten' with the political arena: 'Something is rotten in the state of Denmark' (I.iv.90).

For Lacan, however, the distinction between the psychological and the political proves to be surprisingly unimportant, as is made clear in a striking passage:

> Hamlet always stops. The very source of what makes Hamlet's arm waver at every moment, is the narcissistic connection that Freud tells us about in his text on the decline of the Oedipus complex: one cannot strike the phallus, because the phallus, even the real phallus, is a *ghost*.
>
> We were troubled at the time by the question of why, after all, no one assassinated Hitler – Hitler, who is very much this object that is not like the others, this object *x* whose function in the homogenization of the crowd by means of identification is demonstrated by Freud. Doesn't this lead back to what we're discussing here? (Lacan, 'Desire', pp. 50–1)

I have to say that I find Lacan's comment about Hitler rather cheap. In the first place, I'm not sure who 'we' are; in the second, while it is true that no one successfully assassinated Hitler, I am not at all convinced that all potential assassins held their hands because they equated Hitler with the phallus. (There were, in fact, eighteen unsuccessful attempts to kill him.) This seems to me an example of the bad effects of psychoanalysis's universalising tendencies, though this is just a personal opinion.

Lacan's second great innovation was to stress the importance of a linguistic perspective on the workings of the unconscious: to quote Nigel Wood in his introduction to Nigel Wheale's essay, 'Lacanian literary criticism derives from the realization that, just as the unconscious might be structured *like* a language, it may be an effect of language' – and that 'It is the very condition of language that it is never able to speak of what it desires to say' (p. 109). Indeed Lacan viewed language as being so constitutive that he felt that Shakespeare was unplayable in French. Despite this attention to language, though, Lacan himself is not easy to read:

Lacan's writing is notoriously difficult, partly because its author intended to imitate the complex processes of repression and evasion which are central to Freud's account of psychical structures. He did this so as to make the reader more conscious of these mechanisms, though whether this strategy can be said to be effective is very debatable. (Wheale, '"Vnfolde your selfe"', p. 112)

There are also other oddities about Lacan's relationship to language. Wheale points out that

Lacan introduces *Hamlet* as 'the drama of an individual subjectivity, and the hero is always present on stage, more than in any other play' . . . this is not in fact accurate, since Richard III has a larger share of his own text than does Hamlet, but the emphasis established the focus of analysis on a subject-in-language. (p. 115)

A similarly cavalier disregard for actual facts can be seen in two other assertions made by Lacan. Firstly, he declares of punning and wordplay that 'Without this dimension, as someone has pointed out, more than eighty per cent of the play would disappear' (Lacan, 'Desire', p. 33). Then, with equal disdain for fact and detail, he goes on to assert that 'from one end of *Hamlet* to the other, all anyone talks about is mourning' (p. 39). It is not, it seems, necessary actually to do any real textual analysis of any conventional kind; sweeping assertions will suffice.

Lacan's third innovation is the idea of the mirror stage. Essentially, this posits that at a certain stage in the infant's development, it will see itself in the mirror and will experience the reflection thus produced as something more ordered, coherent and pleasing than is offered by its own still inchoate sense of self. This literal experience of the mirror will produce a need for metaphorical mirroring in which an individual will regard other people as offering a reflection of what he or she would really like to be. For Lacan, the dynamic of the mirror stage is what is underpinning the duel scene in *Hamlet*: 'The dependence of his desire on the Other subject forms the permanent dimension of Hamlet's drama' (Lacan, 'Desire', p. 12), and 'What is expressly articulated in the text – indirectly, it is true, i.e., within a parody – is that at this point Laertes is for Hamlet his double [*semblable*]', because 'The one you fight is the one you admire most. The ego ideal is also, according to

Hegel's formula which says that coexistence is impossible, the one you have to kill' (p. 31).

These, then, are for Lacan the co-ordinates which must be added to the older, simpler Freudian criteria to make possible a genuine psychoanalytic reading of *Hamlet*. He begins his account of the play provocatively, announcing that 'As a sort of come-on, I announced that I would speak today about that piece of bait named Ophelia, and I'll be as good as my word' (p. 11) (the reference to 'today' derives from the fact that what we have here is in fact an [edited] transcript of one of the famous seminars held by Lacan). However we soon see that this is not merely a meretricious piece of attention-grabbing, for Lacan does in fact have a good reason for speaking of Ophelia as bait: he has read the original source texts of Shakespeare's play, in which the Ophelia-figure does indeed act as the bait in the trap which the Claudius-figure sets for Hamlet. He has further noted that 'Shakespeare's play contains one shift in the plot that distinguishes it from previous treatments of the story, including both the narratives of Saxo Grammaticus and Belleforest and the other plays of which we possess fragments. This shift involves the character Ophelia' (p. 11). This shows that Lacan does pay some atttention to the protocols of literary criticism, as too when he notes of Ophelia's reference to 'dead men's fingers' that 'The plant in question is the *Orchis mascula*, which is related to the mandrake and hence to the phallic element. You'll find "dead men's fingers" in the *Oxford English Dictionary*' (p. 23). Generally, however, he is careless on this score, saying blithely that 'I don't recall now what astute commentator pointed out that Hamlet cannot possibly believe that it's Claudius, because he's just left him in the next room' (p. 51). Writing 'I don't recall who said that . . .' will certainly not score you marks in your own essays, and it is one of the aims of this book to show that there is a good reason why that is so. Literary criticism does not come out of a void; it is the product of particular circumstances and agendas which lead particular critics to prioritise some aspects of the text and its contexts and disregard others. (For instance, a critic sufficiently committed to recovering the historical background of *Hamlet* to have visited Kronborg Castle, the model for Elsinore, would know that there is a back staircase which would indeed have allowed Claudius to arrive in the Queen's room before

Hamlet, and since Shakespeare's own company – including, perhaps, Shakespeare himelf – had played at Kronborg Castle, Shakespeare could be expected to have known so.) Lacan's own blindness to the fact that every critical statement reveals a position might well seem to give warrant to Stephen Greenblatt's warnings about the universalising claims of psychoanalysis.

Lacan certainly does make such universalising claims. For him, psychoanalysis is essentially a science: he observes grandly that 'human life could be defined as a calculus in which zero was irrational', which sounds so authoritative that it seems impossible to question it (although a professor of mathematics whom I consulted for help about this replied, 'I have no idea what he means, in fact I doubt that he has any idea what he means'). It seems suggestive that the Jungian Coursen should also use a similar tactic when he writes of Cordelia that 'her scorn is a well-directed sneering at the calculus of self-interest Lear has encouraged' ('"Age Is Unnecessary"', pp. 81–2); here too, it seems, it is being slyly suggested that psychoanalysis either is, or is analagous to, mathematics, and so provides paradigms and truth-value which supersede detail. Lacan's analysis of *Hamlet*, therefore, must be subordinated to exemplifying the truths told by psychoanalysis, so that what he is interested in primarily is

> the extent to which the play is dominated by the Mother as Other [*Autre*], i.e., the primordial subject of the demand [*la demande*]. The omnipotence of which we are always speaking in psychoanalysis is first of all the omnipotence of the subject as subject of the first demand, and this omnipotence must be related back to the Mother. (Lacan, 'Desire', p. 28)

Extrapolating from this to *Hamlet*, Lacan might well be seen as finding only what he expected to find, which is that

> This desire, of the mother, is essentially manifested in the fact that, confronted on one hand with an eminent, idealized, exalted object – his father – and on the other with the degraded, despicable object Claudius, the criminal and adulterous brother, Hamlet does not choose. (p. 12)

This passage does also, I think, suggest that, despite the far more elaborate network of concepts that he brings to bear, there are certainly times when Lacan sounds very like Freud, and indeed not all that unlike A. C. Bradley. Lacan claims, for instance, that Gertrude 'does not choose because of something present inside her, like an instinctive voracity' (p. 12), which seems to take us straight back to Bradley's view of Gertrude as being like a sheep in the sun; and he declares that 'Shakespeare's poetic skill doubtless guided him along the way, step by step, but we can also assume that he introduced into the play some observations from his own experience, however indirectly' (p. 11), which does not seem to represent much of an advance on Freud's and Ernest Jones's models of the processes of creativity.

At least one aspect of Lacan's analysis of *Hamlet* certainly does move beyond Freud, though, because Lacan does not merely confine his attentions to Gertrude; he is also very interested in Ophelia, whom he defines as 'the object *a*' – a difficult concept best approached through Lacan's own explanation of it:

> With respect to the object *a*, at once image and pathos, the subject feels himself to be in an imaginary situation of otherness. This object satisfies no need and is itself already relative, i.e., placed in relation to the subject . . . the object takes the place, I would say, of what the subject is – symbolically – deprived of. (p. 15)

What the subject is deprived of is, Lacan goes on, the phallus – by which he means not an individual penis but the conceptual symbol of the Law – and this is what Ophelia represents for Hamlet. It is sometimes alleged that Lacan proposed that Ophelia's name was in fact derived from 'phallus', but in fact he explicitly dismisses this idea: 'I wouldn't want to encourage you to produce the sort of hogwash that psychoanalytic texts are full of. I'm just surprised that nobody's pointed out that Ophelia is *O phallos*, because you find other things equally gross, flagrant, extravagant' (p. 20). Nevertheless, he does say that

> Ophelia is at this point the phallus, exteriorized and rejected by the subject as a symbol signifying life.
> 'What is the indication of this? There's no need to resort to the etymology of "Ophelia." Hamlet speaks constantly of one thing: child-bearing. (p. 23)

Again, though, whatever theoretical insights there are here are, for me at least, vitiated by the absolute failure to ground them effectively in engagement with the actual text of the play, because I would need an awful lot of quotation to convince me that Hamlet speaks constantly of child-bearing, and Lacan makes no attempt to offer any at all.

Despite its clearly identifiable weaknesses, however, Lacanian criticism has been very influential, and even the sceptical Nigel Wheale suggests that

> Of all critical-theoretical approaches to literature, the psychoanalytic consideration of drama ought to be one of the most useful for comparing and contrasting our text-based readings of a work with the often starkly different responses which we feel in the theatre, or when watching a recorded version of a play. A practical application of a Lacanian approach to *Hamlet* might therefore be found in comparing the experience of watching the play in performance with the intense intersubjectivity of the analytic relationship itself. ("'Vnfolde your selfe'", pp. 124–5)

STOP and THINK

- What can a Lacanian approach offer that other psychoanalytic approaches cannot?
- What might some of the weaknesses and drawbacks of a Lacanian approach be? Is it, for instance, always likely to lead to a flattening of history, or to overly schematic readings, or can these be avoided?

The new concepts that Lacan added to the existing psychoanalytic repertoire – of the unconscious being structured like a language, of the mirror stage, and of the subject – certainly offered new possibilities for psychoanalytic interpretation. You might also feel, though, that they take it further away from the personal experiences of the individual which ultimately underpinned Freud's work, and allow less scope for creative individual interpretation. In the wake of Lacan's work, psychoanalysis has moved even further from the Freudian emphasis on the individual.

Post-Lacanian psychoanalytic approaches

Many recent psychoanalytic critics have sought to transcend the traditional limitations of the approach. One oft-repeated complaint is that psychoanalysis postulates a 'normal' sexual development which simply does not fit the experience of many people and which they may indeed find it offensive to have put forward as the 'norm'. It is also often said to lead to gender stereotyping: thus 'Feminist critics . . . have suggested that Lacan's theory repeats the narrative structure of the Freudian family romance: the relation to the feminine is repressed as the subject moves into the imaginary and symbolic; thus, in the very process by which the (male) subject is constituted, "woman" becomes an object' (Armstrong, *Shakespeare in Psychoanalysis*, p. 93). To counter this, many later critics have paid deliberate attention to non-heteronormative elements in Shakespeare's plays. Thus William Kerrigan switches from the traditional attention to parent/children relationships to the psychoanalytic resonances of sibling interactions instead, something which had first been brought to prominence by Freud's one-time disciple Alfred Adler (1879–1937), but which disappeared from classical Freudian theory after Freud's falling out with Adler. Kerrigan argues that

> Fraternal rivalry, the 'primal eldest curse' of *Hamlet*, is one of those outlets. Shakespeare writes the success story of a 'band of brothers' in *Henry V*, then he relates the failure of a conspiracy of brothers in *Julius Caesar*, and then – assuming the correctness of the Evans chronology – he writes *As You Like It*, which opens in a world torn by fraternal strife. ('Female Friends and Fraternal Enemies in *As You Like It*', p. 184)

John Guillory similarly shifts attention from the more well-worn approaches to *Hamlet* when he writes of 'Hamlet's repeated return to the subject of dirt, which constitutes one of the more obsessional thematics in the play' ('"To please the wiser sort"', p. 91), while Jonathan Goldberg focuses on the anal rather than the Oedipal when he claims that 'To put it crudely, Coriolanus hurls shit at the plebeians because he experiences their words as shit hurled at him' ('The Anus in *Coriolanus*', p. 262).

Concerted attempts have also been made to remedy the traditional inattention of psychoanalysis to material and historical frameworks.

Thus when Janet Adelman begins her analysis of infantile anger in Shakespeare's plays, she is careful to observe that 'the infantile fantasies that Shakespeare invokes to empower his fictions would themselves have been shaped by the actual conditions of infancy and reformulated in adulthood according to the terms provided by his culture' (*Suffocating Mothers*, p. 4). Paradoxically, however, changing critical fashions have also meant that there is one material circumstance which cannot now be mentioned: Roland Barthes's influential theory of the death of the author, building on W. K. Wimsatt's and Monroe Beardsley's attack on 'The Intentional Fallacy', has made it taboo now in literary criticism to speculate on the intentions or personality of the author himself or herself, with the result that Shakespeare the man has virtually disappeared from psychoanalytic criticism of Shakespearean plays. For Adelman, therefore, agency must be relegated to the background; thus she writes of Old Hamlet and Claudius that 'The highly charged word "grossly" . . . hovers indeterminately between the two men . . . and in its indeterminacy, it associates both Claudius and Old Hamlet with the gross possession of Gertrude's unweeded garden' (p. 21) and declares '*Fall/fault/foutre*: the complex bilingual pun ['foutre' is the French for 'to fuck'] registers the fantasy that moves under the surface of Hamlet's meditation' (p. 23). Here the words float free of their authors, and it need be of no concern to us whether Shakespeare himself could ever have conceived of the new meanings and elaborate puns which we may now hear in them.

It has proved difficult, however, for psychoanalytic critics to renounce the author entirely. As Philip Armstrong perceptively comments,

> Working in a critical context in which authorial psychobiography has become anathema, Adelman avoids attributing . . . psychic structures to the author himself: the subject of the plays' psychoanalytic work is never explicitly identified, and can thus be taken to be Shakespeare, the reader or audience member, the masculine subject in early modern culture, or the subject of patriarchy in general. Nevertheless, *Suffocating Mothers* follows the plays in the presumed chronological sequence of their production, articulating complex relationships between them in such a way that, just as they did for Freud, [Ernest] Jones and [Otto] Rank, each text comes to represent a particular 'session' in a series of therapeutic interventions, by means of which their masculine subject works out his own Oedipal dilemmas. (*Shakespeare in Psychoanalysis*, p. 186)

By Armstrong's account, then, this is effectively psychoanalysis of the author by stealth.

Armstrong himself has done much to advance the range of possibilities offered by psychoanalytic criticism, and to combat its traditional areas of blindness. His sophisticated introduction to the subject, which is both readable and theoretically alert, intriguingly offers to bring together 'two approaches to *The Tempest* which, despite their apparent disparity in method and intention, have proven surprisingly symmetrical: the postcolonial and the psychoanalytic' (p. 167). This would have been inconceivable to the first wave of psychoanalytic critics, for whom the inner workings of the mind were the be-all and end-all, but for Armstrong,

> the nuclear family, the bourgeois individual, capitalism and colonialism are contemporaneous and demonstrably complicit cultural developments. In their simplest forms both the colonial and the psychoanalytic narratives describe an agency that seeks separation from an environment which nurtures but threatens to suffocate it and reconstitution on new ground, in its own terms, answerable to its own authority. For psychoanalysis, this mastery can only ever remain an illusion, combining a nostalgic memory of childhood with a childish anticipation of a potency not yet attained, according to the paradigm, for example, of the Lacanian mirror stage. In a similar way colonial ideology articulates the memory of a past golden age of European culture with the anticipation of its future utopian restoration in a new location. (p. 171)

This is not so much psychoanalysis of the author as psychoanalysis of the entire material culture which has conditioned him – and also, to some extent, of psychoanalysis itself, which is no longer seen as absolute truth but as something which is open to question and analysis. A hundred years after its inception, then, psychoanalysis may finally be coming of age. It is no longer axiomatic that it should be regarded as the antithesis of any kind of historicism; indeed, as I shall show in the next chapter, it may not even be as far removed from New Historicism as Stephen Greenblatt's attack on it suggested.

STOP AND THINK

- Given the new areas covered by more recent approaches, can you think of anything for which psychoanalytic criticism of

Shakepeare can still not account or which it is likely to over-look, or is it now a fuller and more comprehensive theory?

• What information would you consider necessary to offer a psychoanalytically oriented account of any particular play or character? Would you, for instance, want to know about the background of the author? Or perhaps about his or her sexuality? Would you want to do historical research into theories of the mind and of human relationships that might have been current at the time of the work's composition?

Further reading

Works discussed in this chapter

Adelman, Janet. *Suffocating Mothers: Fantasies of Maternal Origin in Shake-speare's Plays*, Hamlet *to* The Tempest (London: Routledge, 1992).

Armstrong, Philip. *Shakespeare in Psychoanalysis* (London: Routledge, 2001).

Coursen, H. R. *The Compensatory Psyche: A Jungian Approach to Shake-speare* (Lanham, MD: University Press of America, 1986).

——. '"Age Is Unnecessary": A Jungian Approach to *King Lear*', *The Upstart Crow* 5 (Fall 1984): 75–92.

Goldberg, Jonathan. 'The Anus in *Coriolanus*', in *Historicism, Psychoanaly-sis, and Early Modern Culture*, edited by Carla Mazzio and Douglas Trevor (London: Routledge, 2000), pp. 260–71.

Greenblatt, Stephen, 'Psychoanalysis and Renaissance Culture', in *Learning to Curse: Essays in Early Modern Culture* [1990] (London: Routledge, 1992).

Guillory, John. '"To please the wiser sort": Violence and Philosophy in *Hamlet*', in *Historicism, Psychoanalysis, and Early Modern Culture*, edited by Carla Mazzio and Douglas Trevor (London: Routledge, 2000), pp. 82–109.

Jones, Ernest. *Hamlet and Oedipus* (London: Victor Gollancz, 1949).

Kerrigan, William. 'Female Friends and Fraternal Enemies in *As You Like It*', in *Desire in the Renaissance: Psychoanalysis and Literature*, edited by Valeria Finucci and Regina Schwartz (Princeton: Princeton University Press, 1994), pp. 184–203.

Lacan, Jacques. 'Desire and the Interpretation of Desire in *Hamlet*', in *Literature and Psychoanalysis: The Question of Reading: Otherwise*, edited by Shoshana Felman (Baltimore and London: The Johns Hopkins University Press, 1977), pp. 11–52.

Tebbetts, Terrell L. 'A Jungian Reading of Othello's Fictive Self', *Publica-tions of the Mississippi Philological Association* (1995): 106–11.

Wheale, Nigel. "'Vnfolde your selfe": Jacques Lacan and the Psychoanalytic Reading of *Hamlet*', in *Theory in Practice: Hamlet*, edited by Peter
J. Smith and Nigel Wood (Buckingham: Open University Press, 1996),
pp. 110–32.

Other works which explore issues touched on in this chapter

Hawkes, Terence. *Shakespeare and the Present* (London: Routledge, 1992).
Offers a survey of the spread of 'presentist' criticism of Shakespeare and
an alternative perspective on the issue of the need to historicise.

Holland, Norman. 'Hermia's Dream', *The Annual of Psychoanalysis* 7
(1979): 369–89; reprinted in *Shakespeare's Comedies*, edited by Gary
Waller (London: Longman, 1991), pp. 75–92. Classic psychoanalytic
account of *A Midsummer Night's Dream*.

Lupton, Julia Reinhard and Kenneth Lupton. *After Oedipus: Shakespeare in
Psychoanalysis* (Ithaca: Cornell University Press, 1993). Intriguing psychoanalytic reading of *Hamlet* and *King Lear*.

Schwartz, Murray M. and Coppélia Kahn, eds, *Representing Shakespeare:
New Psychoanalytic Essays* (Baltimore and London: Johns Hopkins University Press, 1980). Though no longer as 'new' as when it first appeared,
this remains a useful volume which covers a good range of plays, including *Hamlet* and *King Lear* and Janet Adelman's now classic essay on
Coriolanus.

Sokol, B. J., ed., *The Undiscover'd Country: New Essays on Shakespeare and
Psychoanalysis* (London: Free Association Books, 1993). Interesting
range of psychoanalytic readings of Shakespeare.

3

New Historicism

New Historicism appeared on the critical scene in the 1980s, so swiftly that even some of its practitioners did not at first know that that was what they were. As Peter Hulme recounts,

> A couple of months after *Alternative Shakespeares* had appeared, Howard Felperin came to Essex to give a departmental seminar. He began by announcing that he was going to talk about New Historicism, and that Essex was an appropriate place for such a talk since the Literature department was home to two new Historicists, Francis [Barker] and myself. We looked at each other in some puzzlement since neither of us had heard this strange phrase before. ('Stormy Weather: Misreading the Postcolonial *Tempest*')

This was in 1985, but New Historicism soon gained so firm a foothold in literature departments, particularly in the United States, that there would very soon be no one who had not heard of it; indeed as early as 1986 Wesleyan University's English department advertised specifically for a New Historicist to fill a vacant post.

So what is New Historicism, and what distinguishes it from 'old' historicism? A good example of 'old' historicism is provided by E. M. W. Tillyard, whose *The Elizabethan World Picture* I discussed in Chapter 1. Tillyard looked at Shakespeare's sources, particularly Hall[e] and Holinshed, and extrapolated from them what he took to be Shakespeare's own 'world-picture'. By contrast, Stephen Greenblatt, most celebrated of the New Historicists, is scathingly dismissive of source study, which he famously characterised as the 'elephant's graveyard' of literary study. For New Historicists, what matters is not whether Shakespeare is definitely known to have read something or not, which is a *sine qua non* of source study, but whether a given idea was 'circulating' in a particular culture at a particular time. So New Historicists study not just Shakespeare but other texts of the period – the more obscure and unusual the better – and read the two together without worrying about whether Shakespeare knew of them directly or not, or indeed without even worrying about whether they were actually written before or after the Shakespearean text on which they are being brought to bear. For New Historicism, Shakespeare is above all a product of his culture, and he is, moreover, merely one voice amongst many which we can hear speaking from it and showing us how it worked. He may be an unusually eloquent voice, but that does not mean that his texts should be afforded any special priority or privilege, and they are of interest more for what they tell us about that culture than for their own sake – an exact reversal of the views held by more traditional literary scholars.

New Historicism is often treated as if it blurred into Cultural Materialism, but I think it is important to separate the two and also to consider the full implications of that separation. It is true that both New Historicism and Cultural Materialism tend to read Shakespeare's plays not in isolation but against other texts or histor-ical episodes, but there are significant differences between them. Typically, New Historicism is American, and Cultural Materialism British; and New Historicism, as I shall explore in this chapter, habitually finds Shakespeare's texts to be pressed into the service of politically quietist ends – Richard Wilson remarks of Stephen Greenblatt's seminal book, which inaugurated New Historicism as a critical practice, that 'Under the shadow of Foucault, each chapter of *Renaissance Self-fashioning* ended in murder or execution, with the subject overpowered by social institutions' (*New Historicism and Renaissance Drama*, p. 7) – while Cultural Materialism generally believes Shakespeare's plays to be genuinely subversive or at least capable of producing subversion. This chapter will, therefore, con-fine itself to readings which are clearly and unequivocally New Historicist in approach, while the next will deal with Cultural Mate-rialism. Above all, I will be looking at the work of the two most famous practitioners of New Historicism, Stephen Greenblatt and Louis Montrose, and a third critic, Leonard Tennenhouse, who, while less prominent than either Greenblatt or Montrose, did produce one particularly influential New Historicist reading of Shakespearean drama. Moreover, I have chosen pieces which have not only been much anthologised in general but which have been reproduced in two particularly significant and widely read collections, Jonathan Dollimore's and Alan Sinfield's *Political Shakespeare* (1985), and Richard Wilson's and Richard Dutton's *New Historicism and Renaissance Drama* (1992). Finally, I will turn to the work of Karen Newman, which has done much to redress the shortcomings identified by the early critics of New Historicism.

New Historicism is also often treated as if it represented a complete break with the past. But, as with so many other things that are new, there is also much in New Historicism that is old. For instance, New Historicism is often regarded as representing a complete break with psychoanalysis. This is unsurprising given Stephen Greenblatt's famous dismissal of psychoanalysis in his essay 'Psychoanalysis and Renaissance Culture', but it is not entirely accurate; as we shall see, Montrose's influential analysis of *A Midsummer Night's Dream* uses psychoanalytic language and techniques, and indeed a crucial bridge between the two approaches was constituted by Joel Fineman, who openly acknowledges in the introduction of his important book *Shakespeare's Perjured Eye* (1986) that he was greatly influenced by Lacan, but also thanks 'The group around *Representations*', the flagship journal of the New Historicism, which was edited from Berkeley, where both Fineman and Greenblatt taught (Fineman, *Perjured Eye*, pp. 44 and ix). Equally, Philip Armstrong suggests a parallel between Otto Rank's view of the psychotherapeutic processes of drama and New Historicism's argument that drama performs a cultural function (*Shakespeare in Psychoanalysis*, p. 29).

Also like psychoanalysis, New Historicism too can be traced to a single founding father, in this case Stephen Greenblatt. But it did not spring fully formed from one man's head. In the first place, many elements of Greenblatt's approach display a clear debt to the work of the anthropologist Clifford Geertz (b. 1926). Geertz was the pioneer of 'thick description', which involves giving the maximum possible amount of detail of any event because this is seen as inherently counterbalancing the historiographical tendency to produce 'grand narratives' – sweeping, all-embracing accounts of historical change, in which local detail is subordinated to the bigger picture –

of which Geertz, like so many other recent critics, has grown suspicious. Thus in arguably his most famous essay, 'Invisible Bullets: Renaissance Authority and its Subversion, *Henry IV* and *Henry V*', we find Greenblatt quoting Geertz in his peroration:

> 'In sixteenth-century England', writes Clifford Geertz, comparing Elizabethan and Majapahit royal progresses, 'the political centre of society was the point at which the tension between the passions that power excited and the ideals it was supposed to serve was screwed to its highest pitch . . . In fourteenth century Java, the centre was the point at which such tension disappeared in a blaze of cosmic symmetry.' ('Invisible Bullets', p. 108)

One might wonder what fourteenth-century Java could possibly have to do with Shakespeare's plays, but the fact that Geertz refers to it apparently legitimates its appearance in Greenblatt here.

Greenblatt's allegiance to Geertz also ensures that the signature technique of New Historicism is the use of the anecdote, an incident which is tiny in itself but which illustrates the workings or assumptions of a particular aspect of a culture and which challenges the force of 'grand narratives' by offering itself as an example of 'la petite histoire', the 'little story' of specific, small-scale events on which the French historians of the *Annales* school had laid such emphasis. (Centred on the journal *Annales d'Histoire Économique et Sociale* [Annals of social and economic history], the *Annales* school (active in France since the late 1920s) were interested in *mentalités* – mentalities or casts of mind – and in small-scale examples of physical or material culture rather than the more traditional historical focus on war, diplomacy and international relations.) Moreover, the anecdotes typically chosen by New Historicists tend to be not only very striking in themselves – such as a story about a man who pretended to be someone else and very nearly deceived a judge, or, as we shall see, an Elizabethan conjurer's erotic dream about Queen Elizabeth – but also new, at least to critics and students of literature. This thus generated both a tremendous sense of excitement and also an impression that New Historicism really did have access to new sources of knowledge and ideas. It also makes New Historicist criticism unusually approachable and easy to read, since the anecdotes are generally recounted with great verve and are so interesting in their own right.

The use of anthropological perspectives in Shakespearean criticism was by no means entirely new: early interest in Sir James Frazer's *The Golden Bough* had led to festival-based readings such as C. L. Barber's *Shakespeare's Festive Comedy* (1959) and the work of the Canadian critic Northrop Frye, which placed considerable emphasis on the redemptive potential of 'the green world' to which the characters of Shakespeare's comedies so often retreat (think of the wood near Athens in *A Midsummer Night's Dream* and the Forest of Arden in *As You Like It*). Other festival-based approaches, such as François Laroque's 1993 *Shakespeare's Festive World*, have been influenced by the Russian critic Mikhail Bakhtin, who drew attention to the importance of popular festivity and particularly of Carnival. The principal difference is that for Greenblatt and those who follow him, the use of anthropology has a fundamentally politicised dimension, as is clearly shown when Peter Stallybrass and Allon White quote Georges Balandier's *Political Anthropology*: 'The supreme ruse of power is to allow itself to be contested *ritually* in order to consolidate itself more effectively' (*The Politics and Poetics of Transgression*, p. 14) – clearly, as we shall see below, precisely the same model as Greenblatt's theory of containment, which suggests that power licenses drama to appear to challenge it, because this functions as a 'letting off of steam' which prevents any real challenge developing.

Anthropology, however, is not the only significant influence on Greenblatt's work. Richard Wilson has pointed out that

> Stephen Greenblatt himself proposes a big bang theory of the origin of New Historicism, with speculation that the lectures of the French social thinker Michel Foucault at Berkeley in October 1980 ignited a theoretical explosion . . . But there is irony in this tribute, since the message Foucault brought to America was that there is no founding moment, because every utterance or event has to be understood as part of something else. Thus, Foucault's thesis that truth is an effect of words and knowledge, the exercise of power, has to be understood itself in the context of the rejection of the totalising drive of Marxism in the aftermath of May 1968. (*New Historicism and Renaissance Drama*, pp. 1–2)

(The allusion to May 1968 refers to the widespread student protests in Paris which brought France to the brink of revolution.)

Finally, it has also been suggested that New Historicism was fundamentally influenced by the failure of American protests against the Vietnam war, which left its leading practitioners convinced of the fundamental futility of political protest, and that New Historicism's typical privileging of containment over subversion is indeed politically quietist for this reason (see the article by Lynda Boose which I have listed in the 'Further Reading'). Thus Tom McAlindon comments that 'If Greenblatt, as seems likely, sees the modern state very much in terms of the government which sacrificed a generation of young Americans to the killing fields of Vietnam, we may have a clue to the extraordinary picture of Hal offered in [his] pages' ('Testing the New Historicism', p. 424), while Walter Cohen remarks that

> if new historicist reductions of Shakespeare to an agent of royal power are hard to defend in the context of the Renaissance, they acquire a certain logic and justification in the context of the present. The social basis for this position is the United States government's mass murder of Indochinese peasants followed first by the failure of the American anti-war movement to achieve any of its radical goals and then by the rightist recovery of the 1980s. ('Political Criticism of Shakespeare', p. 36)

In New Historicist readings, in short, existing modes of power always triumph in the end.

Influential though it has been, New Historicism has not been without its critics. It has been accused both of ignoring gender issues and of fetishising and reifying power. Charges have also been levelled by Tom McAlindon and others that leading New Historicists, most notably Greenblatt himself, falsify history in the service of argument. In his famous and much reprinted article, 'Invisible Bullets: Renaissance Authority and its Subversion, *Henry IV* and *Henry V*', Greenblatt claims that the Renaissance political historian and theorist Niccolò Machiavelli uses the figure of Moses to present Old Testament religion as fundamentally fraudulent; McAlindon counters that 'in this section of the *Discourses* Machiavelli is neither considering the origin of religion nor voicing a negative attitude to it' ('Testing the New Historicism', p. 413), and that Greenblatt is thus fundamentally misrepresenting Machiavelli because 'Greenblatt's circuitous and entirely incorrect identification of Machiavelli with the juggling-Moses theory of politics, religion, and "the origin of European culture and belief" greatly enhances his claim that a common discourse of power is detectable in Renaissance non-dramatic texts' (pp. 414-15). Similarly, Greenblatt claims that the Elizabethan scientist and mathematician Thomas Harriot, who sailed out to join England's first attempt at an American colony in Roanoke, produced or began to produce 'a glossary, the beginnings of an Algonkian–English dictionary, designed to facilitate further acts of recording and hence to consolidate English power in Virginia', 'with its Algonkian equivalents for fire, food, shelter' ('Invisible Bullets', pp. 96 and 100); McAlindon counters simply that 'This information is incorrect. Included in the serial descriptions of "merchantable commodities" given at the start of the *Report* [Harriot's account of his time in Virginia] are some vegetable and mineral items for which there is no word in English, and whose names had to be transcribed. But there is no glossary anywhere in the *Report*; and nowhere is there any glossing of the three words cited (or any such)' ('Testing the New Historicism', pp. 418–19).

A final point to make about the potential limitations of New Historicism is that, just like psychoanalysis, it has found some plays more amenable to its methods than others. Particularly influential have been Montrose's and Tennenhouse's analyses of *A Midsummer Night's Dream* and Greenblatt's of *Henry IV* and *Henry V*. By contrast, other plays, such as *Richard III*, *Titus Andronicus* and *Romeo and Juliet*, have been left largely untouched by New Historicism, although all three have been made into important and well-received films, which suggests that there certainly are ways in which they can be made to speak to our own culture and to contemporary concerns – but then New Historicism does tend to read plays according to a very highly codified and very prescriptive formula, which may well seem inimical to the ambiguity and plural possibilities inherent in the medium of film. New Historicism has a number of clearly marked characteristics; indeed to some extent it is at least as much a set of practices and critical manoeuvres as it is a theory. In the first place, as D. G. Myers observes, it 'is unified by its disdain for literary formalism' ('The New Historicism in Literary Study', p. 27), so that one of its most characteristic techniques is to treat works of very different genres in the same essay. Indeed Leonard Tennenhouse begins his analysis of *A Midsummer Night's Dream* by arguing for the

radical inappropriateness of traditional generic categories as applied
to Shakespeare's plays:

> What if . . . we were to show that a play such as *Henry VIII* uses non-
> dramatic material much more the way such material was used in
> dramatic romance and tragicomedy than as it was used in the chronicle
> histories of the 1590s? And what if the histories written under
> Elizabeth represented political problems and resolved them in terms
> resembling the romantic comedies and the Petrarchan lyrics of the
> same period? Would we not have to rethink our notion of artistic genre,
> if these Elizabethan and Jacobean literary forms were found to resem-
> ble contemporaneous strategies of political argumentation more than
> they resembled each other? ('Strategies of State and Political Plays',
> p. 109)

In such a case, Tennenhouse claims, 'We would have to conclude
that what we now call Renaissance literature displayed its politics
as it idealised or demystified specific forms of power, that such a
display rather than a work's transcendence or referentiality, was
what made it aesthetically successful' (p. 110). To put this another
way, we would effectively have to conclude that there is no such
thing as literature at all, or at least that it is inseparable from history
and from forms of political writing.

The second distinctive feature of New Historicism is that,
because it is committed to this theoretical premise, New Historicism
insists on the textuality of history as well as of literature. Richard
Wilson and Richard Dutton have termed this 'the notion that has
come to characterise New Historicism: a theoretical awareness of
both "the historicity of texts and the textuality of history"' (*New
Historicism and Renaissance Drama*, p. x), and Wilson writing on his
own has declared that 'In its modish refusal to distinguish fact from
fantasy, New Historicism reverts to the metaphysics of *The Name of
the Rose* [a detective novel by Umberto Eco which is set in a
medieval monastery and mingles fact with fiction]' (*Will Power*, p. 8)
– though Jean E. Howard more charitably concurs with Greenblatt
that 'it seems necessary to abandon the myth of objectivity and to
acknowledge that all historical knowledge is produced from a partial
and a positioned vantage point' (*New Historicism and Renaissance
Drama*, p. 26).

STOP and THINK

• Is it either possible or desirable to attempt a recovery of the historical context(s) within which Shakespeare wrote? If it were
possible, would this conflict with pressing Shakespeare into
service to make points about current politics? Do you consider
either or both of these aims to be legitimate?

We can certainly discover a great deal about the material and ideological culture in which Shakespeare wrote, though the evidence
can be contradictory and it is not always clear how much weight
should be placed on it. It is not always easy to be sure, though, of
the relationship between a particular cultural belief or artefact
and any given individual. For instance, one phenomenon of obvious cultural importance in the early twenty-first century is the
mobile phone, but I know plenty of people who do not have one.
I think a useful concept in this connection is the idea of something
– an idea or an object – being 'culturally available'. For instance,
my grandmother believed that the colour green was unlucky, so
that is an idea that is culturally available to me; but I do not myself
happen to share it, and am indeed fond of green. Similarly, belief
in horoscopes is culturally available to all of us, but that does not
help us to predict whether any individual in our culture will or will
not believe in them. However, I don't see any difficulty or contra-
diction in the diachronistic approach of wanting both to situate
Shakespeare in his own time and also to be aware of what he may
mean in ours, both of which seem to me to be perfectly valid
enterprises.

Stephen Greenblatt: 'Invisible Bullets'

Stephen Greenblatt's 'Invisible Bullets' reads both parts of *Henry
IV* and *Henry V* against the Elizabethan scientist and mathematician Thomas Harriot's 1585–86 visit to Virginia to suggest that
'Shakespeare's Henry plays, like Harriot in the New World, can be
seen to confirm the Machi[a]vellian hypothesis of the origin of
princely power in force and fraud even as they draw their audience
irresistibly towards the celebration of that power' (p. 85). What
Greenblatt means by this reference to Machiavelli, as I have

sketched above, is that he sees both Harriot and Machiavelli as sus-
pecting that religion is merely a fraud, with Moses the most famous
practitioner of that fraud. Although there are different versions of
this sentence in existence, the one reproduced in Wilson's and
Dutton's important collection reads, '[Machiavelli's] *The Prince*
observes in its bland way that if Moses's particular actions and
methods are examined closely, they do not appear very different
from those employed by the great pagan princes' (p. 85). The essay
then proceeds in what rapidly became established as standard New
Historicist mode, and draws what became equally rapidly established as the standard conclusion: that in the case of Harriot 'the
subversiveness which is genuine and radical – sufficiently disturb-
ing so that to be suspected of such beliefs could lead to imprison-
ment and torture – is at the same time contained by the power it
would appear to threaten. Indeed the subversiveness is the very
product of that power and furthers its ends' (p. 89). Moreover, this,
it seems, is true not only of the plays which Greenblatt analyses in
this essay but of all Shakespeare's work: 'Shakespeare's plays are
centrally and repeatedly concerned with the production and containment of subversion and disorder' (p. 94); and so, in the words
which have become virtually the mantra of New Historicism,
'There is subversion, no end of subversion, only not for us' (p. 108).

Greenblatt also maintains that the Henry plays provide confir-
mation of the other principal supposition of New Historicism,
which is that literature does not exist in a privileged and separate
realm of its own but is fundamentally connected to the political
world 'outside' it:

> theatrical values do not exist in a realm of privileged literariness, of
> textual or even institutional self-referentiality. Shakespeare's theatre
> was not isolated by its wooden walls, nor was it merely the passive
> reflector of social and ideological forces that lay entirely outside of it.
> (p. 97)

This, he suggests, is proved by the 'fact' that '*1 Henry IV* itself
insists that it is quite impossible to keep the interests of the theatre
hermetically sealed off from the interests of power. Hal's characteristic activity is playing or, more precisely, theatrical improvisation'
(p. 97).

One might well feel, though, that for all the elaborate theoretical trappings which have gone to producing it, this is hardly a very startling new insight into Hal's character. Indeed in many ways this most modern of critics can often sound alarmingly old-fashioned, as when he comments that in one of the comic interludes in *Henry IV, Part Two*, 'We may find, in Justice Shallow's garden, a few twilight moments of release from this oppressive circumstantial and strategic constriction, but Falstaff mercilessly deflates them – and the puncturing is so wonderfully adroit, so amusing, that we welcome it' (p. 39). There seems little to distinguish this from a far older type of criticism, now denigrated as 'liberal humanism'. In a blind reading test, I would assign this passage, on stylistic grounds, to a Victorian critic, magisterial in his use of 'we', and benign in his willingness to find pleasure even in the deflating of what he had previously found pleasurable. The only phrase here which could not have been uttered by a Victorian critic is 'oppressive circumstantial and strategic constriction'. There is more zest in Greenblatt's invocation of Harriot's glossary of Algonquin vocabulary as a parallel to Hal's acquisition of the canting language used by rogues and ruffians, but ultimately he can push this analysis no further than the play's Earl of Warwick has already done for him, in a passage which Greenblatt quotes:

> The Prince but studies his companions
> Like a strange tongue, wherein, to gain the language,
> 'Tis needful that the most immodest word
> Be look'd upon and learnt, which once attain'd,
> Your Highness knows, comes to no further use
> But to be known and hated. So, like gross terms,
> The Prince will in the perfectness of time
> Cast off his followers. (IV.iv–68–78)

Certainly in this section of his analysis, it looks to me as though Greenblatt is revealing about the play only what it has already said clearly.

Greenblatt argues, then, that *Henry IV* and *Henry V*, far from being in any sense unique or transcendent works of art, merely reveal the same truths about Renaissance culture as are (he says) already to be found in Machiavelli and Harriot: that power, in order to further its own ends, gives temporary licence to the subversive and the carnivalesque, but ultimately contains them, and that by doing this power is greatly assisted in its fundamental project of furthering its own position. For Greenblatt, Henry V's treatment of Falstaff is simpy a way for Shakespeare to register this profound truth.

STOP and THINK

- Do you find Greenblatt's argument convincing?
- Does it matter if Machiavelli and Harriot do not actually say what Greenblatt says they say, or is his analysis valid anyway?

Personally, I find Greenblatt's argument interesting, elegant, but not convincing. I do not think that 'power' triumphs in the second tetralogy (and I have reservations about reifying 'power' in this way in the first place). It is true that the rule of kings continues, but it is also true that different groups are beginning to find a voice which will ultimately allow them to be represented. The majority of the individual members of the working class in *Henry V* may die, but the points they have made need not be dismissed or forgotten, and every time the play is produced they speak anew. As for the second question, while I can see the point that the idea expressed by Harriot may be 'culturally available' even if it is not to be specifically found in Harriot, I do think that accuracy matters in questions of quotation and representation of evidence, for on them all scholarly standards depend.

Louis Montrose: New Historicism meets psychoanalysis

Like so many other New Historicist analyses, Louis Montrose's account of *A Midsummer Night's Dream* begins with an anecdote. In a break with tradition, however, Montrose's anecdote concerns a dream – a semi-erotic dream about Queen Elizabeth which the Elizabethan 'conjurer' Simon Forman recorded that he had had. As the editorial comment in the Wilson and Dutton anthology observes, 'Such a psychoanalytic approach is unusual for New Historicism which generally concurs with Foucault's dismissal of Freud' (p. 109). However, Montrose's agenda is not traditionally psychoanalytic. It is true that he begins his analysis proper with the comment that 'Within the dreamer's unconscious, the "little elderly woman" who was his political mother may have been identified with the mother who had borne him' (p. 110), but this proves to be an essentially throwaway remark. Montrose goes on to outline his project in terms of which Freud could never have conceived: 'My concern is not to psychoanalyze Forman but rather to emphasize the historical specificity of psychological processes, the politics of the unconscious. Whatever the place of his dream in the dreamer's interior life, the text in which he represents it to himself allows us to glimpse the cultural contours of a psyche that is both distinctively male and distinctively Elizabethan' (p. 111).

Unlike traditional psychoanalysts, then, Montrose sees the psyche as historically conditioned:

> A fantasy of male dependency upon woman is expressed and contained within a fantasy of male control over woman; the social reality of the player's dependency upon a queen is inscribed within the imaginative reality of the dramatist's control over a queen. Both Forman's private dream-text and Shakespeare's public play-text embody a culture specific dialectic between personal and public images of gender and power; both are characteristically *Elizabethan* cultural forms. (p. 113)

Moreover, Shakespeare's play is Elizabethan in a double sense, for it not only reflects Elizabethan culture but also helps create it:

> This is not to imply that *A Midsummer Night's Dream* is merely an inert product of Elizabethan culture. The play is rather a new *production* of Elizabethan culture, enlarging the dimensions of the cultural field and altering the lines of force within it. Thus, in the sense that the royal presence was itself represented within the play, it may be said that the play henceforth conditioned the imaginative possibility of the queen. (p. 113)

Finally, as is characteristic of New Historicism, *A Midsummer Night's Dream*, in Montrose's account, directs its shaping of events and motifs to fundamentally conservative ends. Specifically, *A Midsummer Night's Dream*, in this reading, works towards the containment and punishment of women. Although 'Shakespeare's text discloses – perhaps, in a sense, despite itself – that patriarchal norms are compensatory for the vulnerability of men to the powers of women' (p. 121), nevertheless 'Shakespeare's royal compliment re-mythologizes the cult of the Virgin Queen in such a way as to sanction a relationship of gender and power that is personally and politically inimical to Elizabeth' (p. 126), working to contain the threatening power of the Queen.

Indeed in Montrose's account *A Midsummer Night's Dream* is barely a comedy at all, but effectively the prologue to a tragedy: 'Regardless of authorial intention, Oberon's blessing of the marriage bed of Theseus and Hippolyta evokes precisely what it seeks to suppress: the cycle of sexual and familial violence, fear, and betrayal begins again at the very engendering of Hippolytus' (pp. 120-1). What Montrose means by this is that in classical mythology, Hippolyta, whom Theseus marries at the close of *A Midsummer Night's Dream*, became the mother of Hippolytus. When Hippolyta subsequently died Theseus married Phaedra, who developed an incestuous passion for her stepson Hippolytus. When Hippolytus rejected Phaedra, she told Theseus that he had attacked her and Theseus therefore arranged the death of his own son, discovering only too late that the young man was in fact innocent of the charges. For Montrose, this story is implicit in *A Midsummer Night's Dream*, and he is able to point to linguistic details such as echoes from Seneca's plays *Hippolytus* and *Medea* to support this, though it is something of a rhetorical flourish to claim so sweepingly that Hippolytus is conceived on the very night that *A Midsummer Night's Dream* closes on. And it is perhaps worth pointing out that when Shakespeare did revisit the events of *A Midsummer Night's Dream* in *The Two Noble Kinsmen*, which he co-authored late in his career with John Fletcher, it was not Hippolytus that he wrote about but Emilia, Hippolyta's sister.

For Montrose, then, the play is no festive comedy but contains dark shadows within it, a nightmare rather than a dream. Its principal achievement is not to offer any kind of escape into fantasy or model of comic resolution in which women and men, and aristocrats and rustics, all win through difficulties and dangers to achieve peace and harmony together, but to face up to some of the most threatening possibilities haunting the male Elizabethan psyche, and to suggest ways of dominating and controlling them.

STOP and THINK

- Do you see *A Midsummer Night's Dream* as a work of fantasy or as a document revealing truths about Elizabethan culture, or both?
- Does its genre affect and/or condition its meaning?

Personally, I would want to answer the second of these questions first. *A Midsummer Night's Dream* is a comedy, and I think genre is always a fundamental determinant of meaning in any Shakespeare play. (Even when it is hard to say what a play's genre *is*, as in the cases of the last plays and the problem plays, I think that in itself is part of the meaning.) As a comedy, the play is likely to need an element of fantasy in order to produce the happy ending, but comedy, as the old saying goes, is a serious business, and there is certainly a layer of harder, more troubling meanings which we can glimpse under the shining surface of the play (if there were not, after all, there would be no need for a comic resolution). So my answer is that it is both a fantasy and a work that mediates cultural uneasinesses, and that that is why it is a great play: it feeds creatively on the tension between darkness and light.

Leonard Tennenhouse and the interest in power

My third example of New Historicist criticism, Leonard Tennenhouse's 'Strategies of State and Political Plays: *A Midsummer Night's Dream, Henry IV, Henry V, Henry VIII*', is not anthologised in Dutton and Wilson, but it does appear in Jonathan Dollimore's and Alan Sinfield's seminal collection *Political Shakespeare: New Essays in Cultural Materialism*, whose significance I will be discussing in the next chapter. Tennenhouse begins with an analysis of *A Midsummer Night's Dream*, although he is interested in the play less for its own sake than as an example of what he sees as a general process: he proposes that 'If we take the example of *Midsummer Night's Dream*, a play surely characteristic of Shakespeare's romantic comedies, we can see that the problem which authority has to master is a problem with authority itself, authority grown archaic' (p. 111). Predictably, what *A Midsummer Night's Dream* illustrates proves to be the inevitability of ultimate containment: the play seems to promise fantasy, subversion and escape, but ultimately it works to support power and to present its continued triumph as inevitable. For Tennenhouse, 'if Theseus authorises certain inversions of power relations by situating them within the framework of festival and art, then it is also true that the introduction of disorder into the play ultimately authorises political authority', and so 'the entire last act of the play . . . theorises the process of inversion whereby art and politics end up in [a] mutually authorising relationship' (p. 112), though it is hard to imagine this being an audience's experience.

In his attempt to establish the ways in which Shakespeare's plays exemplify what Tennenhouse sees as the truth about history, which is that power always triumphs and that there can be no genuine subversion, Tennenhouse paints with an unusually broad brush for a historian. He argues, for instance, that 'It cannot be accidental that the *Henriad*, which produces Shakespeare's most accomplished Elizabethan monarch, should also produce his most memorable figure of misrule' (p. 121). Obviously this fits Tennenhouse's thesis well: the king most successful in achieving containment must necessarily be the king most successful in producing the illusion of subversion. Therefore, he sees Shakespeare's treatment of Henry V as 'hagiography' (p. 120). But many, many readers and viewers have noticed the degree to which we are actually invited to perceive Hal as flawed and compromised rather than any kind of saint, and 'Elizabethan monarch' is, furthermore, a very odd term to apply to a man who reigned from 1413 to 1422. However, Tennenhouse sees little difference between different historical periods, writing for instance that

> Speaking for many in Parliament, [the Jacobean MP] Sir Henry Neville told the king, 'Where your Majesty's expense groweth by Commonwealth, we are bound to maintain it, otherwise not'. To challenge the mystical identification of the political body with the inherited power of blood was to pave the way, semiotically, for the day when, as Jacques Donzelot [a twentieth-century historian] puts it, 'the state was no longer the end of production, but its means: it was the responsibility of the state to govern social relations, in such a manner as to intensify this production to a maximum by restricting consumption'. (p. 119)

Surely the twentieth-century Donzelot's theory was well outside the range of possible meanings envisaged by the seventeenth-century

Sir Henry Neville, but for Tennenhouse both men and their ideas are fundamentally manifestations of the same laws of historical process. Even more striking is the fact that, when Tennenhouse does talk about moments of specific historical change, he does not consider their causes, as when he discusses the debate about Elizabeth I's marriage:

> Her use of her sexuality – which includes her refusal to marry – indicates the degree to which Elizabeth maintained her political identity as the source of economic benefits, the patron of patrons, over and above that which descended upon her as legitimate bearer of blood. Her first two Parliaments frequently pressed her to resolve the succession question either by marrying and having issue or by naming her successor, but she refused to do either ... After 1571 the debate moved from Parliament to the Inns of Court and into polemical tracts as well where it split predictably along religious and nationalist lines. (p. 114)

There is no explanation of what events in the year 1571 might have produced so marked and startling a change. (In fact, the 1571 Parliament concentrated primarily on legislation aimed to counter the threat to Elizabeth which had been created by the Pope's excommunication of her the previous year.)

Tennenhouse does explain why he ignores specific events and prefers to see Shakespeare's career in terms of a general, broadly based cultural and aesthetic shift which demarcates the reign of James from that of Elizabeth: to see Shakespeare's history plays 'as overt political texts that can be interpreted by reference to the historical source material [e.g. Holinshed and Hall] ... testifies to a belief in the distinction between literature and politics and so serves the interests of modern society by imposing this belief on the past' (p. 109). While he advances his own politically correct credentials here, however, his own account is in fact no less mystifying than those he demonises, for it offers no explanation of agency or process, but merely postulates shifts in sensibility so widespread as to be unanalysable, and consquently, presumably, unstoppable by any consciously willed means: 'With the ascension of James we are not entering new semiotic territory even though there appears to be a widespread attempt on the part of the literate classes to revise the problematics of power' (p. 110). What does this mean? Who were 'the literate classes' (and how, incidentally, might gender as well as class affect their literacy), what was the state of their apprehension of concepts such as 'the problematics of power', how did they arrive at this group decision, how was it disseminated, and why? When the leaders of the Easter Rising seized the Dublin Post Office in 1916, or when any *coup*-organising general worth his salt commandeers the local television and radio stations, they show themselves acutely aware of one thing of which Tennenhouse appears to have a rather shaky grasp: you need to know *precisely* what, and where, the lines of communication are, before any sort of change can be effected. (A similar blindness to pragmatics is identified in Greenblatt's work by Michael Bristol, who comments shrewdly that 'New Historicism seems weakest in its attempt to present an account of state power by means of a cultural poetics' (*Shakespeare's America, America's Shakespeare*, p. 206).)

It is a rich irony, then, that, for Tennenhouse, the crucial issue raised by all these plays is forms of power, specifically genealogical entitlement versus juridical role. For Tennenhouse, the fundamental question being addressed by the five plays he discusses is the succession to the Crown of England. This, he claims, had been treated as effectively personal property by Henry VIII when he willed the succession to the descendants of his preferred younger sister Mary, Duchess of Suffolk, rather than to those of his elder one, Margaret, Queen of Scotland. Taking at face value the claim that 'When in her last hours Elizabeth finally named her successor, James VI of Scotland seemed the obvious choice particularly since he had been reared a Protestant' (p. 114) (which is in fact problematic, since other accounts present Elizabeth as past speech but as making a gesture which was interpreted as assent when James was named), Tennenhouse argues that she reinstated the principle of succession according to the rules of primogeniture. Elizabeth I, he declares, 'used her power as a patron to affect the power of the ruling families and thus set economically-based political authority in opposition to that based on blood' (p. 112); and when, dying, she named her successor, she thus 'acted in accordance with a view of the crown as an object of property, which was therefore dispensed according to the will of its owner. By naming James rather than an English claimant, however, she also acted according to the law of primogeniture'

(p. 114). With the settling of this question, Tennehouse declares, history plays fell out of favour because their modes of argument and characteristic techniques no longer addressed a burning question, and so when Shakespeare did return to the form of the chronicle history play, in the late and collaborative *Henry VIII*, it more closely resembles his romances rather than his earlier history plays.

However, it could well be objected that by naming James as her successor (if indeed she did so) Elizabeth was not (as Tennenhouse implies by picking up on his earlier construction of an opposition between inheritance and primogeniture in the will of Henry VIII) restoring a principle of primogeniture. The Suffolk line, which Henry had favoured over the Stuart one, had no surviving members of indisputably legitimate birth. The Suffolk heiress Lady Catherine Grey had married the Earl of Hertford and borne him two sons, but no witness to the marriage could ever be found and neither the Earl nor Lady Catherine knew the name of the priest who had married them, so the legitimacy of the children remained in doubt. James VI's double descent from not one but two marriages of Margaret Tudor, elder daughter of Henry VII, gave him the highest remaining quotient of Tudor blood in the land, thus making him the only likely heir. The choice of Elizabeth's successor was thus surely less a question of principle than of practicalities. The entire situation was problematic – as a modern Tudor historian comments, 'when Richard of York claimed the Crown in the teeth of King Henry VI in 1460 . . . no law had decided whether the Crown was a title or a property, and the issue had to be resolved by wager of battle' (David Loades, *The Politics of Marriage: Henry VIII and His Queens*, p. 3). Given the appalling history of battles of varying decisiveness which followed, any attempt to clarify the issue definitively by a subsequent monarch would have seemed remarkably ill-advised, and as a result in the sixteenth century 'the succession in England was governed not by law but by custom' (Loades, p. 3).

If Elizabeth I did indeed name or assent to the naming of James, then, her decision, made on her deathbed, in a seriously debilitated state, could well be seen less as a fully weighed constitutional statement – especially in view of her notorious refusal to indicate her successor earlier – but more as an action circumscribed by custom, and perhaps by a sense that she was actually doing little more than ratify an assumption which had long been shared by many of her councillors. Indeed the extent to which James' succession was considered the most probable outcome is best illustrated by the uncertainty surrounding the question of whether or not Elizabeth *did* name him: the evidence that she did so is – suitably enough – essentially an anecdote, and one, moreover, told by an interested party, a fact which Tennenhouse passes over in silence.

STOP and THINK

- Are history and literature separate categories? Is it, for instance, possible to study literature from the past without studying the history of the period in which it was written?
- Can history ever be 'true'? Or are all accounts biased in some way or another? If so, could literature tell us as much about the past as history?
- Does genre matter when we are studying literature?

Although Shakespearean critics of many persuasions turn freely to history for evidence to support their case, history and literature remain separate disciplines, taught separately in universities (and while literary critics now frequently cite historians, historians are much less likely to cite literary critics). It is certainly important to be aware of the nature of the texts which provide us with historical evidence – to consider the point of view, the relationship of the narrator to events, any possible bias, and so on – and here the skills of the literary critic might indeed come in useful, but the phenomenon of Holocaust denial should also teach us the dangers of failing to realise that some things are facts. And genre does matter, I think. Comedies and tragedies work in different ways, and a history play works in different ways from a history book, and, when New Historicism treats the one alongside the other, it is in danger of losing sight of that.

Later developments: New Historicism meets gender

After increasingly bitter attacks on New Historicism by feminist and other scholars, most famously in a public argument at the 1986 World Shakespeare Congress in Berlin (see the introduction to Jean

E. Howard and Marion F. O'Connor, eds, *Shakespeare Reproduced*),
New Historicism's traditional inattention to women did at last begin
to be addressed. A notable example of this tendency is Karen
Newman's article 'Renaissance Family Politics and Shakespeare's
The Taming of the Shrew', published in the prestigious journal
English Literary Renaissance. Newman's reading of the play opens,
characteristically enough, with an anecdote:

> Wetherden, Suffolk. Plough Monday, 1604. A drunken tanner,
> Nicholas Rosyer, staggers home from the alehouse. On arriving at his
> door, he is greeted by his wife with 'dronken dogg, pisspot and other
> unseemly names.' When Rosyer tried to come to bed to her, she 'still
> raged against him and badd him out dronken dogg dronken pisspott.'
> She struck him several times, clawed his face and arms, spit at him and
> beat him out of bed. Rosyer retreated, returned to the alehouse, and
> drank until he could hardly stand up. Shortly thereafter, Thomas
> Quarry and others met and 'agreed amongest themselfs that the said
> Thomas Quarry who dwelt at the next howse ... should ... ryde
> abowt the towne upon a cowlestaff [a staff or pole on which two people
> carry a vessel] whereby not onley the woman which had offended
> might be shunned for her misdemeanors towards her husband but
> other women also by her shame might be admonished to offence in
> like sort.' Domestic violence, far from being contained in the family,
> spills out into the neighborhood, and the response of the community
> is an 'old country ceremony used in merriment upon such accidents'.
> (p. 86)

(To explain briefly what is happening here: Quarry and the others
are effectively mounting a 'skimmington ride', a kind of noisy pro-
cession enacted by neighbours to show their disapproval of what
they consider an inappropriate marriage or inappropriate marital
behaviour, in this case the dominance of the wife over the husband
(there is a famous example of a skimmington ride in Thomas
Hardy's *The Mayor of Casterbridge*).) There is much in Newman's
analysis that has become familiar in New Historicist criticism: we
are presented not only with an anecdote, but with one recounted
with a vividness accentuated by the use of the historic present and
of interspersed dialogue. Newman also carries on along traditional
lines, and indeed openly declares her critical affiliations by invoking
Louis Montrose:

> The entire incident figures the social anxiety about gender and power which characterizes Elizabethan culture. Like Simon Forman's dream of wish-fulfillment with Queen Elizabeth, this incident, in Louis Montrose's words, 'epitomizes the indissoluably political and sexual character of the cultural forms in which [such] tensions might be represented and addressed'. (p. 87)

This interestingly suggests the rapidity with which Montrose (whose analysis of *Dream* had first appeared in *Representations* only three years earlier) had become established as an authority.

It is unsurprising, therefore, that *The Taming of the Shrew* should seem, in Newman's analysis, much the same thing as *A Midsummer Night's Dream* does in Montrose's:

> The events of Plough Monday 1604 have an uncanny relation to Shakespeare's *The Taming of the Shrew* which might well be read as a theatrical realization of such a community fantasy, the shaming and subjection of a shrewish wife. (p. 87)

Moreover, as the use of the word 'uncanny' suggests, Newman also follows Montrose in using the discourse of psychoanalysis:

> In his paper 'Hysterical Phantasies and their Relation to Bi-Sexuality' (1908), Sigmund Freud observes that neurotic symptoms, particularly the hysterical symptom, have their origins in the daydreams of adolescence. 'In girls and women,' Freud claims, 'they are invariably of an erotic nature, in men they may be either erotic or ambitious.' A feminist characterological re-reading of Freud might suggest that Kate's ambitious fantasies, which her culture allows her to express only in erotic directions, motivate her shrewishness. (p. 96)

It is clear, though, that Newman is using Freud less as a guide than as a figure whose ideas might themselves be critiqued and interrogated, and this is developed even further when she goes on to suggest that

> Instead of using Freud to analyze Kate's character, a critical move of debatable interpretive power, we might consider the Freudian text instead as a reading of ideological or cultural patterns. The process Freud describes is suggestive for analyzing the workings not of character, but of Shakespeare's text itself. No speech in the play has been more variously interpreted than Kate's final speech of women's submission. In a recent essay on the *Shrew*, John Bean has conveniently

assigned to the two prevailing views the terms 'revisionist' for those who would take Kate's speech as ironic and her subservience as a pretense, a way of living peaceably in patriarchal culture but with an unregenerate spirit, and the 'anti-revisionists' who argue that farce is the play's governing genre and that Kate's response to Petruchio's taming is that of an animal responding to 'the devices of a skilled trainer'. Bean himself argues convincingly for a compromise position which admits the 'background of depersonalizing farce unassimilated from the play's fabliau sources,' but suggests that Kate's taming needs to be seen in terms of romantic comedy, as a spontaneous change of heart such as those of the later romantic comedies. (pp. 96–7)

The position which Newman endorses here constitutes a radical departure from the traditional New Historicist inattention to literary form. In another significant detour from mainstream practice, Newman also invokes the feminist psychoanalytic critic Luce Irigaray:

We know, then, in a way we never know about the other comedies, except perhaps *The Merchant of Venice*, . . . that Kate has continued to speak. She has not, of course, continued to speak her earlier language of revolt and anger. Instead she has adopted another strategy, a strategy which the French psychoanalyst Luce Irigaray calls mimeticism. Irigaray argues that women are cut off from language by the patriarchal order in which they live, by their entry into the Symbolic which the Father represents in a Freudian/Lacanian model. Women's only possible relation to the dominant discourse is mimetic. (p. 98)

And indeed Newman's article generally emphasises the woman's perspective on events. She argues that 'Significantly, Sly is only convinced of his lordly identity when he is told of his "wife" . . . the Induction suggests ironically how in this androcentric culture men depended on women to authorize their sexual and social masculine identities' (p. 88). And she also contends that Kate's 'sexual puns make explicit to the audience not so much her secret preoccupation with sex and marriage, but what is implicit in Petruchio's wooing – that marriage is a sexual exchange in which women are exploited for their use-value as producers' (p. 94).

Most startling of all, however, is Newman's willingness to see the play as potentially subversive, which is a marked departure from New Historicism's traditional interpretative preference of finding that drama works ultimately to produce containment. Early in the essay, she suggests that 'in the Induction, these relationships of power and gender, which in Elizabethan treatises, sermons and homilies, and behavioral handbooks and the like were figured as natural and divinely ordained, are subverted by the metatheatrical foregrounding of such roles and relations as culturally constructed' (p. 88). Later, a similar idea provides the peroration of her argument:

> Representation contains female rebellion. And because the play has no final framing scene, no return to Sly, it could be argued that its artifice is relaxed, that the final scene is experienced naturalistically. The missing frame allows the audience to forget that Petruchio's taming of Kate is presented as a fiction.
>
> Yet even with its missing frame and containment of woman through spectacle, the *Shrew* finally deconstructs its own mimetic effect if we remember the bisexual aspect of the representation of women on the Elizabethan and Jacobean stage. Kate would have been played by a boy whose transvestism, like Thomas Quarry's in the Wetherden skimmington, emblematically embodied the sexual contradictions manifest both in the play and Elizabethan culture. The very indeterminateness of the actor's sexuality, of the woman/man's body, the supplementarity of its titillating homoerotic play . . . foregrounds its artifice and therefore subverts the play's patriarchal master narrative by exposing it as neither natural nor divinely ordained, but culturally constructed. (p. 100)

Newman here pays attention to form, to gender, and to the material circumstances of production; though she does indeed read *The Taming of the Shrew* as a document which casts light on its culture, she has also remembered that it is a play, and a play staged in a theatre which structurally marginalised women. Just like psychoanalysis, then, New Historicism can be seen to have responded to its critics and to have become gradually more attentive to those things it had initially overlooked. However, as I shall show in the next chapter, its interest in the material circumstances of performance and production still remains less than that of cultural materialism, and the approaches are also politically different.

STOP and THINK

- If New Historicism, at least in Newman's work, has finally started to take account of gender, does it present any remaining methodological problems?
- What do you think are the strengths and weaknesses of New Historicism as an approach to Shakespearean drama?

Further reading

Works discussed in this chapter

Fineman, Joel. *Shakespeare's Perjured Eye: The Invention of Poetic Subjectivity in the Sonnets* (Berkeley: University of California Press, 1986).

Greenblatt, Stephen. 'Invisible Bullets: Renaissance Authority and its Subversion, *Henry IV* and *Henry V*', in *New Historicism and Renaissance Drama*, edited by Richard Wilson and Richard Dutton (London: Longman, 1992), pp. 83–108.

Hulme, Peter. 'Stormy Weather: Misreading the Postcolonial *Tempest*', *Early Modern Culture* 1.3. Online: http://eserver.org/emc/1-3/hulme.html.

McAlindon, T. 'Testing the New Historicism: "Invisible Bullets" Reconsidered', *Studies in Philology* 92.4 (Fall 1995), pp. 411–38.

Newman, Karen. 'Renaissance Family Politics and Shakespeare's *The Taming of the Shrew*', *English Literary Renaissance* 16.1 (1986): 86–100.

Stallybrass, Peter and Allon White, *The Politics and Poetics of Transgression* (London: Methuen, 1986).

Tennenhouse, Leonard. 'Strategies of State and Political Plays: *A Midsummer Night's Dream, Henry IV, Henry V, Henry VIII*', in *Political Shakespeare: Essays in Cultural Materialism*, edited by Jonathan Dollimore and Alan Sinfield, 2nd edition (Manchester: Manchester University Press, 1994), pp. 109–28.

Other works which explore issues touched on in this chapter

Armstrong, Philip. *Shakespeare in Psychoanalysis* (London: Routledge, 2001). Excellent account of the uses, history and limitations of psychoanalytic readings of Shakespeare.

Barber, C. L. *Shakespeare's Festive Comedy* (Princeton: Princeton University Press, 1959). Now dated but still classic account of Shakespeare's early comedies as festive and life-enhancing.

Boose, Lynda E. 'The Family in Shakespeare Studies; or – Studies in the Family of Shakespeareans; or – The Politics of Politics', *Renaissance*

Quarterly 40 (1986): 707–41. A very interesting account of the genesis of New Historicism and a consideration of what its origins might mean for it.

Cohen, Walter. 'Political Criticism of Shakespeare', in *Shakespeare Reproduced: The Text in History and Ideology*, edited by Jean E. Howard and Marion F. O'Connor (London: Routledge, 1987), pp. 18–46. A consideration of the differences between UK-based and US-based political criticism of Shakespeare.

Greenblatt, Stephen. 'Psychoanalysis and Renaissance culture', in *Learning to Curse* (London: Routledge, 1990). The standard account of the historicist case against psychoanalysis.

Howard, Jean E. 'The New Historicism in Renaissance Studies', in *New Historicism and Renaissance Drama*, edited by Richard Wilson and Richard Dutton (London: Longman, 1992), pp. 9–32. Survey of the field.

Howard, Jean E. and Marion O'Connor, eds, *Shakespeare Reproduced* (London: Merhuen, 1987). The introduction offers insight into some of the tensions affecting the Shakespeare community in the years after the politicising of Shakespeare criticism.

Laroque, François. *Shakespeare's Festive World: Elizabethan Seasonal Entertainment and the Professional Stage*, translated by Janet Lloyd (Cambridge: Cambridge University Press, 1991). Recovers valuable information about the seasonal patterns and expectations of the early modern world.

Myers, D. G. 'The New Historicism in Literary Study', *Academic Questions* 2 (Winter 1988–89): 27–36. An overview of the rise of New Historicism.

Wilson, Richard. *Will Power: Essays on Shakespearean Authority* (Hemel Hempstead: Harvester Wheatsheaf, 1993). Sharp, elegant, and provocative historicised accounts of a range of Shakespearean plays.

Wilson, Richard and Richard Dutton, eds, *New Historicism and Renaissance Drama* (London: Longman, 1992). A valuable collection of essays illustrating New Historicist approaches to Renaissance plays.

4

Cultural Materialism

The issue of appropriation, which I introduced in Chapter 1 – of whether Shakespeare's texts belong to their own historical moment or can be appropriated for use in ours – becomes particularly acute in relation to Cultural Materialism. This approach first leapt to prominence with the publication of *Political Shakespeare* in 1985, because, although I have already discussed some essays from that volume under the rubric of New Historicism, the volume's editors, Jonathan Dollimore and Alan Sinfield, openly identified its dominant approach as Cultural Materialist. *Political Shakespeare* has so far sold over 16,000 copies, and Cultural Materialism is now well established as the dominant approach in UK universities. Sean McEvoy's *Shakespeare: The Basics*, for instance, declares at the outset that

> In this book I follow one type of criticism, which happens to be the one you are most likely to meet at university. It is probably the most influential, too. This approach always sets the plays firmly in the context of the time in which they were written *and* in the time in which they are read. It is also influenced by certain feminist ideas. Different versions of the approach are known as *new historicism* and *cultural materialism*. (p. 7)

Although McEvoy seems here almost to elide them, it is important to reiterate that there are fundamental differences between the two approaches. Above all, the major difference is that New Historicism, as I stressed in the last chapter, tends to find containment; Cultural Materialism tends to find subversion. New Historicism therefore presents itself as a way to chart and understand Shakespearean plays with regard to the political situation in the time when they were written; Cultural Materialism presents itself as a way of using Shakespeare's plays to change the current political situation.

A consequence of this, and a major difference between the two approaches, is that although both stress the necessity of contextualisation, New Historicism tends to read Renaissance plays largely in the light of other Renaissance documents, whereas Cultural Materialism is much more likely to adduce *contemporary* contexts (the first wave of Cultural Materialists, for instance, often referred to the political doctrine of Thatcherism and its consequences, particularly the year-long miners' strike of 1984). In the introduction to his useful collection *Materialist Shakespeare* (1995), Ivo Kamps explains the reason for this difference:

> Historian Hayden White observes that although both new historicism and cultural materialism aim to understand the literary text in its socio-cultural field, new historicist practice has a distinctly synchronic [across time] emphasis, whereas Marxist materialism is also concerned with the '"diachronic [through time]" aspects of the relationship between literature and the "cultural system"' ... New Historicism, White argues apropos of Louis Montrose, reorients the focus of historical criticism along 'the axis of intertextuality' ... In practice this means that new historicism links a number of roughly contemporaneous 'texts' ('dreams, popular or aristocratic festivals, denunciations of witchcraft, sexual treatises, diaries and autobiographies, descriptions of clothing, reports of disease, birth and death records, accounts of insanity') into 'the *synchronic* text of a cultural system'. (p. 6)

Finally, another difference which has been proposed between the two camps is that whereas 'the affective intensity of the language in which critics debate the Shakespearean text in Britain is an index of the degree to which they are connected (and cathected [libidinally or emotionally charged]) psychologically and existentially to the culture which is their polemical object', American critics, 'ever since Eliot and the New Critics established the principle of aesthetic distance ... as a *sine qua non* of literary study, ... have tended to repress the political nature of our activity as critics ... the most effective means by which this depoliticization was achieved in American criticism was by the repression of an affective response that might provide the energy for a politically engaged criticism' (Don E. Wayne, 'Power, Politics, and the Shakespearean Text', p. 52). Put simply, this means that the protocols of British academic life allow critics of Shakespeare both to care about the texts and the uses to which they can be put and to show this openly, without being accused of undue subjectivity or of a stifling closeness to the text, whereas the American tradition is to preserve a greater emotional distance.

Political Shakespeare: a landmark text

The foreword to the first edition of *Political Shakespeare* began as follows:

> The break-up of consensus in British political life during the 1970s was accompanied by the break-up of traditional assumptions about the values and goals of literary criticism. Initially at specialised conferences and in committed journals, but increasingly in the main stream of intellectual life, literary texts were related to the new and challenging discourses of Marxism, feminism, structuralism, psychoanalysis and poststructuralism. It is widely admitted that all this has brought a new rigour and excitement to literary discussions. At the same time, it has raised profound questions about the status of literary texts, both as linguistic entities and as ideological forces in our society.
>
> Some approaches offer a significant alternative to traditional practice; others are little more than realignments of familiar positions. But our belief is that a combination of historical context, theoretical method, political commitment and textual analysis offers the strongest challenge and has already contributed substantial work. Historical context undermines the transcendent significance traditionally accorded to the literary text and allows us to recover its histories; theoretical method detaches the text from immanent criticism which seeks only to reproduce it in its own terms; socialist and feminist commitment confronts the conservative categories in which most criticism has hitherto been conducted; textual analysis locates the critique of traditional approaches where it cannot be ignored. We call this 'cultural materialism'. (p. vii)

This was a very surprising introduction for its time. The opening sentence refers to politics, which are normally considered a concern divorced from literature and the 'ivory tower' of academe, as though they were a fundamental condition of literary response. It also situates that response within both a time and a place, implying that human nature is not stable and transhistorical but conditioned and constructed by specific places and circumstances.

After this initial introduction, the prefatory material to the volume goes on to explain further what Cultural Materialism means:

> 'Materialism' is opposed to 'idealism': it insists that culture does not (cannot) transcend the material forces and relations of production. Culture is not simply a reflection of the economic and political system, but nor can it be independent of it. Cultural materialism therefore studies the implication of literary texts in history. A play by Shakespeare is related to the contexts of its production – to the economic and political system of Elizabethan and Jacobean England and to the particular institutions of cultural production (the court, patronage, theatre, education, the church). Moreover, the relevant history is not just that of four hundred years ago, for culture is made continuously and Shakespeare's text is reconstructed, reappraised, reassigned all the time through diverse institutions in specific contexts. What the plays signify, how they signify, depends on the cultural field in which they are situated. That is why this book discusses also the institutions through which Shakespeare is reproduced and through which interventions may be made in the present.
>
> Finally, cultural materialism does not pretend to political neutrality. It knows that no cultural practice is ever without political significance – not the production of *King Lear* at the Globe, or at the Barbican [theatre in London], or as a text in a school, popular or learned edition, or in literary criticism, or in the present volume. Cultural materialism does not, like much established literary criticism, attempt to mystify its perspective as the natural, obvious or right interpretation of an allegedly given textual fact. On the contrary, it registers its commitment to the transformation of a social order which exploits people on grounds of race, gender and class. (p. viii)

Cultural Materialism undoubtedly has many strengths. In the first place, it offers a valuable understanding of the processes by which Shakespeare has acquired his present iconic status. It has also done much to demystify and reveal the ideological premises of both its own and earlier readings of Shakespeare, taking issue particularly with E. M. W. Tillyard's view that Shakespeare was a natural conservative:

> Tillyard was concerned to expound an idea of cosmic order 'so taken for granted, so much part of the collective mind of the people, that it is hardly mentioned except in explicitly didactic passages'.

> The objection to this is not that Tillyard was mistaken in identify-
> ing a metaphysic of order in the period, nor even that it had ceased to
> exist by the turn of the century (two criticisms subsequently directed
> at him). The error, from a materialist perspective, is falsely to unify
> history and social process in the name of 'the collective mind of the
> people'. (p. 5)

This response does not simply take issue with Tillyard's conclu-
sions; it also unpacks the assumptions which inform them. This
uncovering of the foundations of a particular critical approach is a
very effective way of demystifying any claims it may have to the
status of fact. Indeed demystification is a key concept for Cultural
Materialism. Cultural Materialist criticism is usually written in
clear, accessible prose; it opposes any attempt to pass off things
which are the products of culture as inherent or natural; and it
always seeks to uncover the background and origins of things. To
that extent, my own approach in this volume, in always trying to elu-
cidate the factors which conditioned particular critical approaches,
is essentially a product of Cultural Materialism.

However, cultural materialism also has features which at least
some academics find unpalatable. In particular, its contextualising
approach requires a decentralising both of Shakespeare and of many
of his characters which many students find to be counter-intuitive.
Students who respond enthusiastically to the poetry of Shakespeare
may perhaps bridle when it is first put to them that they should look
at the politics of his works and of their reception; students who feel
that Shakespeare 'speaks to' them may not want to be told that his
voice can be heard properly only when it is put in the context of his
own culture.

Another point to make about cultural materialism is that, like
other theories we have looked at, it too clearly finds certain plays
particularly amenable to its suppositions – two of the essays in *Political Shakespeare* were on *Measure for Measure*, and two more on
Henry IV and *Henry V* – but tends to have little to say about others.
Cultural materialists are particularly silent on the subject of the
romances, though *The Tempest* does come in for discussion; indeed
Walter Cohen declares that 'the British critics find everything about
Shakespeare potentially progressive except the romances and especially *The Tempest*, whose connection with the origins of empire

seems to be more than they can stomach' ('Political Criticism of Shakespeare', p. 37).

STOP and THINK

- Is there a danger that, if we adopt a Cultural Materialist approach, we will effectively end up studying history rather than literature? If so, does it matter? And can you think of any particular factor or factors which might make plays such as *The Winter's Tale* or *Pericles* more resistant to a cultural materialist analysis than histories or problem plays?

The romances are in many ways the most dream-like of Shakespeare's plays, and sometimes seem to share something of the peculiar logic of dreams. One would not be surprised, then, if they were to prove more amenable to psychoanalysis than to Cultural Materialist analysis. Another factor may be that the romances do not really represent the materiality of their own culture to any great degree (with the partial exception of *The Tempest*); whereas, as we shall see, a play such as *Measure for Measure* offers us a realistic-seeming picture of the seamier side of Shakespeare's London, *The Winter's Tale* gives us instead the Delphic oracle and a bear, *Pericles* stages a series of phantasmagoric journeys in the classical Mediterranean, and *Cymbeline* offers a heady mixture of fairy-tale motifs with a Roman invasion story. If we pay too great an attention to contextual matters, of course, we might find, as with New Historicism, that we end up subordinating the study of things like the generic, formal and linguistic features of Shakespeare's plays and poems to the study of the ways in which they were bound to their own culture and the ways in which they may be used to influence ours. But I think we can certainly see, in the work of the critics I am about to discuss, some persuasive and fruitful arguments for the importance of cultural contexts.

Dollimore and Sinfield: literature and power

Both the editors of *Political Shakespeare* were also the authors of essays in the collection. Jonathan Dollimore contributed a piece on

'Transgression and Surveillance in *Measure for Measure*'. The opening sentences of this read:

> In the Vienna of *Measure for Measure* unrestrained sexuality is ostensibly subverting social order; anarchy threatens to engulf the State unless sexuality is subjected to renewed and severe regulation. Such at least is the claim of those in power. Surprisingly critics have generally taken them at their word even while dissociating themselves from the punitive zeal of Angelo. ('Transgression and Surveillance in *Measure for Measure*', in *Political Shakespeare*, p. 72)

Dollimore suggests here that he is going to offer an entirely new reading, one which will somehow cut through the mystifications which have managed to ensnare other critics. He then seems to go on to hint at what kind of reading this might be:

> But consider now a very different view of the problem. With the considerable attention recently devoted to Bakhtin and his truly important analysis of the subversive carnivalesque, the time is right for a radical reading of *Measure for Measure*, one which insists on the oppressiveness of the Viennese State and which interprets low-life transgression as *positively* anarchic, ludic, carnivalesque – a subversion from below of a repressive official ideology of order. What follows aims (if it is not too late) to forestall such a reading as scarcely less inappropriate than that which privileged 'true' authority over anarchic desire. Indeed, such a reading, if executed within the parameters of some recent appropriations of Bakhtin, would simply remain within the same problematic, only reversing the polarities of the binary opposition which structures it (order/chaos). I offer a different reading of the play, one which, perhaps paradoxically, seeks to identify its absent characters and the history which it contains yet does not represent. (p. 73)

During the course of this passage, Dollimore performs a remarkable volte-face, since his initial gesturing towards Bakhtin proves to be merely a prelude to what he is *not* going to do. Instead he is, rather like psychoanalysts, going to focus on what is *not* there.

The element which is, in Dollimore's view, conspicuously absent from the play turns out, eventually, to be direct representation of the prostitutes, but this will not become apparent until the very end of his essay. Instead, what he concentrates on is the means by which the citizens of Vienna are policed:

> Whatever subversive identity the sexual offenders in this play possess
> is a construction put upon them by the authority which wants to con-
> trol them; moreover control is exercised through that construction.
> Diverse and only loosely associated sexual offenders are brought into
> renewed surveillance by the State; identified in law as a category
> of offender (the lecherous, the iniquitous) they are thereby demonised
> as a threat to law. Like many apparent threats to authority this one in
> fact legitimates it: control of the threat becomes the rationale of
> authoritarian reaction in a time of apparent crisis. Prostitution and
> lechery are identified as the causes of crisis yet we learn increasingly
> of a corruption more political than sexual (see especially v.i.316ff).
> Arguably then the play discloses corruption to be an effect less of
> desire than authority itself. It also shows how corruption is down-
> wardly identified – that is, focused and placed with reference to low-
> life 'licence'; in effect, and especially in the figure of Angelo,
> corruption is displaced from authority to desire and by implication
> from the rulers to the ruled. (p. 73)

Here we have something like the New Historicist idea that power
covertly licenses limited subversion in order to bolster its own position. This, Dollimore says, is typical of the way authority operates
in the early modern period:

> The same process of displacement occurs throughout discourses of
> power in the period . . . one of the many royal proclamations attempt-
> ing to bring vagabonds under martial law asserts that 'there can grow
> no account of disturbance of our peace and quiet but from such refuse
> and vagabond people' . . . and this despite the fact that the proclama-
> tion immediately preceeding this one (just six days before) announced
> the abortive Essex rebellion. (p. 80)

This is certainly a neat point, but more traditional scholars might
well feel that it is one marred by an error which it is surprising to
find in an academic book: 'preceeding' for 'preceding'. Although
this is presumably the result of poor proof reading rather than an
inability to spell, it is nevertheless symptomatic of what Cultural
Materialism's detractors have alleged against it, which is that it is
inattentive to detail, and prone both to inaccuracy and to suborning
evidence for its own purposes. One might well, for instance, com-
plain that Dollimore's assertion that 'it is Isabella's fate to be
coerced back into her socially and sexually subordinate position – at
first illicitly by Angelo, then legitimately by the Duke who "takes"

her in marriage' (Dollimore, p. 83) entirely ignores the fact that the ending of the play is actually left open. Isabella makes no reply to the Duke's proposal of marriage, and although it is perfectly true that many productions are likely to suggest her assent by having her take his proferred hand, it is equally true that by no means all have done so.

Even more contentious is Dollimore's account of the episode in II.i of *Measure for Measure* in which Escalus, Angelo and another, unnamed Justice are called upon to adjudicate in a complex dispute concerning Elbow, a constable, and two men whom the constable is apparently accusing of a crime, the pimp Pompey Bum and the foolish young gentleman Master Froth. It proves very difficult to get to the bottom of the case, not least because Elbow begins by introducing Pompey and Froth as 'benefactors' when he really means 'malefactors' (II.i.49). Indeed when matters are still not much clearer after nearly a hundred lines of dialogue, Angelo loses patience altogether and says to Escalus,

> This will last out a night in Russia
> When nights are longest there. I'll take my leave,
> And leave you to the hearing of the cause,
> Hoping you'll find good cause to whip them all.

> (II.i.128–31)

So Angelo departs. Escalus, however, not only stays until the end of the proceedings but has a private word with all parties afterwards, advising Master Froth to stay away from tapsters and Pompey to make sure that he does not get into trouble again. It is in this context that he then has the conversation with Elbow to which Dollimore refers:

> ESCALUS   Come hither to me, Master Elbow. Come hither, master
> constable. How long have you been in this place of constable?
> ELBOW   Seven year and a half, sir.
> ESCALUS   I thought, by your readiness in the office, you had contin-
> ued in it some time. You say, seven years together?
> ELBOW   And a half, sir.
> ESCALUS   Alas, it hath been great pains to you; they do you wrong to
> put you so often upon't. Are there not men in your ward sufficient
> to serve it?

ELBOW   Faith, sir, few of any wit in such matters. As they are chosen,
    they are glad to choose me for them. I do it for some piece of money,
    and go through with all.
ESCALUS   Look you bring me in the names of some six or seven, the
    most sufficient of your parish.
ELBOW   To your worship's house, sir?
ESCALUS   To my house. Fare you well.

(II.i.245–60)

Finally, Escalus ends his morning by inviting the other judge
present to come home to dinner with him.

What has happened here? For Dollimore, that question is easy
to answer:

> In II.i. we glimpse briefly the State's difficulties in ensuring the levels
> of policing which the rulers think is required. Escalus discreetly
> inquires of Elbow whether there are any more officers in his locality
> more competent than he. Elbow replies that even those others who have
> been chosen happily delegate their responsibility to him. (pp. 80–1)

Escalus, this seems to imply, is a rather sinister figure whose
primary motivation is ensuring what he takes to be good policing,
and the phrase 'the levels of policing which the rulers think is
required' further suggests that what he is aiming to secure is in fact
an excessive level of surveillance and control. But policing does have
to happen, and it would indeed be possible to suggest that Escalus,
whose name is derived from 'scale' and so connotes an idea of
balance, is in fact administering it with a notably light hand. He is
not only obviously contrasted with the supercilious Angelo but is
also a kindly, engaged figure who goes well beyond the call of duty
in attempting not only to deal with this incident but to forestall
future ones which, as he well knows, can, under the new regime,
only end in serious trouble. It is certainly true that Escalus's notion
of justice is influenced by material considerations, as we clearly see
in his exchange with Froth:

ESCALUS   Where were you born, friend?
FROTH   Here in Vienna, sir.
ESCALUS   Are you of forescore pounds a year?
FROTH   Yes, an't please you, sir.

(II.i.183–6)

There is, clearly, one law for the rich and another for the poor. However, Escalus also takes the trouble to warn the lower-class Pompey that the judicial system is changing and that he needs to take care. Equally, it is of course true that Pompey has no possible livelihood except his present occupation of pimp, and that Escalus's warning to him does not address that fundamental inequality. Escalus is a man dispensing justice according to what he sees as his own duty, not one challenging the deep-seated and widespread injustices which we might now feel make a mockery from the outset of all the judicial procedures in the play.

We should not, however, assume that Shakespeare would have shared those views. The opening sentence of the introduction to my Penguin copy of *Measure for Measure*, edited by J. M. Nosworthy, is 'No play of Shakespeare's more amply vindicates the claim that "he was not of an age but for all time" than does *Measure for Measure*' (p. 7). This seems to me a woefully misleading and restricting view of the play. Perhaps Shakespeare will indeed last, if not for the grandiose 'all time', then at least for the foreseeable future, but that should not blind us to the fact that he was very firmly the product of 'an age', specifically one in which King James VI and I was proposing tightened controls of brothels very similar to those which Shakespeare's Angelo is so eager to enforce – but also one which had very different concepts of social justice from our own. However much I may differ from Dollimore's assessment of Escalus, I am at least grateful to Cultural Materialism for, I hope, making such sentences as Nosworthy's impossible to write in the future, and for making me fully aware of their limitations.

And it is of course in the light of such statements as this that, for Cultural Materialism, arguments about the finer nuances of the text do not ultimately matter, because what is important is the big picture, and the political project which it serves. Dollimore, for instance, remarks on

> the question of the Duke's choice of *religious* disguise. As I've argued elsewhere, there was considerable debate at this time over the 'Machiavellian' proposition that religion was a form of ideological control which worked in terms of internalised submission. Even as he opposes it, Richard Hooker cogently summarises this view; it represents religion as 'a mere politic devise' and whereas State law has 'power

over our outward actions only' religion works upon men's 'inward cogitations . . . the privy intents and motions of their heart'. Armed with this knowledge 'politic devisers' are 'able to create God in man by art'.

The Duke, disguised as a friar, tries to reinstate this kind of subjection. (p. 81)

Here Machiavelli is pressed into service just as he was for Greenblatt, with only a pair of inverted commas between him and the fact that it is difficult to locate this precise formulation anywhere in his text, and the Elizabethan theologian Richard Hooker can be adduced to further an argument which was in fact the direct contrary of his own. Along similar lines, Dollimore writes that 'What [Michel] Foucault has said of sexuality in the nineteenth and twentieth centuries seems appropriate also to sexuality as a sub-category of sin in earlier periods: it *appears* to be that which power is afraid of but in actuality is that which power works through' (p. 85). The fact of some fairly significant differences between the nineteenth and twentieth centuries and the early modern period can be overlooked here because it is so much less material than the fact that Shakespeare can be used to score a direct political hit against the workings of power.

Eventually, Dollimore does reveal the absent focus at which he had hinted in the beginning of the essay:

In pursuing the authority–subversion question, this chapter has tried to exemplify two complementary modes of materialist criticism. Both are concerned to recover the text's history. The one looks directly for history in the text including the historical conditions of its production which, even if not addressed directly by the text can nevertheless still be said to be within it, informing it. Yet there is a limit to which the text can be said to incorporate those aspects of its historical moment of which it never speaks. At that limit, rather than constructing this history as the text's unconscious, we might instead address it directly. Then at any rate we have to recognise the obvious: the prostitutes, the most exploited group in the society which the play represents, are absent from it. Virtually everything that happens presupposes them yet they have no voice, no presence. And those who speak for them do so as exploitatively as those who want to eliminate them. Looking for evidence of resistance we find rather further evidence of exploitation. (pp. 85–6)

I said earlier that whereas New Historicism typically found containment in Renaissance texts, Cultural Materialism typically found
subversion. Dollimore here might well appear to prove me wrong,
especially since he has earlier written that 'By means of the Duke's
personal intervention and integrity, authoritarian reaction is put
into abeyance but not discredited: the corrupt deputy is unmasked
but no law is repealed and the mercy exercised remains the prerogative of the same ruler who initiated reaction' (p. 83). For Cultural
Materialists, however, what matters is not so much the effect which
texts produced in their own period but the effects to which they can
be made to contribute now – and those effects can indeed be subversive. This will be even clearer in a later essay in *Political Shakespeare*, by Dollimore's co-editor Alan Sinfield.

Alan Sinfield's incisive essay in *Political Shakespeare* is called
'Give an account of Shakespeare and Education, showing why
you think they are effective and what you have appreciated about
them. Support your comments with precise references'. It
addressed the question of how Shakespeare was taught and examined in schools in England and Wales, something to which univer-
sity-level specialists had generally paid little previous attention. It
opened with the provocative declaration that 'Any social order has
to include the conditions for its own continuance, and capitalism
and patriarchy do this partly through the education system' (p. 158).
This is not only a bold statement but one which might, at first
glance, seem counter-intuitive: surely, we might think, education is
a liberalising force, which creates opportunities for those who
would otherwise lack them? For Sinfield, however, it is no such
thing. In the first place, he argues that pupils from less 'cultured'
backgrounds are discriminated against in the study of literature,
and that it functions in effect as a tool to legitimise and perpetuate
the views of the middle classes. In the second, he contends that
'While Literature is made to operate as a mode of exclusion in
respect of class, it disadvantages girls by including them' (p. 160)
because humanities students tend to enter less well-paid jobs and
therefore 'girls are condemned to a relatively low position in the
job market' (p. 161).

It might well seem at this point that the study of literature is in
fact thoroughly pernicious, and that to undertake it is to be entirely

co-opted into the maintenance of an unjust social system. Sinfield insists, however, that this need not be so: 'In education Shakespeare has been made to speak mainly for the right; that is the tendency which this book seeks to alter' (p. 159). Later, he expands on this:

> Shakespeare does not have to work in a conservative manner. His plays do not have to signify in the ways they have customarily been made to . . . It is partly a matter of reading them differently – drawing attention to their historical insertion, their political implications, and the activity of criticism in reproducing them . . . And it is also a matter of changing the way Shakespeare signifies in society: he does not have to be a crucial stage in the justification of elitism in education and culture. He has been appropriated for certain practices and attitudes, and can be reappropriated for others. (p. 161)

And the final conclusion of the essay is that

> Socialists may challenge these appropriations of Shakespeare. The plays may be taught so as to foreground their historical construction in Renaissance England and in the institutions of criticism, dismantling the metaphysical concepts in which they seem at present to be entangled, and especially the contruction of gender and sexuality. Teaching Shakespeare's plays and writing books about them is unlikely to bring down capitalism, but it is a point for intervention. (p. 178)

It is, at this point, worth pointing out that all the exam questions which Sinfield discusses and critiques in this chapter were set in 1983; that the type of question set now, nearly twenty years later, is very different; and that *Political Shakespeare* and other books like it were a motivating force in bringing about that change. To that extent, Sinfield is certainly right to point out that change is possible, and it is worth reiterating that this belief that criticism is a genuine social force is both the keynote of Cultural Materialism and the thing which primarily sets it apart from New Historicism. As Richard Wilson observes in his critique of New Historicism, 'When the Berliners razed the wall, when the Romanians stormed the TV studio, when the Czechs elected a playwright President, people learned that history is not necessarily a Kafkaesque prison' (*New Historicism and Renaissance Drama*, p. 16).

What, then, was the exact nature of these exam questions which Sinfield finds so efficacious in the perpetuation of the existing social order? Sinfield's first objection is that 'Almost invariably it is assumed that the plays reveal universal "human" values and qualities and that they are self-contained and coherent entities; and the activity of criticism in producing these assumptions is effaced' (p. 162). This takes us back to Cultural Materialism's standard charge of mystification: the cultural, Sinfield alleges, is being passed off as natural and hence unalterable. Secondly,

> In the examination questions almost no reference is made to the diverse forms which the play has taken and may take – to scholarly discussions about provenance, to the conditions under which it has been transmitted, to the different forms it takes today, from school editions to stage, film and TV productions. Even the occasional question about staging is liable to involve the assumption that there is a true reading behind the diverse possibilities (pp. 162–3)

This too could be seen as a form of mystification: the play is assumed to have a transcendent essence which exists independently of the material circumstances and conditions of its production and reproduction, and it is presumably partly because of this that the view 'That the text is to be regarded as coherent, either in terms of action or of dramatic effect, is frequently insisted upon' in the exam questions (p. 163).

The last and perhaps the most surprising of Sinfield's charges, however, concerns not the play at all but the students who take the exam:

> The examination papers construct Shakespeare and the candidate in terms of individuated subjectivity through their stress upon Shakespeare's free-standing genius, their emphasis on characterisation, and their demand for the candidate's personal response. (p. 164)

To this many teachers of literature must plead guilty, for many of us do indeed hunt the student's personal response as the most desirable of all quarries. Sinfield's objection to this process is twofold. In the first place, it is a central tenet of Marxist thought that there is no such thing as an entirely independent subjectivity, and that the belief in it is a result of false consciousness: 'The twin manoeuvres of bourgeois ideology construct two dichotomies: universal versus historical and individual versus social. In each case the first term is privileged, and so meaning is sucked into the universal/individual polarity, draining it away from the historical and the social – which is where meaning is made by people together in determinate conditions, and where it might be contested' (p. 165). Secondly, Sinfield points out that the response is not really personal at all, but directly produced by teachers' insistence on the value and appropriateness of certain sorts of comments and interpretative strategies – and it is certainly true that, however much I may encourage students to tell me what *they* think, I do not want them to reply that they think *Hamlet* is really about skiing, or about the problems suffered by long-distance lorry drivers. The personal, in short, is acceptable only when it accords with existing ideas. At its worst, then, the giving of a 'personal response' could perhaps be seen as nothing more than a mystification of the parrot-fashion repetition of teachers' own views.

STOP and THINK

- Why are *you* studying literature? Do you think it is that doing so makes you likely to earn less than graduates in other disciplines? If you think that's probably true, does it matter? And do you believe that studying literature has, or can have, a political impact?

Personally, I studied English at university because it excited and engaged me more than any other subject, and it continues to do so. I'm not sure I did realise that studying an arts subject might well limit my earning power – I was too young and naive to think about such things – but I don't think I would have cared if I had. Nor did I, in those days, ever imagine that the study of literature could have a political impact. I do believe now that it can, though. I believe Margaret Thatcher was wrong to say that there is no such thing as society; and I think that each individual person who leaves our university English course – and I hope and expect that the same is true of all other university English courses – has at the very least been encouraged to think criticially and independently, and to understand that texts do not have one single meaning. If that does not lay the foundations for an intelligent and responsible political nation, maybe nothing will. Certainly for the next theorist I will consider, the politics of meaning is crucial.

Terence Hawkes and the politics of meaning

My third example is Terence Hawkes. Hawkes has been one of the most consistently provocative and indefatigable of the Cultural Materialists. However, though he has been influential, this seems often to have been almost against his will. Whereas Alan Sinfield writes clearly, openly states his theoretical position, and seems genuinely to want to inform and educate his reader, Hawkes is typically mischievous and teasing. He is notorious for his interventions on the global electronic discussion list SHAKSPER, where he usually posts deeply sarcastic messages purporting to state the exact opposite of what he actually believes in, a tactic which often bamboozles innocents who fail utterly to detect his irony. A typical exchange was in January 2000, and concerned Susan Cooper's children's book *King of Shadows*, which focused on a boy player in Shakespeare's company. After some enthusiastic praise of the book was posted on SHAKSPER, Hawkes wrote, quoting the original post, "King of Shadows is clearly a masterpiece. "One of the lovely things to watch is the way Nat moved from being awed by Shakespeare to becoming his friend." Am I alone in thinking that a Golden Quill cannot be long delayed?' The unfortunate poster of the original message, totally unaware that she was being sent up, only won herself further scorn when she replied 'Dear Terence Hawkes: I'm so glad you enjoyed the book'.

Hawkes's 1992 collection of essays *Meaning by Shakespeare* gives hardly any more interpretative guidance to the reader. The titles of the seven chapters are 'By', 'Or', 'Shakespeare and the General Strike', 'Take me to your Leda', 'Slow, slow, quick quick, slow', 'Lear's maps', and 'Bardbiz'. Only one of these flags up emphasis on any particular play, and even when we start reading the essays their focus is not always immediately apparent. The essay on 'Shakespeare and the General Strike' opens with a quotation from Rudyard Kipling's 'The Glory of the Garden':

Our England is a garden full of stately views,
Of borders, beds and shrubberies and lawns and avenues,
With statues on the terraces and peacocks strutting by;
But the Glory of the Garden lies in more than meets the eye.

(p. 42)

There is no indication, either at the beginning or anywhere else in the essay, of what the relevance of this quotation might be. By the end it will probably be clear to most readers that what Kipling's poem represents is a version of the kind of complacent, pious, Establishment England that Hawkes's essay is designed to expose and criticise. I can, though, imagine readers who would remain mystified by the excerpt from the poem, and even those who see its relevance might benefit from an explicit engagement with what kinds of thing Kipling might have meant by 'The Glory of the Garden' – especially since such an engagement would, as it turns out, have been germane to the theme of Hawkes's argument.

Matters do not become very much clearer when we move on to the main body of the essay. It begins with the subheading 'Criticism on strike', and goes on:

There is a particular statue in the centre of the city of Cardiff whose inscription has always seemed to me to offer a text suitable for the most stringent critical analysis. Its six words are pithy and pointed. 'John Cory', it says, 'Coal-Owner and Philanthropist'. (p. 42)

Hawkes's point is that this is effectively oxymoronic, since property is theft and thus no coal-owner could be a philanthropist, and he goes on to explain that, like the statue, he too proposes to bring together two ostensibly oxymoronic terms, because he believes that Art and Politics are not separate:

Of course, the trap of essentialism lies in wait for the unwary critic here. 'Art', it can be said, has no necessary commitment to binding, bonding, affirmation. Any work can be *read* in an oppositional mode, or to a subversive purpose. Equally, a 'strike' often generates bonding amongst its participants: it can and does develop its own kind of affil-iative unity. These are important considerations. However, my focus here is on ways in which the world is experienced and understood as meaningful in terms of the 'common sense which all cultures habit-ually and uncritically endorse as the basis of existence'. And Art – particularly the art of Shakespeare – is certainly understood by our society on that 'common-sense' level as wholly capable of unsullied transcendence over the everyday sphere of profit margins, market forces, redundancies and wage settlements. Strikes, on the same level, are deemed to be quintessentially of that world and in it. The separation seems absolute. But the central concern of this essay is not just to confirm that this is the way things appear to be. It also – and in so doing – implies a challenge to and a questioning of that arrangement. Perhaps what it calls for is a strike against common sense. (p. 43)

What I find surprising about this is the sweepingness of the statements to which it is prepared to commit. It is a bold and almost certainly unverifiable assertion, for instance, to declare that 'all cultures' 'habitually and uncritically endorse [common sense] as the basis of existence', and I am not even sure I know what it means. Equally difficult to verify would be the bald assertions about what 'society' thinks about Shakespeare and strikes. Perhaps more to the point, there is no attempt to verify them, or to provide substantiating evidence of any sort.

After this preamble, Hawkes does finally declare what his main subject of interest in the essay will be: *Coriolanus*. However, no sooner has the play itself seemed briefly to come into focus than it immediately retreats into the background again:

Some scholars argue that it possibly bears some imprint of the the riots of 1607–8 in the Midlands. The fundamental opposition it constructs between patricians and plebeians, and the involvement in that of an arrogant and charismatic military hero whose final march to sack Rome is stayed only by the pleas of his mother, suggests links with various aspects of post-Renaissance class conflict.

Certainly, by the nineteenth and early twentieth centuries the play regularly seems to chafe against the boundaries of that 'Art' category to which common sense so earnestly wants to consign it. (p. 44)

Whatever meanings *Coriolanus* may have had for its original audience are not Hawkes's concern (though he does provide a footnote reference for anyone wishing to follow up the question of its possible relation to the riots of 1607/8); he is interested in what it has come to mean, or been made to mean, since, so that he passes on almost immediately to the reference to the play in Charlotte Brontë's *Shirley*, and subsequently to uses of it in the early twentieth century, and particularly the production of the play at Stratford-upon-Avon in 1926, the year of the General Strike.

When Hawkes turns to the General Strike, his previous reticence and concentration on generalities disappears, and he gives a clear and detailed account of the political situation in 1926, and especially of the growth of fascism in Britain. He makes a number of interesting points about the conjunction of *Coriolanus* and this particular historical moment, and he has uncovered some very telling evidence about the presence of at least one actual fascist among the governors of the Shakespeare Theatre. Again, though, the emphasis is solely on what *Coriolanus* might have meant in the twentieth century. Particularly striking is Hawkes's comment on Coriolanus' decision to 'banish' his fellow Romans:

> Absolute, even heroic, self-commitment in the face of a contemptible world in this manner, assertion of the individual solitary will as the ultimate and only valid instrument of power and morality, has of course been a feature of a range of political stances in Europe since the early modern period and is probably specifically linked with the thinking of Nietzsche. (pp. 52–3)

To say in the same breath that a phenomenon dates from the early modern period and that it is linked with Nietzsche (who was born in 1844 and died in 1900) seems very odd indeed. However, since in the next paragraph we find Coriolanus being compared to Hitler (p. 53), transhistoricism is obviously the order of the day.

The fact that *Coriolanus* was susceptible to right-wing readings and appropriations, however, does not mean that those are the only possible meanings which can be made of it. Indeed, in the standard manoeuvre of Cultural Materialism, Hawkes explicitly exonerates the play itself from ideological collusion with the Shakespeare Theatre's co-option of it: 'in fact, a contradictory case can easily be discerned, deployed no less forcefully in the play, which questions whether true independence is ever possible and suggests to the contrary that human beings are inescapably involved in mutuality and defined by reciprocity' (p. 54). Hawkes does not propose that the oppositional reading is the only one; indeed he suggests that it is no more and no less tenable than its own opposite – 'It isn't that it can be "read" in a number of ways. It is that it can't be coherently read in any single way' (p. 55). Nevertheless, for Hawkes, *Coriolanus*, and indeed all of Shakespeare's plays, lies open for us to make of it the meanings which best suit our own purposes. As the title of his book, *Meaning by Shakespeare*, implies, the meaning is not something controlled by Shakespeare, but produced by us.

STOP and THINK

- Do you see Cultural Materialism as the product of a specific historical moment?
- How do you think such an approach might be deployed in the future?

Further reading

Works discussed in this chapter

Dollimore, Jonathan and Alan Sinfield, eds. *Political Shakespeare: Essays in Cultural Materialism*, [1985], 2nd edition (Manchester: Manchester University Press, 1994).

Hawkes, Terence. *Meaning by Shakespeare* (London: Routledge, 1992).

Wayne, Don E. 'Power, Politics, and the Shakespearean Text: Recent Criticism in England and the United States', in *Shakespeare Reproduced: The Text in History and Ideology*, edited by Jean E. Howard and Marion F. O'Connor (London: Routledge, 1987), pp. 47–67.

Wilson, Richard and Richard Dutton, eds. *New Historicism and Renaissance Drama* (London: Longman, 1992).

Other works which explore issues touched on in this chapter

Cohen, Walter. 'Political Criticism of Shakespeare', in *Shakespeare Reproduced*, edited by Jean E. Howard and Marion F. O'Connor (London: Methuen, 1987), pp. 18–46. Particularly interesting on the different practices in the UK and the USA.

Evans, Malcolm. *Signifying Nothing: Truth's True Contents in Shakespearean Texts* (London: Harvester Wheatsheaf, 1986). Brilliant, playful analyses of a wide range of Shakespearean texts.

Kamps, Ivo. *Materialist Shakespeare: A History* (London: Verso, 1995). An excellent selection of Cultural Materialist analyses with a sound introduction.

McEvoy, Sean. *Shakespeare: The Basics* (London: Routledge, 2000). Extremely student-friendly and a good introduction to Cultural Materialist analysis.

Wilson, Richard. *Will Power: Essays on Shakespearean Authority* (Hemel Hempstead: Harvester Wheatsheaf, 1993). Although I mentioned this in the last chapter, the essay on *Coriolanus* would be particularly appropriate for consideration here too.

5
New factualisms

If New Historicism has been accused of historical inaccuracy and of being cavalier with facts and details, the same cannot be said of the group of approaches which I am here calling the 'new factualisms', which are typically characterised by a positively daunting degree of engagement with minutiae. Essentially, 'new factualisms' boil down to three broad areas. Firstly, there has recently been a considerable flurry of concentration on unearthing new features of Shakespeare's own biography. Secondly, there is a growing interest in attribution studies; one of the most controversial elements of Shakespearean studies in recent years has been the attempt to use computers to attribute new works to Shakespeare or to question the reliability of existing attributions, and other approaches, such as linguistic analysis, have also been used in the attempt to determine the boundaries of the Shakespeare canon. Finally, it is not only the composition of the canon but also that of individual plays which has been called into question, this time by the increasing quantity and sophistication of the current interest in Shakespearean editing – a topic which might seem dry, but is actually the subject of some of the liveliest and most heated debates in Shakespeare studies today. In this chapter, I will examine each of these three topics in turn.

The 'new biography'

In the recent flurry of research into Shakespeare's life, particular attention has been paid to two interrelated questions: firstly, the issue of whether Shakespeare might have been a Catholic, and secondly the question of whether he might, therefore, have been the 'William Shakeshaft' who spent time in the recusant household at Hoghton Tower in Lancashire ('recusant', which comes from the Latin *recusare*, to refuse, being the term for Catholics who refused to attend the services of the Church of England, which was compulsory at the time). The suggestion is an old one, but the question was comprehensively reopened by E. A. J. Honigmann in his book *Shakespeare: The 'Lost Years'*, first published in 1985 and then updated and reissued in 1998. Honigmann explains that 'Shakespeare's lost years are usually said to extend from 1585, when he disappears from the Stratford records, to 1592' (p. 1). Various possible suggestions have been made for what he may have been doing during that period, often based on what seem to be particular kinds of experience or knowledge which scholars have fancied that they can detect in his plays: these range from the suggestion that he served as a soldier in the Netherlands with the Earl of Leicester to the idea that the many Italian settings of his plays mean that he must have travelled there. Honigmann, however, is inclined to give most credence to John Aubrey's suggestion that Shakespeare in his youth had been a schoolmaster in the country, because although Aubrey was writing well after Shakespeare's death (around 1681), his informant, William Beeston, was the son of Christopher Beeston, who had worked with Shakespeare. On the basis of this, Honigmann suggests that Shakespeare went to Hoghton Tower in Lancashire, and since Hoghton Tower was the home of recusants, this would mean that Shakespeare must, in his youth at least, have been a Catholic, since no one who was not would have been trusted in such a household.

Both these suggestions are still hugely controversial, and both also raise large further questions. In the first place, there are epistemological issues. The evidence suggesting that Shakespeare may have been a Catholic is fragmentary, and amenable to widely differing interpretations and constructions: essentially, it comes down to the putative Hoghton connection, to some possible family connections through his mother with the Ardens of Park Hall (who were certainly Catholic) and to the fact that in the late eighteenth century a workman claimed to have found concealed in the roof of the Shakespeare house in Stratford a copy of the Spiritual Testament of St Carlo Borromeo, a Catholic manual, belonging, it is alleged, to

Shakespeare's father John. The evidence connecting Shakespeare to Hoghton Tower is slimmer still. The will of Alexander Hoghton, drawn up on 3 August 1581 and proved on 12 September of that year, mentioned a William Shakeshafte in a context suggesting that he was a player; Shakespeare's grandfather seems to have used the names Shakespeare and Shakeshaft interchangeably; and John Cottam, a master of Shakespeare's school, had strong Lancashire connections and was the brother of a recusant priest, so he could have effected an introduction to the Hoghtons.

Ideally, one would want more evidence than this, both for Shakespeare's Catholicism and also for the alleged Hoghton connection, especially given the fact that Shakeshaft is a common Lancashire name. In both cases, however, no new information seems likely to emerge. We need, therefore, to consider how much evidence, and of what kind, we want to see before we are prepared to act on it or form theories on its basis. We need too to consider whether we are prepared to accept internal evidence from Shakespeare's works as well as the patchy surviving external evidence, and, if so, how much weight it will bear. Finally, we need to consider how much difference it would make to our view of Shakespeare's works if we were prepared to accept the idea that he either was a Catholic himself or at least had Catholic sympathies.

It might be as well, before we proceed, to consider what it actually meant to be a Catholic in Elizabethan England. After Henry VIII's break with Rome in the 1530s, English Catholics were increasingly beleaguered. There was a brief respite for them during the reign of the Catholic Mary I (1553–58), and when Elizabeth I succeeded in 1558 she had little personal interest in persecuting them, but after the publication of Pope Pius V's Bull 'Regnans in Excelsis' in 1570, which excommunicated Elizabeth and exonerated any Catholic who assassinated her, Catholicism became virtually synonymous with treason. Nevertheless, many people, to varying degrees, continued to practise or at least remained sympathetic to the Old Religion. Women seem to have been particularly faithful to it, perhaps because the legal penalties for Catholicism – principally heavy fines – were less likely to be levied on them, and in some cases heads of families seem to have conformed with the Anglican settlement, presumably to avoid fines and loss of property, while other members of the family remained more or less openly Catholic. Shakespeare's elder daughter Susanna seems to have been one such Catholic woman; at any rate she was fined for not attending church, which is often an indication of Catholicism.

It may be difficult in this secular age to understand why Catholicism continued to command such loyalty. However, spiritual matters were generally taken very seriously in the sixteenth century, and there were very significant doctrinal differences between Protestanism and Catholicism. Perhaps the most important of these was that Catholics believed that, on death, the human soul could go to one of three destinations, Hell, Heaven or Purgatory. Those in Purgatory still had a chance of reaching Heaven, particularly if their loved ones on earth were willing to say prayers for them and spend money on intercessory masses. Protestants, on the other hand, believed that the spiritual destiny of the soul was decided irrevocably at the point of death. To die when not in a state of grace was therefore a fearful thing, and, even more alarmingly, the followers of John Calvin further maintained that the destiny of the soul was decided even *before birth*: all humans are at birth predestined to be either of the Elect or of the Damned, and nothing can alter this. This is so much less attractive than the 'second chance' theory of Catholicism that it is no wonder that many people clung to the comfort of Purgatory and of the intercessory saints. By contrast, Protestants paid little heed either to saints or to the Virgin Mary, something which, it has often been suggested, was a particular blow to women, who were thus deprived of all role models, and this may be another reason why women seem to have been particularly loyal to Catholicism. Other differences between the faiths included the fact that Catholics believed that during Communion the wine and the bread literally become the body and blood of Christ, by an essentially miraculous process known as transubstantiation, while Protestants thought that the wine and the bread were merely symbolically the body and blood ('consubstantiation'). Indeed Protestants did not believe that miracles still took place at all; for them, miraculous events had occurred only in biblical times, and the age of miracles was now past.

Since to be a Catholic in Elizabethan England was dangerous, it might seem very controversial to seek to align Shakespeare with this persecuted, underground religion. However Michael Davies has made the provocative suggestion that

> The principal benefit this Catholic Shakespeare offers . . . [is that] it effectively releases the reader or critic from the interpretative burden of having to consider Shakespeare in relation to any religious background. Because the Catholic Shakespeare is essentially secular, having had to create his own religious vacuum, then this version of the Bard ostensibly provides the perfect excuse not to engage with Shakespeare in terms of the far more difficult and potentially more radical tenets of, say, Protestant, Reformed, and Calvinist doctrine – that is, of the orthodox beliefs of his time. As such, the Catholic Shakespeare merely serves to justify the traditional erasure of theological history and historicity from Shakespeare's plays in a way that would be unthinkable for practically any other writer of the same period. What would evidently be far more distubring, what would present a far more potent challenge to the canonised Shakespeare, is not a Catholic Bard at all, therefore, but a Protestant, if not a Calvinist one . . . This version of Shakespeare would, finally, be historically specific and canonically subversive in a way that the Catholic Shakespeare simply is not. But for this reason alone, quite unsurprisingly, critics have traditionally found the idea of a Protestant Shakespeare largely unthinkable, if not utterly abhorrent – and one might suspect that this will remain the case for some time. ('On This Side Bardolatry', p. 39)

For Davies, then, the idea of Shakespeare's Catholicism has been so readily embraced because it is not in fact radical at all, but allows us to disregard difficult issues like the roles of grace and faith in Lutheran theology and the complexities of the Calvinist doctrines of election and predestination.

There are some plays in the Shakespeare canon which we might indeed be tempted to read differently if we were sure that they were written from a Catholic perspective. A particularly notable example is *Hamlet*. Catholics and Protestants held quite different views on ghosts: Catholics, who believed in Purgatory, were prepared to accept the existence of ghosts, while Protestants, who thought that there was no intervening state between Heaven and Hell, were not. A Catholic reading of *Hamlet* would therefore allow for the Ghost to be really, as it claims, the spirit of Hamlet's father. A Protestant reading could allow it to be nothing more than a deceptive or malignant spirit. This is potentially always an issue with Renaissance plays which feature ghosts, but it is particularly acute in *Hamlet*, because Hamlet himself has been educated at Wittenberg, famous (or notorious, depending on your perspective) as the place where Martin Luther pinned up his ninety-five theses on the church door and so inaugurated the Reformation (and also the university of Marlowe's Doctor Faustus). And there are a number of references within *Hamlet* to issues connected with the Reformation, most notably Hamlet's remark about the body of Polonius, 'A certain convocation of politic worms are e'en at him' (IV.iii.19–20), which is a clear allusion to the 1521 Diet of Worms which outlawed Luther.

Even if I were sure that Shakespeare himself was a Catholic, however, I would still see *Hamlet* as a play which dramatised religious uncertainty rather than as a play with a thesis which was peddling religious certainty. In this case particularly, but in Renaissance drama in general, it seems to be that the most important thing is to grasp what were the various religious positions available at the time rather than to undertake the probably futile enterprise of seeking to determine what Shakespeare's own religious convictions might have been. Moreover, religion in the sixteenth and seventeenth centuries was an immensely complex area, interwoven with questions of national identities and political beliefs as well as theological convictions, and I do not think we should be quick to pin any simple labels on Shakespeare.

There are some plays in the Shakespearean canon which are rather difficult to read from a Catholic perspective, perhaps most notably *King John*, which represents the monarch as something of a hero for his vigorous defiance of the Pope. Honigmann suggests that the strongly anti-Catholic tone of many of Shakespeare's earlier plays is attributable to the desire of Ferdinando Lord Strange, whom he sees as Shakespeare's patron, to put distance between himself and his embarrassing Catholic relatives by establishing his credentials as a patron of unimpeachably Protestant drama (pp. 118–19). Honigmann thinks also that Shakespeare changed his religion later, pointing to the effect of the attempted invasion of the Armada in disillusioning English Catholics (p. 122), making many of them put their country before their faith. One may well feel, however, that it smacks of special pleading to suggest that the more anti-Catholic something appears to be, the closer to Catholicism it must therefore really be.

King John, though, is a bit of an isolated instance in the Shakespearean canon. Other plays are more amenable to a Catholic reading, and perhaps most particularly *King Lear*. It has long been established that Shakespeare took the names of the devils in *King Lear* from Samuel Harsnett's book *A Declaration of Egregious Popish Impostures*, a wildly hostile and rabidly anti-Catholic account of some supposed exorcisms. There were good reasons why Shakespeare should have been interested in this: Honigmann points to the Lancashire connections of Harsnett's material (p. 124), and Shakespeare knew, or at least knew of, one of the exorcists in the case which Harsnett described, Robert Dibdale, who came from Stratford (Brownlow, *Shakespeare, Harsnett, and the Devils of Denham*, p. 108). F. W. Brownlow, however, has recently argued that Shakespeare's interest in the case went well beyond that, and that *King Lear* is in fact a considered and thoroughgoing response to Harsnett: 'Shakespeare read Harsnett *before* he wrote *Lear*, and the reading so affected his conception of the central themes, scenes, and characters of the play that it may have been the determining influence upon his decision to write the play at all' (p. 118). In particular, he notes that 'Two modern Catholic scholars have seen in Edgar's performance an allusion to the plight of hunted missionary priests' (p. 119). These outlawed Catholic priests, of whom Edmund Campion was perhaps the most famous, trained at seminaries abroad and then returned to England at the risk of their lives to minister to existing Catholics and try to convert new ones. Their lives of danger and disguise might indeed seem to be similar to Edgar's, and since Edgar is a character to whom we are presumably likely to be sympathetic, it might therefore be deduced that the play seeks to evoke sympathy for the missionary priests also. If that were to be accepted, we would have to see a *King Lear* with a sharply focused political and religious subtext, and that would be a very different play from either the absurdist one of Jan Kott or the 'universal' one of a Jungian critic.

STOP and THINK

• Is there anything in the Shakespearean works you know which might suggest to you that he was Catholic? Is it valid to use

Shakespeare's works as evidence for his possible Catholicism? Does an author's biography matter for study of his works?

As we have seen, Shakespeare's plays and poems have been made to yield support for all sorts of theories and meanings, so it is no surprise that they do contain lines which can be read as sympathetic to Catholicism. There is a famous reference in one of his sonnets to 'Bare ruin'd choirs, where late the sweet birds sang', which seems to refer to the monasteries which lay in ruins after the Dissolution, and which are still so notable a feature in many parts of England. But I have already suggested that even in Shakespeare's poems – and certainly in his plays – it may well be the voice of a speaker that we are hearing rather than the voice of Shakespeare himself. This is one of the reasons why it is usually considered unsafe and unproductive to read an author's work solely or substantially in the light of his or her biography. Another is that the author does not control or generate all the meanings that a work may have for its readers and viewers. And you could say many things about the life of any particular author which would be both completely true and completely immaterial to the analysis of his or her work. If you go to Stratford-upon-Avon, for instance, you can learn a lot of facts about Shakespeare's life and see a lot of houses and objects connected with him, but I am not at all sure that all of these together will get you anywhere useful in interpreting his work. Indeed, as we will see in the next section, we might want to be wary in general of linking an author's texts too closely to his or her supposed biography, because we might just be wrong about who the author actually was.

Attribution studies

The second area which I want to consider under this rubric of 'new factualisms' is the proposed expansion or redefinition of the canon by means of computer testing. Attribution studies have a long history, but the earliest attempts to ascribe new works to Shakespeare or delete others from his canon often relied on supposed parallel passages and verbal echoes, which is a subjective and imprecise approach and so soon came to be regarded with suspicion. In the late twentieth century, however, the considerable strides forward in humanities computing and programming encouraged many scholars to try to develop ways in which the borders of the Shakespearean canon could be 'scientifically' established.

One of the most controversial of these attempts was by Donald Foster. Foster designed a computer database called SHAXICON, which, he claimed, was able to identify Shakespearean authorship. Despite promises to do so, Foster has not yet made the program publicly available, but its basic mode of procedure was firstly to identify roles in the plays which he thought that Shakespeare himself had played, such as Egeus in *The Comedy of Errors* or the Ghost in *Hamlet*; secondly to isolate any particularly rare words which occur in these roles; and then finally to correlate the dates of known revivals of the plays containing those roles with the recurrence of those rare words in other work which Shakespeare is known or thought to have been writing at the time of the revival, on the basis that Shakespeare will have been reminded of that rare word by the fact that he is acting the part which contains it. On this basis, in 1996 Foster stunned the literary world by confidently attributing to Shakespeare the authorship of an obscure and uninspiring funeral elegy for the Devonshire gentleman William Peter, who died in 1612. Foster had in fact first attempted to make this case thirteen years before, in his book *Elegy by W.S.: A Study in Attribution*, but now he presented it far more forcefully in an article in *PMLA* (*Publications of the Modern Language Association of America*), in some ways a flagship journal for literary studies, and certainly a very prominent one. The attribution caused a furore, not least because everyone, including Foster himself and his most ardent supporters, concurred that the 'Funeral Elegy' was a very bad poem, one which it would be quite astonishing to find the mature Shakespeare writing at roughly the same time as *The Tempest*, when he was clearly at the height of his powers. To illustrate the point, here are its opening lines:

> Since Time, and his predestinated end,
> Abridg'd the circuit of his hopeful days,
> While both his Youth and Virtue did intend
> The good endeavors of deserving praise,
> What memorable monument can last
> Whereon to build his never-blemish'd name

But his own worth, wherein his life was grac'd –
Sith as that ever he maintain'd the same?

This is pretty dreary stuff, and certainly does not compare well with the lyricism and verbal inventiveness of *The Tempest*. It is notable, for instance, that all these lines are perfectly regular iambic pentameters, producing an unbroken de-dum-de-dum pattern which threatens to produce instant sleep and is quite anathema to the typically quirky, inventive versification of late Shakespeare.

Nevertheless, the 'Elegy' subsequently appeared under Shakespeare's name in, amongst other places, the prestigious *The Norton Shakespeare* (1997), which is very widely read by American undergraduates. Indeed, since the attribution was in general much more readily accepted in the USA than in Britain, it seemed briefly as if we were to have *two* Shakespeares, an American and a British one. Then, without warning, both Foster and his chief supporter Richard Abrams publicly (and generously) retracted their support for the Elegy, declaring themselves convinced by the much more old-fashioned parallel-passage study of Gilles Monsarrat which attributed it to John Ford, who later became one of the most prominent of the Caroline playwrights but who at the time of the composition of the 'Elegy' was still only a young man and might, therefore, well be expected to write something so gauche and undeveloped.

The literary world could breathe freely again secure in the knowledge that it did not have to accept a Shakespeare capable of perpetrating verse as leaden as that of the 'Elegy', but others of the borders of the canon still continue to be assailed. Although SHAXICON will presumably not receive another outing, other forms of computer-assisted analysis remain firm in allotting *Edward III* to Shakespeare, and it was performed by the Royal Shakespeare Company with his name on it in 2002, although many scholars still feel that only one scene of the play 'sounds' Shakespearean.

In essence, *Edward III* reads very much like a dry run for *Henry V*, since it tells a story of English success in France against apparently hopeless odds. It opens rather flatly. As in *Henry V*, the English are being goaded by the French, but for me Prince Edward's response lacks the rhetorical fire of Henry V's:

> Defiance, Frenchman? We rebound it back,
> Even to the bottom of thy master's throat.
> And, be it spoke with reverence of the King,
> My gracious father, and these other lords,
> I hold thy message but as scurrilous.
> And him that sent thee, like the lazy drone,
> Crept up by strength unto the eagle's nest;
> From whence we'll shake him with so rough a storm,
> As others shall be warned by his harm. (I.i.89–97)

'Scurrilous' uses up a lot of the line for no very striking effect; 'As others shall be warned by his harm' is a very feeble threat; and the passage as a whole lacks the inventiveness both of vocabulary and versification so typical of Shakespeare. Not until the entry of the Countess of Warwick does the verse loosen, the language begin to become luxuriant, and the tone become flexible and playful. This is how her husband introduces her to the king:

> Even she, my liege; whose beauty tyrants fear,
> As a May blossom with pernicious winds,
> Hath sullied, withered, overcast, and done. (I.ii.95–7)

It is true that 'done' is flat, but then it is *theatrically* flat, in that it allows Warwick to register awareness that his rhapsody over his wife's beauty is perhaps inappropriate in public – not to mention impolitic, since the king promptly proceeds to fall in love with her and try to tempt her to adultery. He does this by sending her a letter, though he takes issue with his clerk over the phrasing of it:

> I did not bid thee talk of chastity,
> To ransack so the treasure of her mind;
> For I had rather have her chased than chaste.
> Out with the moon line, I will none of it;
> And let me have her likened to the sun. (II.i.152–6)

Here, the liveliness of tone, the interest in simile, and even the awful pun on 'chased' and 'chaste' seem to me typically Shakespearean, and so too does the inventiveness and enjambement of the Countess's subsequent reproof to the king that 'To be a king is of a younger house / Than to be married' (II.i.263–4). In short, I feel that this scene is by Shakespeare, but that the rest of the play is not.

A 'feeling', however, does not seem much to put against the scientific-seeming claims to certainty of computer-assisted approaches. The journal *Notes and Queries*, for instance, regularly publishes pieces which venture well outside the normal boundaries of literary criticism in their use of techniques such as stylometry and letter-frequency counting. Thus Thomas Merriam claims that the relative frequency of the letter 'O' can be used to distinguish between texts by Shakespeare and texts by Marlowe:

> Such testing is quite possible thanks to advances in computers since 1988. With a 33 megahertz 486DX microcomputer, using a SNOBOL programme, the 26 letters in a play can be tallied in two minutes. The play should be prepared by stripping speech prefixes and repetitive stage directions such as 'Enter', 'Re-enter', 'Aside', 'Exit', 'Exeunt'. The task can be performed in about 20 minutes with various search-and-replace techniques. Because of the great number of letters involved, 100,000 in a large play, letter frequencies are tolerant of failure to purge the texts of all possible distortions. ('Letter Frequency as a Discriminator of Authors', p. 468)

Few literary scholars will be able to respond to this, because most will be hopelessly lost after the first sentence. Certainly when Merriam goes on to suggest, on the basis of this methodology, that the three parts of *Henry VI* and *Titus Andronicus* may well be by Marlowe rather than by Shakespeare, I have no idea whether this is plausible or not. All I can do is revert to 'feeling', which in this case says that bits of *Henry VI* do indeed seem Marlovian but that *Titus Andronicus* has a verve and playfulness much more characteristic of early Shakespeare. But I do not expect anyone else to take such 'hunches' seriously.

There is an interesting contrast here with the methodologies of art history, where connoisseurship in the recognition of a master's style is regularly used to make secure attributions. In literary studies, however, very few people would confidently claim that they could 'hear' Shakespeare, and to do so would certainly not boost their job prospects.

To some extent, the question of attribution also intersects with that outermost reach of Shakespearean criticism, the dreaded Authorship Question. Everyone has heard the rumours that the works of Shakespeare were not really written by Shakespeare at all, but by Sir Francis Bacon, or Queen Elizabeth I, or Christopher Marlowe, or Edward de Vere, Earl of Oxford, or (more rarely) by William Stanley, Earl of Derby. People who believe in any of these alternative candidates are known collectively as 'anti-Stratfordians', and they tend to believe that 'Stratfordian' scholars, as they derisively name us, are engaged in a world wide conspiracy to suppress the truth in order to keep our jobs. It is certainly true that 'Stratfordians' tend to steer well clear of 'anti-Stratfordians', but it is not because they are engaged in a global conspiracy; it is because they know perfectly well that there is no evidence worth the name that Shakespeare was anyone but Shakespeare. All too often, what is offered as evidence is in fact an unpleasant mixture of conjecture, innuendo and assertion, as in the following passage from an attempt by John Baker to prove that Shakespeare was really Marlowe:

> *Now we can leap over to the plays.* In the introduction we've pointed out the vilification of Marlovians by the Stratfordian establishment. We return thus to the *Times Literary Supplement*, which vilified the research of the Cambridge political historian Lilian Winstanley (1921). Winstanley's study of the ascension of James IV [*sic*: he means James VI, and presumably he also means 'accession' rather than 'ascension'] appeared under the title: *Hamlet and the Scottish Succession*. In considerable detail Ms. Winstanley proved 'Shakespeare' had been to Scotland, knew James and intimate details concerning his family, including Arabella Stuart, as evidenced throughout *Hamlet*. Indeed she demonstrates how the play, at root a diplomatic docudrama, was written in order to urge James to become a better ruler by prodding him to be more decisive. This trail is thus all we need to know to understand that Marlowe not only survived 1593, but continued to work for the Cecils and did so at the side of King James IV. Marlowe, not Shakespeare. Everything else is simply additional nails in the Stratfordian coffin. Here's how the syllogism runs: The author of *Hamlet* knew James. Of the candidates, only Marlowe knew James. Thus Marlowe wrote *Hamlet*.
> (John Baker, *The Case for Authorship of the Works Attributed to William Shakespeare*, p. 9)

So wild speculations mutually reinforce each other and the case is 'proved'. We can probably also be confident that Elvis Presley is alive and well and living on Mars.

STOP and THINK

- Would you be more willing to go and see a play if it was advertised as being by Shakespeare?
- Are you prepared to credit the intuition of a critic (or your own), or do you believe that computer-assisted analysis is likely to prove more reliable?

There is no doubt that Shakespeare is a bigger box-office draw than, say, Beaumont and Fletcher, or even than Marlowe. For one thing, Shakespeare's plays are far more likely to appear on school syllabuses, and so to attract school audiences to the theatre. But anyone with much experience of going to see Renaissance plays knows that there can be terrible productions of even the greatest of plays, while conversely there have been some spectacularly successful productions of little-known plays of the period, most notably at the Swan Theatre in Stratford, which specialises in resurrecting the lost repertoire of the Elizabethan and Jacobean stages. As we shall see in Chapter 8, 'Shakespeare' is not an infallible badge of quality when it comes to theatre productions. As for the second question, I suspect the answer to this will depend on whether you, like me, feel faint when you see numbers. However, as I shall show in the next section, the study of Shakespeare does sometimes depend on a willingness to engage with unfamiliar methodology.

Editing

In her book *Unediting the Renaissance*, Leah Marcus remarks that

> On the average page of the usual multi-volume Shakespeare edition, the playtext is separated from the historical and explanatory notes by what Thomas L. Berger has amusingly termed the 'band of terror' and Lewis Mumford and Edmund Wilson had earlier derided as 'barbed wire' – a bristling hedge of textual notes that are incomprehensible to the average reader and therefore serve as a forbidding barrier between the 'text itself' above the band of terror and culturally variable questions of meaning taken up in the historical notes beneath the barrier. (p. 72)

Thus if I open my Arden 2 *Hamlet* at random, I find, underneath the page on which the Player King breaks off his speech in tears, the following set of notes:

> 515. whe'er *Capell* (whe'r); where *Q2, F.* 516. Prithee] Q2; Pray you *F.*
> 517. of this] *Q2; not in F.* 519. you] *Q2;* ye *F.* 520. abstract] *Q2;*
> Abstracts *F, Q1.* 522. live] *Q2, Q1;* liued *F.* 524. bodkin] *Q2;* bodykins
> *F.* much] *Q2; not in F;* farre *Q1.* 525. shall] *Q2;* should *F, Q1.*
> 531. *To First Player] As they follow Polonius, Hamlet detains and steps*
> *aside with I Player. White.*

The page in question has only nineteen lines on it, yet it has generated six lines of tightly packed and densely abbreviated textual notes. It is little wonder if students shy away in horror from such unpromising-looking information; I certainly did so myself until well after my postgraduate days. In the first place, I could not understand any of it, and, in the second, I could not see what it could possibly have to do with anything the text might mean.

In recent years, however, this deeply unpromising-looking topic has emerged as one of the most exciting and hotly debated of all areas of Shakespearean study. It is not even as difficult as it looks to understand. The 'Q's and 'F's with which the *Hamlet* notes are so liberally sprinkled mean nothing more complicated than 'Quarto' and 'Folio', and those two terms refer simply to the size of the page on which a given text was printed: thus *Hamlet* originally appeared in a quarto (i.e. small) version, now known as Q1; then came a significantly different version of the play, also published in quarto, and therefore known as Q2; and finally there was the version of the play, a little different from Q2 and very different from Q1, which was published in the First Folio which Shakespeare's colleagues Heminges and Condell brought out after his death in 1623, and which is therefore known as F.

In many cases, such as that of *The Tempest*, the Folio represents the only known version of a Shakespearean play, and so there is no question of textual disagreements between different versions. This applies to eighteen plays – very nearly half the canon. But in other cases, most notably *Hamlet* and *King Lear*, there are two or maybe three versions of a play, and the differences may be very substantial indeed. It is the nature and significance of those differences that is most hotly debated in editing theory, and the magnitude of what may be at stake is well illustrated by two comments made by academics asked to adjudicate on the merits of an article by Michael Warren which examined some of the differences between the Quarto and Folio versions of *King Lear*: 'In 1976 a *PMLA* referee for Michael Warren's seminal essay on *King Lear* advised that it "should not be published anywhere"; a decade later one referee of an article by Steven Urkowitz wrote that "This sort of thing must be discouraged"' (Gary Taylor, 'The Rhetorics of Reaction', p. 34).

How can something apparently so dry-seeming possibly have become so controversial? At least part of the answer to this lies in the observation made by Leah Marcus in her book *Unediting the Renaissance* that 'Because of the sheer weight of erudition involved, if for no other reason . . . editing has tended to be a profoundly conservative activity. To an extent that few of us recognize, our standard editions are shaped by nineteenth-century or even earlier assumptions and ideologies' (p. 5). Marcus's 'if for no other reason' rather slyly insinuates that she thinks that there probably are other reasons, and certainly editing, like everything else, has its own history which, in turn, has shaped for it its own distinctive set of agendas. Marcus notes that

> The great nineteenth-century philological enterprise was made possible by the French Revolution and other similar disruptions, which caused a flood of early books and manuscripts to pass out of the possession of royal and noble households and into public archives where they became available for research. (p. 19)

Subsequently,

> The American treasurer for the Malone Society has made the interesting suggestion that the New Bibliography and its antecedents can be understood in part as a reaction to the experiences of wartime, first in Britain, then in America. Immediately after each major war, there was a burst of bibliographical activity which is only partly explicable in terms of a lifting of wartime restraints on scholarly activity. (p. 19)

'The New Bibliography' is used here to refer to the labours of men such as W. W. Greg before the Second World War and Fredson Bowers after it, who, where there were textual variants, sought to establish a 'copy-text' as the basis for the edition of a play, with its readings being privileged and others being regarded as deviants or variations. Marcus sees the impulse of the New Bibliographers as being to keep an 'ideal' text safe from the ravages of history, and notes that

> One of Bowers's final essays on Shakespeare and the printinghouse refers repeatedly to the 'veil' of print: for Bowers, despite all his erudition about printinghouse practices, it was the editor's business to lift that veil, go beyond particular embodiments of the text to an 'ideal' version approximating Shakespeare's intent – we learn about printinghouse practices only to transcend them. (p. 30)

The trouble is, of course, that one person's 'ideal' is another person's nightmare. As Marcus points out, 'In the late nineteenth century, F. J. Furnivall expressed a fervent hope that Shakespeare was not responsible for "all the women's rant" in *Titus Andronicus*, the *Henry VI* trilogy, and *Richard III*' (p. 101). Furnivall was too good a scholar to find only what he wanted to find, but nevertheless it is clear that the temptation is there, and that the way was open for some readings to become 'good' and others to be relegated to 'bad' for a variety of reasons. Thus one of the most notable consequences of the shift in favour of the New Bibliography was the utter disgrace of many of the early quarto editions of Shakespeare, which now became known as the 'Bad' Quartos. It is in order to rehabilitate the Bad Quartos that Marcus proposes her strategy of 'unediting', and although she concedes that 'If modern scholars, students, and general readers were suddenly deprived of all the historical, linguistic, and literary investigation that lies behind the average standard edition, we would find ourselves crippled and disoriented' (p. 4), she does nevertheless propose that we should pass the dreaded frontier of 'the band of terror' and see what really lies behind the ordered, tidy editions in which we read Shakespeare.

People who have never considered textual matters before might well be surprised at how many aspects of the Shakespearean text can be brought into question. Take, for instance, the example I cited above:

> 515. whe'er *Capell* (whe'r); where *Q2*, *F*. 516. Prithee] *Q2*; Pray you *F*. 517. of this] *Q2; not in F*. 519. you] *Q2;* ye *F*. 520. abstract] *Q2;* Abstracts *F, Q1*. 522. live] *Q2, Q1;* liued *F*. 524. bodkin] *Q2;* bodykins *F.* much] *Q2; not in F;* farre *Q1*. 525. shall] *Q2;* should *F, Q1*.

531. *To First Player*] *As they follow Polonius, Hamlet detains and steps aside with I Player. White.*

What this means is that, of the nineteen lines printed on the page, seven exist in different versions. In some cases the differences are so small as to appear negligible (though a careful close reading might well be able to attach significance to even the tiniest); in others, though, there is a large gulf – 'bodkin' means a needle or (metaphorically) a dagger, and Hamlet has wondered not long ago about whether he should make his quietus with a 'bare bodkin'; 'bodykins' is more likely to be a diminutive of 'body', something else with which the play – which after all features a scene in a graveyard – is much concerned. Which should we read here? Similarly, in a much more famous crux in *Hamlet*, does the Prince condemn his flesh as 'too too solid' (F), 'too too sallied' (Q1 and Q2), or 'too too sullied' (modern editorial reconstruction of what 'sallied' might have meant)?

Traditional methods of editing Shakespeare aimed to provide clear and definitive answers to these sorts of questions. Thus, for example, an editor might argue that since Hamlet wishes his flesh would melt, he is more likely to think it 'solid' – a good opposite to something which is melting – rather than 'sullied' or 'sallied'. On other occasions, an editor might use his (or very rarely her) knowledge of Elizabethan handwriting styles to argue, for instance, that a 'd' had probably been read as a 'b', or rely on what he or she knew of typesetting practices to show that one particular letter was especially likely to be substituted for another. (On a QWERTY keyboard, for instance, it is much more likely that 'qere' is a mistake for 'were' than for 'here', since *q* and *w* are adjacent, and *h* is a long way away; similarly, we can reconstruct the ways in which Elizabethan type was stored and set.)

Marcus's point, however, is that, historically, not all editorial decisions have been made on grounds of typesetting practice or handwriting styles. She begins by taking an example from *The Tempest*, where the witch Sycorax is said to have blue eyes. This seems somewhat surprising, since every other piece of information we are given about Sycorax seems designed to underline her ugliness, evil and foreignness, yet we associate blue eyes with beauty, innocence, and familiar racial identities. Marcus notes that 'In nearly all modern editions, "blew ey'd," "blue-ey'd," or "blue-eyed" is glossed in a way that cancels out its potential for disrupting the self–other binary that has characterized most readings of the play' (p. 6), by which she means that since we tend to regard blue eyes as normal and indeed attractive, and Sycorax is clearly not meant to be either, modern editors have generally found some way of explaining 'blue-eyed' as having some meaning other than the obvious one, and specifically a meaning which does not force us to confront the fact that Sycorax might be in any way like ourselves. Often, for instance, the blueness is ascribed to the eyelid, where it would seem much more alien, rather than to the eye. Other attempts have also been made to explain it away: the celebrated Shakespeare editor John Dover Wilson, for instance, suggested emending the text to 'blear-ey'd' on palaeographical grounds (that is, on the basis of his knowledge of contemporary handwriting styles). Marcus, however, claims that 'In fact, the idea that Sycorax could not possibly be blue eyed in our usual sense of the term seems to have been hatched around mid-century along with the dissemination of Charles Darwin's theory of evolution' (pp. 7–8) – Daniel Wilson's 1873 *Caliban: The Missing Link* was the first text to call Sycorax 'blear-eyed' – and notes that the Shakespeare scholar Horace Howard Furness 'made the interesting suggestion that some of the positive connotations associated with blue eyes in recent Anglo-American culture were in Shakespeare attached to gray eyes' (p. 12). Maybe, then, the text is right and it is our ideas about its meaning that are wrong. Similarly, Marcus argues that 'For a broad stream of Freudian critics beginning with Freud himself and his disciple Ernest Jones, Hamlet is the English Oedipus – unable to kill Claudius because of his own repressed desire for his mother and covert identification with Claudius as the man who has won her away from his father. That interpretation is far less available in Q1, in which most of Hamlet's "diseased" language is not present and in which most of his sexual anguish seems to relate to the breach with Ofelia rather than repressed desire for his mother' (p. 142).

There are many other similar examples of passages in Shakespeare that we ought perhaps to read very differently from the way we do now. Terence Hawkes, for instance, points out that though we read in *Coriolanus* 'like an eagle in a dovecote, I / Flutter'd your Volsces in Corioles' (V.vi.114–15), the First Folio has 'flatterd'd'. Hawkes claims that '"Flatter'd" makes perfect sense and needs no emendation if we accept the arguments . . . about Coriolanus's actual relation to his enemies and to society at large. The word suggests a much more complex interactive engagement with the Volscians than the imperiously dismissive "flutter'd".' Hawkes further points out that Shakespeare often uses 'flatter'd' but never elsewhere 'flutter'd' and argues that

> 'flatter'd' bespeaks a kind of baffled reciprocity and . . . acknowledges
> a degree of impotent mutuality, even whilst it manifests the wholesale
> hostility to which Coriolanus is undoubtedly committed. In this
> sense, 'flatter'd' is not simply different from 'flutter'd', it offers a
> completely opposed dimension of meaning. To refuse that dimension
> is deliberately to choose to impose a single and specific reading on the
> indeterminacy and multiplicity fostered by the First Folio text.
> (*Meaning by Shakespeare*, pp. 53–4)

Until very recently, however, it was extremely difficult to bear such indeterminacy in mind without interrupting the flow of one's reading to rummage through 'the band of terror' in case it noted variant readings. With the potential revolution in editorial procedures that hypertext and the internet have made possible, though, that is no longer the case, and a number of projects are already working on ways in which more than one version of a text can be displayed.

The play which has been most affected by the growing tendency towards 'unediting' is *King Lear*. This exists in two very different versions: a quarto, published in 1608, and the First Folio, published in 1623. (There is also a 1619 quarto, but that differs only slightly from the 1608 one.) In 1608, the play is called a History, suggesting that its primary importance lies in its truth (and the story of King Lear was indeed regarded as true); in 1623, it is called a Tragedy, suggesting that it is to be read primarily in terms of its aesthetic and moral force. In 1608, Edgar speaks the closing lines; in 1623, Albany does. There are also numerous other differences, some as major as the omission of whole scenes, and as a result, there is an increasing move to treat *King Lear* not as one play but as two. Similarly, the prestigious Arden Shakespeare series is about to bring out an edition of *Hamlet* which will contain three separate texts of the play – Q1, Q2 and F.

So what happens if we 'unedit' *King Lear*, or if we edit it differently? In her article '*Cor.*'s Rescue of Kent', in the important collection edited by Gary Taylor and Michael Warren, *The Division of the Kingdoms: Shakespeare's Two Versions of* King Lear, Beth Goldring begins by boldly asserting that 'Small textual changes can have large effects in the dramatic structure of Shakespeare's plays' (p. 143). She focuses her argument on two speech prefixes in the Folio version of the play: '*Alb. Cor.* Deare Sir forbeare', which appears in the Folio when Lear is about to attack Kent and has no parallel in the Quarto; and '*Cor.* Heere's *France* and *Burgundy*, my Noble Lord', a line which the Quarto gives to Gloucester. Editors who follow the Folio usually assign both these lines to Cornwall, but Goldring argues that they should belong to Cordelia:

> Cordelia is admirably suited to speaking these lines and defending Kent. Her speech in this first scene is already marked by the combined formality and intensity of feeling which will characterize it throughout the play. She has already called Lear either 'my Lord' or 'Good my Lord' four times in twenty-one lines … 'Deare Sir forbeare' is extreme language in her mouth, both in the intensity of its protest against Lear's action and the extremity of feeling it manifests towards Lear. Love and outrage combine in simple eloquence.
>
> No character has more reason than Cordelia to come to Kent's aid. Even if Kent's primary concern is, as he says, with Lear's safety, it is still Cordelia's inheritance that he is defending, and some action on her part is demanded in response. (p. 148)

A close study of the language pattern of the play and a new awareness that the play as we read it is merely an editorial construct thus leads Goldring to challenge the received text in ways that, if we accept her arguments, would bring about a definite change in our understanding of a major character in the play.

In editing studies as in attribution and the question of Shakespeare's possible Catholicism, then, the emergence of new facts about Shakespeare's life or about printing-house practices and textual transmission is central to the attempt to construct readings of his works. In the next chapter, I will look at an approach which is in some respects entirely opposite, because, for gender studies and queer theory, what matters is not so much what can be proved about Shakespeare's own historical moment as what can be speculated about, guessed at, or imagined.

STOP and THINK

• Are you convinced by Goldring's arguments that to give these lines to Cordelia is more dramatically fitting than to give them to Cornwall?

• Is dramatic fittingness an appropriate criterion in editing? Are there others more important?

• Are you happy to entertain the idea that a play can exist in more than one version?

• Would you rather read a version where the editor has already made all the textual decisions, or would you welcome indeterminacy?

Further reading

Works discussed in this chapter

Brownlow, F. W. *Shakespeare, Harsnett, and the Devils of Denham* (Cranbury, N.J.: Associated University Presses, 1993).

Davies, Michael. 'On This Side Bardolatry: The Canonisation of the Catholic Shakespeare', *Cahiers Elisabéthains* 58 (2000): 31–47.

Foster, Donald. *Elegy by W.S.: A Study in Attribution* (Newark: University of Delaware Press, 1989).

——. 'A *Funerall Elegy*: W[illiam] S[hakespeare]'s "Best-Speaking Witnesses"', *PMLA* 111 (96): 1080–95.

Hawkes, Terence, *Meaning by Shakespeare* (London: Routledge 1992).

Honigmann, E. A. J. *Shakespeare: The 'Lost Years'*, 2nd edition (Manchester: Manchester University Press, 1998).

Marcus, Leah S. *Unediting the Renaissance: Shakespeare, Marlowe, Milton* (London: Routledge, 1996).

Merriam, Thomas. 'Letter Frequency as a Discriminator of Authors', *Notes and Queries* 41.4 (December 1994): 467–9.

Monsarrat, Gilles. 'A *Funerall Elegy*: Ford, W. S. and Shakespeare', *Review of English Studies* 53 (2002): 186–203.

Taylor, Gary. 'The Rhetorics of Reaction', in *Crisis in Editing: Texts of the English Renaissance*, edited by Randall M. Leod (New York: AMS Press, 1994).

——, and Michael Warren. *The Division of the Kingdoms: Shakespeare's Two Versions of* King Lear (Oxford: The Clarendon Press, 1983).

Other works which explore issues touched on in this chapter

Cloud, Random, '"The Very Names of the Persons": Editing and the Invention of Dramatick Character', in *Staging the Renaissance: Reinterpretations of Elizabethan and Jacobean Drama*, edited by David Scott Kastan and Peter Stallybrass (New York: Routledge, 1991), pp. 88–96. Interesting account from one of the most versatile and provocative theorists of edition, who also refers to himself as Randall McLeod and various other variants of that name; as As Randall M. Leod, for instance, he has edited *Crisis in Editing: Texts of the English Renaissance* (New York: AMS Press, 1994).

Dutton, Richard, Alison Findlay and Richard Wilson, eds. *Theatre and Religion: Lancastrian Shakespeare* (Manchester: Manchester University Press, 2004); Dutton, Richard, Alison Findlay and Richard Wilson, eds. *Region, Religion and Patronage: Lancastrian Shakespeare* (Manchester: Manchester University Press, 2004). Two volumes of essays from the first academic conference held to explore seriously the possibility that Shakespeare's 'lost years' were spent at Hoghton Tower in Lancashire.

Kastan, David Scott, 'The Mechanics of Culture: Editing Shakespeare Today', in *Shakespeare After Theory* (London: Routledge, 1999). Comments on the current interest in editing and speculates on the causes.

Murphy, Andrew, '"Tish ill done": *Henry the Fift* and the Politics of Editing', in *Shakespeare and Ireland: History, Politics, Culture*, edited by Mark Thornton Burnett and Ramona Wray (Basingstoke: Macmillan, 1997), pp. 213–34. Useful 'worked example' of the difference editorial decisions can make.

Vickers, Brian. *'Counterfeiting' Shakespeare: Evidence, Authorship, and John Ford's 'Funerall Elegy'* (Cambridge: Cambridge University Press, 2002). Vigorous and densely argued attack on Donald Foster and his methodology.

6

Gender studies and queer theory

When it comes to approaches to Shakespeare which have been influenced by either gender studies or queer theory, it might well seem that anything goes. Such approaches have come an astonishingly long way since the relatively unsophisticated analyses found in *The Woman's Part*, the book whose publication in 1980 inaugurated feminist criticism of Shakespeare and of which one of the editors, Gayle Greene, later commented:

> In the late seventies when I and my coeditors were asked to submit names of readers for our anthology *The Woman's Part: Feminist Criticism of Shakespeare*, we had difficulty coming up with the names of two senior Shakespeareans who would not trash the idea of a feminist reading of Shakespeare; what we encountered again and again was the response I have described – that we were desecrating something sacred ('How dare we call Othello hysterical!'). When by the early 1980s our book was published and we'd achieved some recognition and were working together with the pleasure and excitement of a just cause, we had become sufficiently threatening to be characterized by a former friend of mine as 'the Shakespeare mafia'; a group of women working together – we had become a 'mafia.' ('The Myth of Neutrality, Again?', p. 27)

Since then, analyses centred on gender have become ever more popular, with some selected landmarks in the field including Juliet Dusinberre's *Shakespeare and the Nature of Women* (1975), Linda Bamber's *Comic Women, Tragic Men* (1982), Lisa Jardine's *Still Harping on Daughters* (1983) and Dympna Callaghan's *Woman and Gender in Renaissance tragedy* (1989), while in the area of queer theory Eve Kosofsky Sedgwick's groundbreaking *Between Men: English Literature and Male Homosocial Desire* (1985) has been followed by works such as Valerie Traub's *Desire and Anxiety: Circulations of Sexuality in Early Modern Drama* (1992), Mario DiGangi's *The homoerotics of Early Modern Drama* (1997) and Bruce Smith's *Shakespeare and Masculinity* (2000).

Such approaches are often very attractive to modern students, seeming to offer them a personal foothold on the text. But the work of Michel Foucault in his epic *History of Sexuality* suggests that previous societies' understandings of sexuality and gender are precisely *not* rooted in our own experiences but require some historicisation of concepts of gender, and these in themselves are subject to change. Moreover, sexuality-based approaches have been subject to other criticisms: Philip Armstrong, for instance, calls Janet Adelman's book *Suffocating Mothers* '"heteronormative" in its psychosexual attitude . . . It is for this reason that feminist object-relations psychoanalytic approaches have been attacked by recent queer critics' (*Shakespeare in Psychoanalysis*, p. 187) (object-relations-based approaches postulate that relationships between humans, from the mother and child relationship onwards, are central to individual human identity and experience). And feminist criticism in particular has been the subject of a number of attacks by Richard Levin, who has repeatedly maintained that though he does accept 'feminist political ideology . . . this did not affect my judgment of those feminist readings, since a just cause cannot justify interpretive faults' ('Ideological Criticism and Pluralism', p. 15) and says doggedly that 'unless they intend to force us into submission – poetics comes from the barrel of a gun? – they will have to persuade us' (p. 19). Along similar lines, Gareth Lloyd Evans, reviewing Barry Kyle's 1982 production of *The Taming of the Shrew* in *Drama*, lamented that

> It will not have escaped the notice of some Shakespearean theatregoers that some of his plays have, in the past few years, not so much been directed as victimised by bands of literary wild eyed mobsters. On nothing but bizarre, fashionable, or totally wrong evidence they hack at the heart and guts of the plays while relieving their less coherent din with cries that Shakespeare shall be revitalised and (wait for it) made to speak to the 20th century.

This is clearly rant, but perhaps a more substantial point to raise against the validity of feminist criticism is that it too has focused on some plays at the expense of the relative neglect of others. Thus Walter Cohen comments that 'The formalist heritage of New Criticism has characteristically involved an interest in the reciprocal relationship between gender and genre, a relationship often understood in terms of *Comic Women, Tragic Men*'; as a result, in feminist criticism of Shakespeare 'Broadly speaking the romantic comedies, the problem plays, and the romances have received sustained, favorable treatment at the relative expense of the histories and tragedies' ('Political Criticism of Shakespeare', p. 23). When it does come to the tragedies, Cohen goes on, 'feminists' recurrent concern with *Othello* and especially *Antony and Cleopatra* has implicitly challenged A. C. Bradley's still hegemonic exclusion of the latter play from the major tragedies' (p. 24).

STOP and THINK

- Can you think of any reason why *Othello* and *Antony and Cleopatra* might be more amenable to feminist criticism than the other tragedies?
- Does it matter for the legitimacy of feminist criticism if some plays are not susceptible to its approaches?

Antony and Cleopatra gives Cleopatra equal billing with Antony in the title, and Antony dies in Act IV, leaving Cleopatra to carry the close of the tragedy entirely on her own. Moreover, Antony and Cleopatra are both notable for their unwillingness to conform to traditional gender roles: indeed it is one of Octavius Caesar's complaints about Antony that he 'is not more manlike / Than Cleopatra, nor the queen of Ptolemy / More womanly than he'. *Othello* does not give as much prominence to Desdemona as *Antony and Cleopatra* does to Cleopatra, but *Othello* is much more concerned with marital relationships and domesticity than Shakespeare's other tragedies, and that is often the focus of feminists' interest in it. As for whether you think it matters if some plays are more amenable to feminist analysis than others, that depends, as with any theoretical perspective, on whether you think that a theory is true, and hence something that *must* be taken account of, or whether you think it merely provides one possible explanatory model.

Boy actors

Feminist readings of Shakespeare can do a number of different things. They can focus particularly on female characters in the plays; they can expose bias within the culture which produced the plays or within the cultures that have since received them; and they can observe features of the plays, their production and their reception which might not have been noticeable from a different perspective. One of the earliest results of developments in feminist criticism was an intense focus on the fact that all the female parts in Shakespeare's plays were acted by boys (or in some cases possibly by men). In 1983 Lisa Jardine published *Still Harping on Daughters: Women and Drama in the Age of Shakespeare*, which represented what was then still a rarity in the field of literary criticism, a book devoted entirely to the representation of women on stage. Much more sophisticated than many of the analyses in *The Woman's Part*, *Still Harping on Daughters* was also even more controversial, because in it Jardine announced that 'Whenever Shakespeare's female characters in the comedies draw attention to their own androgyny, I suggest that the resulting eroticism is to be associated with their *maleness* rather than with their femaleness' (p. 20). For Jardine, the crucial fact about the representation of women on the Renaissance stage was that they were played by males, and she examined antitheatrical tracts of the period to show that this was the source of a large part of the uneasiness felt about theatre by the people whom we now loosely lump together as Puritans, because they saw these cross-dressed boys as arousing illicit sexual urges in the adult men who attended plays. This was an idea which she later developed in subsequent work on *Twelfth Night* in particular, arguing provocatively that

> in the early modern period, erotic attention – an attention bound up with sexual availability and historically specific forms of economic dependency – is focused upon boys and women in the *same* way. So that, crucially, sexuality signifies as *absence of difference* as it is inscribed upon the bodies of those equivalently 'mastered' within the

early modern household, and who are placed homologously in relation to that household's domestic economy. ('Twins and Travesties',
p. 28)

At first sight the fear that the men who frequent early modern play-
houses might view the boy actors in an eroticised way might seem a
rather perverse one, for we would now be likely to assume that the
majority of men are heterosexual. But one of the major effects of the
explosion of work on sex and gender in the Renaissance has been
to call into question the whole idea that heterosexuality and homosexuality, as we now understand them, actually existed in the early
modern period. The words 'homosexual' and 'heterosexual' certainly did not, and many critics would argue that the concepts and
patterns of behaviour associated with those words not only did not
exist, but were in fact entirely antithetical to the kinds of sexual identity available in Renaissance England, where, they argue, sexual
identities were envisaged as being on a continuum rather than a
bifurcated choice, so that the fact that a man might desire women did
not stand in the way of his also desiring boys. Moreover, it is not only
sexual identities but gender ones which many critics of the period see
as fluid, for they point to the existence in medical theory of a 'one-
sex model' which postulated that male and female genitalia were
essentially mirror images of each other, and that it was possible for
changes to occur or to be effected to them which would actually mean
that a person would cross from one gender to the other.

It is this idea which lies behind a remarkable story recounted by
Stephen Greenblatt:

> In September 1580, as he passed through a small French town on his
> way to Switzerland and Italy, Montaigne was told an unusual story
> that he duly recorded in his travel journal. It seems that seven or eight
> girls from a place called Chaumont-en-Bassigni plotted together 'to
> dress up as males and thus continue their life in the world.' One of
> them set up as a weaver, 'a well-disposed young man who made friends
> with everybody,' and moved to a village called Montier-en-Der. There
> the weaver fell in love with a woman, courted her, and married. The
> couple lived together for four or five months, to the wife's satisfaction,
> 'so they say.' But then, Montaigne reports, the transvestite was recog-
> nized by someone from Chaumont; 'the matter was brought to justice,
> and she was condemned to be hanged, which she said she would
> rather undergo than return to a girl's status; and she was hanged for

using illicit devices to supply her defect in sex.' The execution, Montaigne was told, had taken place only a few days before.

I begin with this story because in *Twelfth Night* Shakespeare almost, but not quite, retells it. ('Fiction and Friction', p. 66)

Greenblatt follows this up with an even more surprising anecdote, telling of how the sixteenth-century French physician Ambroise Paré

recounts the story of 'a fifteen-year-old peasant girl who one day was 'rather robustly' chasing her swine, which were going into a wheat field. As Marie in midpursuit leaped over a ditch, 'at the very moment the genitalia and male rod came to be developed.' After consulting with physicians and the bishop, Marie changed her name to Germain. (p. 81)

Greenblatt suggests, then, that not only was the one-sex model believed in in Shakespeare's day, but that Shakespeare is in some sense drawing on it in *Twelfth Night*.

The question of belief in the one-sex model is controversial. It was energetically advanced by Thomas Laqueur, who argued in his book *Making Sex* (1990) that the one-sex model remained dominant until as late as the eighteenth century, but this has been challenged by other historians. Nevertheless, there is no doubt that belief in the one-sex model remained an option intellectually available in the early modern period. It is because of our awareness of this, as well as for other reasons, that C. L. Barber's 1959 comment on *Twelfth Night* that 'The most fundamental distinction the play brings home to us is the difference between men and women' (*Shakespeare's Festive Comedy*, p. 245) is now much less likely to be accepted than it was when he made it.

STOP and THINK

- Have you ever seen a production of a Shakespearean play in which a female character was played by a male performer, or vice versa? If not, can you imagine one?
- Is it possible to disregard the actual gender of the performer, or will it always be a factor?
- It is common nowadays for plays and films to cast black actors in rôles originally written for white ones. Could cross-gender casting work in the same way as 'colour-blind' casting?

As it happens, there have recently been several opportunities for critics and audiences to experience the effects of gender-blind casting. For instance, as part of the 2003 Shakespeare's Globe season, an all-female *Richard III* was performed, starring Kathryn Hunter in the title role. Reviewing the production in *The Guardian*, Lyn Gardner wrote:

> The big question was: what would an all-female production do to this play? Surprisingly little, is the answer. Of course, certain lines about male ambition and the like come to the fore, but in the case of Hunter you entirely forget that she is a woman playing a man.
>
> Subconsciously, perhaps, you take in the ironies, particularly in the scenes where Richard comes face to face with his most spitting adversaries, all of whom are women – Lady Anne, the widowed Elizabeth, and Queen Margaret. In the last role, Linda Bassett gives the one performance that gives Hunter a run for her money.
>
> But in general, the gender reversal is no more difficult for an audience to accept than is the suspension of disbelief that makes us feel that we have been whisked back to the 15th century. Mind you, I did miss that little erotic tingle that Richard himself so often engenders. There are also moments in some of the lamer performances when you think of a school play at some posh girls' school.

I would agree with Gardner about the effect of this production: in Kathryn Hunter's performance, at least, gender was not an issue. The experience of watching Hunter suggested, to me and others, that it might similarly have been possible to ignore cross-gender casting on the Renaissance stage, but this must remain speculation.

Political feminisms

For Catherine Belsey, writing two years after Lisa Jardine, this possibility of questioning the very existence of gender difference is a property not only of Shakespeare's culture but also of his plays, for she announces in her article 'Disrupting Sexual Difference: Meaning and Gender in the Comedies' that 'I want to suggest that

Shakespearean comedy can be read as disrupting sexual difference, calling in question that set of relations between terms which proposes as inevitable an antithesis between masculine and feminine, men and women' (p. 171). She, too, suggests that cross-dressing disrupts the whole idea of gender difference (pp. 182–3), and this is doubly important because, for Belsey, disruption of difference allows for an explicitly politicised reading which has ramifications well beyond the question of gender:

> The problem with the meanings that we learn – and learn to produce – is that they seem to define and delimit what is thinkable, imaginable, possible. To fix meaning, to arrest its process and deny its plurality, is in effect to confine what is possible to what is. Conversely, to disrupt this fixity is to glimpse alternative possibilities. A conservative criticism reads in quest of familiar, obvious, common-sense meanings, and thus reaffirms what we already know. A radical criticism, however, is concerned to produce readings which challenge that knowledge by revealing alternative meanings, disrupting the system of differences which legitimates the perpetuation of things as they are. The project of such a criticism is not to replace one authoritative interpretation of a text with another, but to suggest a plurality of ways in which texts might be read in the interests of extending the reach of what is thinkable, imaginable or possible. (p. 171)

Thus such a reading is a political – specifically a Marxist – tool:

> a close reading of the texts can generate a more radical challenge to patriarchal values by disrupting sexual difference itself. Of course, the male disguise of these female heroines allows for plenty of dramatic ironies and double meanings, and thus offers the audience the pleasures of a knowingness which depends on a knowledge of sexual difference. But it can also be read as undermining that knowledge from time to time, calling it in question by indicating that it is possible, at least in fiction, to speak from a position which is not that of a full, unified, gendered subject. (p. 184)

Belsey's argument here is thus like that of the twentieth-century German playwright Bertolt Brecht in his challenge to realist drama. Realism, Brecht argues, is a politically deadening force because it leads us to believe that what we see happening must always inevitably happen like that, and so restricts our sense of what is possible, persuading us that attempts to change are doomed. To push at the frontiers of realism is thus a step towards effecting (political) change in the world. As with Cultural Materialism, this wider political commitment has tended to be a feature of British rather than American criticism; thus Walter Cohen comments on 'probably the most serious limitation of current American feminist accounts of Shakespeare – an inadequate use of historical materials, with the inevitable foreclosure of a promising mode of ideological critique within a tradition that understands its purpose to be ideological critique' ('Political Criticism of Shakespeare', p. 24), while Kate Chedgzoy writes from a British perspective that 'feminist criticism of Shakespeare characteristically weaves between past and present, driven by a commitment both to intervene in contemporary cultural politics and to recover a fuller sense of the sexual politics of the literary heritage' (*Shakespeare, Feminism and Gender*, p. 4).

The third highly influential feminist voice of the 1980s was that of Kathleen McLuskie. In her essay 'The Patriarchal Bard: Feminist Criticism and Shakespeare: *King Lear* and *Measure for Measure*', in the seminal collection *Political Shakespeare*, McLuskie refused any blanket or overarching idea of feminist criticism, declaring that 'feminist criticism can only be defined by the multiplicity of critical practices engaged in by feminists' (p. 88). She was, however, prepared to be much more prescriptive about what feminist criticism should *not* be. Firstly, she criticises the essentialism of critics such as Marilyn French and Linda Bamber (p. 89), who set up a rigid, transhistorical idea of what women are (and implicitly should be) like. Secondly, she deplores what she sees as a different kind of historical blindness, that which sees Shakespeare himself as sharing modern-day feminist sensibilities. Rather than co-opting Shakespeare as a supporter of feminism, she suggests instead reading the plays as 'the products of an entertainment industry which, as far as we know, had no women shareholders, actors, writers, or stage hands. His women characters were played by boys and, far from his plays being an expression of his idiosyncratic views, they all built on and adapted earlier stories' (p. 92).

McLuskie discusses two plays from this perspective, *Measure for Measure* and *King Lear*. In both cases, she argues that it is in fact impossible to read the play from a feminist perspective. For instance, at a crucial point in *Measure for Measure*, Angelo begins to feel desire for Isabella, and asks, 'What's this? What's this? Is this her fault or mine? / The tempter, or the tempted, who sins most?' (II.ii.162–3). McLuskie observes of this, 'A feminist reading of the scene may wish to refuse the power of Angelo's plea, may recognise in it the double bind which blames women for their own sexual oppression. However to take up that position involves refusing the pleasure of the drama and the text, which imply a coherent maleness in their point of view' (p. 97). For McLuskie, then, 'Feminist criticism of this play is restricted to exposing its own exclusion from the text. It has no point of entry into it, for the dilemmas of the narrative and the sexuality under discussion are constructed in completely male terms' (p. 97).

For McLuskie, to be excluded from the aesthetic pleasures offered by *Measure for Measure* is ultimately not particularly serious, because it belongs to the lesser genre of comedy or problem play. What is far graver, she argues, is that women are also precluded from the aesthetic delights offered by the culturally much more prestigious genre of tragedy, because 'the human nature implied in the moral and aesthetic satisfactions of tragedy is most often explicitly male' (p. 98). Above all, in *King Lear*,

> The action of the play, the organisation of its point of view and the theatrical dynamic of its central scenes all depend upon an audience accepting an equation between 'human nature' and male power. In order to experience the proper pleasures of pity and fear, they must accept that fathers are owed particular duties by their daughters and be appalled by the chaos which ensues when those primal links are broken. Such a point of view is not a matter of consciously-held opinion but it is a position required and determined by the text in order for it to make sense. It is also the product of a set of meanings produced in a specific way by the Shakespearean text and is different from that produced in other versions of the story. (p. 98)

McLuskie thus finds it impossible to offer a feminist reading of *King Lear*:

> When Lear enters, bearing his dead daughter in his arms, we are presented with a contrasting emblem of the natural, animal assertion of family love, destroyed by the anarchic forces of lust and the 'indistinguished space of woman's will'. At this point in the play the most stony-hearted feminist could not withhold her pity even though it is

called forth at the expense of her resistance to the patriarchal relations
which it endorses. (p. 102)

Nor is it possible to find any kind of circumventory reading which
ignores these issues, because

> A feminist reading of the text cannot simply assert the countervailing
> rights of Goneril and Regan, for to do so would simply reverse the
> emotional structures of the play, associating feminist ideology with
> atavistic selfishness and the monstrous assertion of individual wills.
> Feminism cannot simply take 'the woman's part' when that part has
> been so morally loaded and theatrically circumscribed. (p. 102)

McLuskie does suggest, however, that there is one possible strategy
left to feminist critics of Shakespeare. Although it is impossible to
read the plays from a feminist perspective, it is possible to comment
on why that cannot be done, and to point out the political consequences of that impossibility – to read texts, in fact, not on their
own terms but in order to expose their ideological underpinnings.
McLuskie therefore concludes by declaring that

> An important part of the feminist project is to insist that the alterna-
> tive to the patriarchal family and heterosexual love is not chaos but the
> possibility of new forms of social organisation and affective relation-
> ships. However, feminists also recognise that our socialisation within
> the family and, perhaps more importantly, our psychological develop-
> ment as gendered subjects make these changes no simple matter.
> They involve deconstructing the sustaining comforts of love and
> family as the only haven in a heartless world. Similarly a feminist
> critique of the dominant traditions in literature must recognise the
> sources of its power, not only in the institutions which reproduce
> them but also in the pleasures which they afford. But feminist criti-
> cism must also assert the power of resistance, subverting rather than
> co-opting the domination of the patriarchal Bard. (p. 106)

Finally, Ann Thompson, in 'Feminist Theory and the Editing of
Shakespeare: *The Taming of the Shrew* Revisited' (reprinted in the
Palgrave Casebook *Shakespeare, Feminism and Gender*), suggests that
feminist approaches could even influence the apparently gender-
neutral activity of editing:

> Editors of Shakespearean texts have always had to choose between
> possible readings, and it is arguable that a feminist editors [*sic*] might

make a different set of choices. In the case of plays that survive in two
or more early printed versions, editors have to choose which version
they see as more 'authoritative'. This choice will depend on a number
of factors including, of course, an argument about the provenance of
each text, but an awareness of gender issues can contribute to such a
choice in the present and help to explain the reasons behind editorial
choices made in the past. At the most obvious level editorial choices
can strengthen or weaken the roles of female characters. (p. 53)

It is undeniably unfortunate that this passage, written by a feminist
about editing and subsequently edited by another feminist, contains
a typographical error ('a feminist editors'), although if anything this
ironically reinforces Thompson's point that editing is important.
Thompson does not advocate a doctrinaire feminism in editing – she
acknowledges, for instance, that the provenance of a text (i.e. where
it comes from and what relationship it bears to the work as the
author left it) is also a vital determinant. As we have seen in the
previous chapter, however, editing can be a matter of ideology as
well as of scholarship, and here a feminist perspective might indeed
make a difference.

Thompson further suggests that

A feminist editor of Shakespeare will . . . usually find that in their
introductions her male predecessors have neglected, distorted and
trivialised topics that are of interest to women. She must interrogate
the assumptions made about gender in the text itself and in the previous transmission and elucidation of the text, drawing on feminist
studies of the ways in which Shakespeare has been reproduced and
appropriated by patriarchal cultures. (p. 55)

Here we come close to the concerns of cultural materialism again; a
feminist editor, Thompson suggests, needs to address not only the
question of what text to print (i.e. what Shakespeare 'originally'
said) but also the question of what he has been made to mean since.
She even suggests that

This approach could also inform and enliven a stage history, often a
rather dull section of an introduction consisting of a dutiful list of
names, dates and places with little to interest non-antiquarian readers.
With *Cymbeline*, for example, one can trace how the idealisation of
the heroine could only have been achieved by radical cutting and
expurgation of the text, beginning with David Garrick's version in

> 1761. Explicit sexual references and references to all but the most
> 'innocent' parts of the human body were routinely omitted. (p. 56)

However, as we shall see in Chapter 8, it is not entirely fair to suggest that stage history is necessarily dull.

Easily the most vociferous opposition to feminist readings of
Shakespeare has come from Richard Levin. In an article called
'Feminist Thematics in Shakespearean Tragedy', published in 1988
in *PMLA* (*Publications of the Modern Language Association of America*), regarded by many as the flagship journal of the profession,
Levin comprehensively attacked feminist readings of Shakespearean tragedy. He began by announcing the rules of engagement
as he saw them:

> I have . . . narrowed the scope of this inquiry to one major trend of the
> movement in this country, which defined itself in 1980–82 in our only
> anthologies of feminist criticism of Shakespeare – *The Woman's Part*
> (Lenz et al.) and two special issues of *Women's Studies* (Greene and
> Swift). Most of the contributors to those anthologies (many of whom
> went on to write other essays and books) shared an interpretive
> approach, which a number of other critics have also employed and
> which I focus on in this investigation. This focus means that I have
> had to exclude those feminist critics who adopt other approaches,
> even though some of them have given us significant studies that may
> be riding the wave of the future. It should be understood, therefore,
> that the following inquiry is meant to refer only to the particular body
> of work produced by this one approach within the larger enterprise of
> feminist criticism of Shakespeare, and to the critics actually named
> here, although I think much of the discussion will also apply to simi-
> lar kinds of feminist criticism in other fields. Because of space limita-
> tions, I have further narrowed my focus to the tragedies, which are
> generally regarded as Shakespeare's greatest achievement and so
> should provide the clearest test of this approach. (p. 125)

Although, in fairness to Levin, I should stress that many of the critics he goes on to cite by name are men, I nevertheless think that
there is a tricksiness here: Levin says first that 'the following inquiry
is meant to refer only to the particular body of work produced by
this one approach within the larger enterprise of feminist criticism
of Shakespeare, and to the critics actually named here', and then
slips in the seemingly throwaway comment that 'I think much of the
discussion will also apply to similar kinds of feminist criticism in

other fields', which certainly saves him a lot of work but does not seem to me to meet the standards of scholarly fair play, since it is surely at least as tendentious as anything he goes on to castigate in the practice of specific feminist critics.

Levin goes on to specify what his objection to this kind of writing is:

> this body of criticism is thematic. These critics agree that the plays are not really about the particular characters who appear there but about some general idea and, consequently, that they are not primarily dramatizations of actions but explorations of or commentaries on or inquiries into or critiques of that idea, which the characters and actions subserve. (p. 126)

Moreover, he continues,

> It is also clear that the themes employed in their interpretations are basically the same. Although the terminology may vary, these critics all find that the plays are about the role of gender in the individual and in society. Moreover, their formulations of this theme usually turn on a polar opposition between two abstractions that are supposed to encompass and divide the world of the play and all human experience. This kind of formula was very common in the older thematic criticism of Shakespeare, which regularly discovered that his plays portrayed the conflict of appearance and reality or reason and passion or the like, so we might expect these new gender thematists to adopt the same strategy, especially since it is implicit in the very concept of gender, which comes in two varieties. Thus their thematic dichotomies usually turn out to be some version of the eternal struggle of yang and yin. Even the readings that make 'patriarchy' the theme are really not an exception, since they always define it in terms of this gender opposition. And that opposition, we must remember, is not between the female and male characters (although there may be some relation to them) but between two abstract entities that can 'conflict' inside one character or outside any character in the thematic ether, just like 'appearance versus reality.' (p. 126)

This may look as though Levin's animus is not in fact against women at all, since he is so careful to specify that the division against which he is inveighing is not one between women and men but one between abstractions which are gendered masculine or feminine. However, a less even-handed note soon returns:

We will not be surprised to learn . . . that in these studies the cause of the tragedy is located not in the particular characters but in one of those two abstractions whose opposition constitutes the theme, nor will we be surprised to learn which one always turns out to be the guilty party. (p. 126)

Levin then turns to irony:

Of course, the characters themselves are unaware of the real cause of their misfortunes (as many of the critics acknowledge), which seems a pity, for if they only knew they might have given us some great last words. When the dying Desdemona is asked by Emilia, 'Who hath done this deed?' she could have answered, 'Nobodie, twas the male order of thinges, farewell.' And the dying Laertes could have ended his confession to Hamlet by exclaiming,

> I can no more; the Patriarchie, the Patriarchie's to blame!

(p. 127)

In fact, Levin has a point here. In *The Woman's Part*, Lorie Jerrell Leininger concludes her analysis of *The Tempest* with a battle cry along very similar lines to those which Levin mocks:

Let us invent a modern Miranda, and permit her to speak a new Epilogue:

'My father is no God-figure. No one is a God-figure. My father is a man, and fallible, as I am. Let's put an end to the fantasy of infallibility.

'There is no such thing as a "natural slave." No subhuman laborers exist. Let's put an end to *that* fantasy. I will not benefit from such a concept represented in any guise, be it Aristotelian, biblical, allegorical, or Neoplatonic . . .

'I cannot give assent to an ethical scheme that locates all virtue symbolically in one part of my anatomy. My virginity has little to do with the forces that will lead to good harvest or greater social justice.

'Nor am I in any way analogous to a foot . . . Neither my father, nor my husband, nor any one alive has the right to refer to me as his foot while thinking of himself as the head . . .

'Will I succeed in creating my "brave new world" which has people in it who no longer exploit one another? I cannot be certain. I will at least make my start by springing the "Miranda-trap," being forced into unwitting collusion with domination by appearing to be a beneficiary. I need to join forces with Caliban – to join forces with all those who are exploited or oppressed – to stand beside Caliban and say,

As we from crimes would pardon'd be,
Let's work to set each other free."

(pp. 291–2)

I think it is certainly possible to read *The Tempest* as inviting us to
see ironies in Prospero's treatment of Caliban and to read Prospero's
concern over Miranda's virginity as odd and possibly pathological.
But 'ironies' would be, for me, the key word here. Drama, and
Shakespearean drama in particular, does not state things; it suggests
them, delicately balancing one fact, one image, one point of view
against another, and inviting us to judge and assess. The ending
which Leininger suggests would, I think, be a far poorer one than
the one which Shakespeare wrote.

This does not, however, complete the list of Levin's objections to
this variety of feminist criticism. He also thinks feminist readings
are fundamentally illogical:

> since gender relations are only one of the components of each 'world,'
> we have no reason to single them out as the basic cause of events.
> Actually, these components cannot be called causes in the usual sense:
> they are necessary *conditions* of the action but are not in themselves
> sufficient to *cause* it. Many of these critics seem to have confused these
> two different kinds of agency.
>
> The distinction may become clearer if we look at some of the
> crucial actions that these readings blame on patriarchy. Novy, for
> instance, devotes some time to arguing that Lear's rejection of
> Cordelia in the opening scenes is based on patriarchal assumptions
> concerning the father–daughter relationship . . . But the witnesses to
> this rejection – Kent, Gloucester, Burgundy, France, even Goneril
> and Regan – all of whom presumably share these patriarchal assump-
> tions, regard his behavior as a shocking abnormality, which must
> mean that, while the assumptions made his behavior *possible* (by giving
> him absolute power over Cordelia), they cannot have *caused* it, for then
> it would appear normal. (p. 127)

Levin goes on to say that

> This attempt to blame the catastrophes on patriarchy is illogical in
> another sense as well, for while it is true that they would not have
> occurred in a non-patriarchal society, it is also true that they would not
> have occurred in a society that was even *more* patriarchal than the one
> we are shown – a society, for instance, where Juliet and Desdemona

could not be married, or Ophelia be courted, without the consent of their fathers, or where Goneril and Lady Macbeth were completely subservient to their husbands (which is just another way of saying that each tragedy could only take place in the specific 'world' depicted in that play). Moreover, if patriarchy is held responsible for the unhappy endings of the tragedies, then it must be equally responsible for the happy endings of the comedies and romances, which are also brought about in patriarchal worlds . . . It seems evident, then, that patriarchy cannot have any causal connection to misery (p. 128)

However it is hard to see how this comment can be reconciled with his later remark on 'the conception of the tragic genre itself that emerges from these studies': 'In most of them I did not find any real sense of the genre as an important determinant of dramatic form and effect' (p. 132). If genre is an important factor, how can it also be the case that patriarchy should have the same effects in both comedy and tragedy?

Levin's final objection to feminist readings is a particularly interesting one, because it raises a much wider theoretical issue:

thematic critics (including these feminist thematists, as we saw) regularly claim that the play [i.e. whichever play they are discussing] is 'exploring' or 'commenting on' the central theme, which implies a conscious purpose. An unintended exploration seems self-contradictory; to adapt E. D. Hirsch's dictum on meaning, there can be no exploring without an explorer. All thematists therefore have the obligation of proving that the play really is intended to be about their theme. And this general obligation becomes even greater in these feminist readings, for they assert that each tragedy is meant to call into question some of the most basic beliefs in the fictional world it dramatizes and in the real world of its author, which ought to place a very heavy burden of proof on them. (p. 133)

Virtually his final point similarly has much wider potential applicability for how we read, not only if or when we read as feminists but from any position:

nobody in these plays ever learns the lesson that these critics say is being taught there. And, except in *Antony and Cleopatra*, there is no suggestion of an alternative society with different assumptions that might serve as a basis for judging them. In view of this lack of evidence, then, it seems more reasonable to conclude that the tragedies are not criticizing their own gender assumptions but just assuming them, along with other conditions underlying the dramatized action, which is their real subject. This does not mean that *we* cannot criticize those assumptions; it only means that we should separate our activity from Shakespeare's. (p. 134)

STOP and THINK

• Do you think Levin's objections to this sort of feminist reading are justified? Are there any counter-objections to be made to his own modes of reading?

I do think Levin is in danger of writing about the characters in the plays as if they were real people rather than dramatic constructs when he says that 'the witnesses to this rejection – Kent, Glouces- ter, Burgundy, France, even Goneril and Regan – all . . . presum- ably share these patriarchal assumptions, [but] regard [Lear's] behavior as a shocking abnormality'. Can we really deduce what people in plays might feel about issues on which they do not (and in this case could not) express any opinion? I think it is also worth noting that Levin's declaration that 'thematists . . . have the oblig- ation of proving that the play really is intended to be about their theme' is fundamentally at odds with Terence Hawkes's con- tention that *we* make the meaning of Shakespeare's plays. This question of whether the meaning is inherently there or whether critics are making it will be even more pertinent when it comes to queer theory.

Queer theory

The introduction of queer theory into Shakespeare studies announced itself with a bang in the opening salvo of Joseph Pequigney's 1992 article 'The Two Antonios and Same-Sex Love in *Twelfth Night* and *The Merchant of Venice*':

The Shakespeare professoriat has a long history of avoiding the topic of homosexuality, and the critics and scholars who have written on these comedies fall into three categories: those – the largest group – who have given this topic no thought; those who are doctrinaire in denying the topic pertinence; and those – a relatively small but recently growing number, many of them feminists – who ascribe homosexual-ity to both the Antonios. The second group always and the third ordinarily are assertive of positions that they think are self-evident and require – or admit of – no proof, so that disagreement rules in the commentary. Moreover, the critics who postulate homoerotic Antonios also maintain that the homoerotic impulses are suppressed; that the love returned by the other is non-erotic; and that the characters are finally ostracized and marginalized. (p. 178)

This is an omission which Pequigney promptly proceeds to remedy by reading both Antonios as overtly homosexual. Thus in *Twelfth Night* Antonio and Sebastian are lovers: 'Antonio will see to it that they "keep company" this night also as he goes off to arrange for their dining and sleeping together at the Elephant, an inn. "There," he says, "shall you have me" (III.iii.42)' (p. 180). This reading is, however, made possible only by disregarding the fact that at the time when Shakespeare wrote, 'have' had no connotation of 'sleeping together' (the verb commonly used for such innuendo was 'know', in the Biblical sense of 'knowing carnally').

Equally tenuous is Pequigney's next piece of evidence:

When he is initially about to depart, Sebastian makes the curious admission that as a companion to Antonio he had always gone by another name, calling himself Roderigo. Why he should do so goes unexplained in both the comedy and the commentary. The alias may be demystified if it is seen as a means to hide his identity, his true name and family connections, during a drawn-out sexual liaison with a stranger in strange lands. When his twin Viola, in male disguise, cor-respondingly goes by an assumed name, Cesario, she gets caught up in novel, and homoerotic, sexual situations. Isn't this an intimation of something analogous happening – as it does – to Roderigo? Then, too, the given name Sebastian recalls the martyr traditionally pictured as a handsome youth – a kind of Christian Adonis – with a nearly nude body pierced by arrows. Our Sebastian is not a martyr, of course, although he once came close to death by drowning; yet like the saint, he is a young male beauty and, again like him, passive, the target of Olivia's as well as Antonio's desires. (p. 181)

Most surprising of all, though, is Pequigney's conclusion. Noting that most critics have imagined that Antonio ends the play partner-less and forlorn, Pequigney contends instead that Sebastian has no intention of forsaking his 'lover':

'Antonio! O my dear Antonio, / How have the hours rack'd and tor-
tur'd me, / Since I have lost thee!' (V.i.216–18). This, the most impas-
sioned speech Sebastian delivers, is hardly the prelude to a rejection;
and, further, with his late dramatic change of fortune, the sole reason
he gives for the separation disappears. The expectation is set up that
in taking a wife Sebastian need not and will not suffer the 'rack and
torture' of losing his male lover. Not the rejected 'poor Antonio' of the
commentary, he is instead the 'dear Antonio' here and hereafter of
lucky Sebastian. Does this imply a *ménage à trois* at Olivia's house?
That's anybody's guess, but a guess about nothing, for once they leave
the stage the characters vanish into thin air. (p. 182)

There is, I think, a bit of a cop-out here. Earlier, Pequigney's argument has depended on treating the characters as if they were real
people in an ongoing story, and this, indeed, he is soon to do again
when he declares that 'Sebastian could never have done what was
necessary to win Olivia, and his only chance was for his sister to per-
form this masculine role for him. Her Cesario makes a lasting
impression' (p. 184). When it comes to confronting the question of
what exactly is going to happen at the end of the play, though, he
retreats into its fictionality.

Alan Sinfield adopts virtually the same strategy as Pequigney
in his article 'How to Read *The Merchant of Venice* Without Being
Heterosexist', reprinted in the Palgrave Casebook *Shakespeare,
Feminism and Gender*, because he too suggests that we need not
necessarily see the 'homosexual' character (suggestively, another
Antonio – the name seems to be associated with same-sex orientation in Shakespeare's mind) as marginalised at the end of the play,
but as about to be incorporated into the Belmont household (p. 129).
In this essay, Sinfield pursues the point Kathleen McLuskie made
about the impossibility of a feminist reading of *King Lear*:

> The question of principle is how readers not situated squarely in the
> mainstream of Western culture today may relate to such a powerful
> cultural icon as Shakespeare. In a notable formulation, Kathleen
> McLuskie points out that the pattern of 'good' and 'bad' daughters in
> *King Lear* offers no point of entry to the ideas about women that a
> feminist criticism might want to develop; such criticism 'is restricted
> to exposing its own exclusion from the text'. This challenge has
> caused some discomfort: must exclusion from Shakespeare be added
> to the other disadvantages that women experience in our societies?

> But it has not, I think, been successfully answered. In this essay I
> pursue the question as it strikes a gay man. (p. 116)

For Sinfield, 'The key critical move' in reading as a gay man 'is to
reject the sentimental notion of Portia as an innocent, virtuous,
"Victorian" heroine' (p. 118). To do this displaces Portia and the
heterosexual wooing story which centres on her, and allows us to see
The Merchant of Venice as suffused with 'an air of homoerotic excess,
especially in the idea of being bound and inviting physical violation
. . . Bassanio introduces Antonio to Portia as the man "To whom I
am so infinitely bound"' (p. 118), and as a play in which, 'as everywhere in the period, we see a traffic in boys who, because they are
less significant, are moved around the employment–patronage
system more fluently than women' (p. 124) – as evidence for which
assertion Sinfield cites Launcelot Gobbo's change of employer and
Jessica's elopement dressed as a boy. He even claims that Portia's
anger over Bassanio's giving away of the ring is in fact based on
sexual jealousy: 'Portia has no hesitation in envisaging a sexual relationship between Bassanio and the young doctor: "I'll have that
doctor for my bedfellow", she declares, recognising an equivalence'
(p. 126). In this account, Portia is not only not at the centre of the
play, she is actually sharing Sinfield's own perspective on it as a story
of same-sex love.

Sinfield's boy-centred reading does not merely displace Portia,
however. In fact he comes close to demonising her, declaring, for
instance, that 'It is to contest Antonio's status as lover that Portia, in
her role of young doctor, demands of Bassanio the ring which she
had given him in her role of wife' (p. 119) and that

> The last act of the play is Portia's assertion of her right to Bassanio.
> Her strategy is purposefully heterosexist: in disallowing Antonio's
> sacrifice as a plausible reason for parting with the ring, she disallows
> the entire seriousness of male love. She is as offhand with Antonio as
> she can be with a guest. (p. 119)

Moreover, Sinfield also seems to draw an implicit parallel between
the strategy he attributes to Portia here and the strategy he attributes
to two recent feminist critics of the play, Janet Adelman and Coppélia
Kahn, who both see Bassanio as moving 'through' a phase of attach-
ment to Antonio before he commits himself to Portia. Sinfield

remarks of this that '[t]o heterosexually identified readers this might not seem an exceptional thought, but for the gay man it is a slap in the face of a very familiar kind' (p. 120). In fact, the critical approaches of both Adelman and Kahn are informed by psychoanalysis as much as by feminism, but nevertheless Sinfield does seem to come dangerously close to misogyny here. No sooner has he done so, however, than he signals a clear retreat from that danger:

> The fault does not lie with Kahn and Adelman (though in the light of recent work in lesbian and gay studies they might want to formulate their thoughts rather differently). They have picked up well enough the mood and tendency of the play, as most readers and audiences would agree. It is the Shakespearean text that is reconfirming the marginalisation of an already marginalised group. (p. 121)

And he also exculpates Portia by declaring that 'while an obvious perspective on the play is resentment at Portia's manipulation of Antonio and Bassanio, we may bear in mind that Portia too is oppressed in hetero-patriarchy, and try to work towards a sex-gender regime in which women and men would not be bound to compete' (p. 131).

Sinfield's analysis raises a fundamental question about feminist, gay and lesbian readings: is it gender or sexual orientation that is the main determinant of identity? This is probably something which can be answered only on a personal basis. Perhaps, if I were a lesbian, I might think that queer theory was a more urgent and valuable approach to Shakespeare than feminism; I might think that a number of major battles for women's rights have now been won, but that lesbians tend to remain invisible and that little or no attention is paid to their possible presence in Shakespeare's plays. And if I were a gay man, I might argue, as Sinfield does, that a feminist reading of Shakespeare's comedies does indeed tend to minimise or overlook entirely the effect that a female character's success may have on male same-sex relationships. Certainly I might conclude from Sinfield's account that there is an inherent tension between queer readings and feminist ones.

In fact, however, it is in the end on a strategy already proposed by a feminist critic that Sinfield eventually falls back, since the possibilities that he ultimately offers for reading *The Merchant* so closely echo those proposed by Kathleen McLuskie for *King Lear*:

> In practice, there are (at least) two routes through *The Merchant* for
> out-groups. One involves pointing out the mechanisms of exclusion
> in our cultures – how the circulation of Shakespearean texts may
> reinforce the privilege of some groups and the subordination of
> others . . . Another involves exploring the ideological structures in
> the playtexts – of class, race, ethnicity, gender and sexuality – that
> facilitate these exclusions. These structures will not be the same
> as the ones we experience today, but they may throw light upon
> our circumstances and stimulate critical awareness of how our life-
> possibilities are constructed. (p. 121)

Sinfield does note that his reading strategy may be considered exclu-
sionary or eccentric, but he also disallows the assumptions which
would underpin any such judgement: 'But (the question is always
put): Is it Shakespeare? Well, he is said to speak to all sorts and conditions, so if gay men say "OK, this is how he speaks to us" – that,
surely, is our business' (p. 130). As one would expect of a Cultural
Materialist, it is implicit here that Sinfield is talking not about what
Shakespeare's plays *mean*, but about what they can be *made to mean*.

Mario DiGangi, in his book *The Homoerotics of Early Modern
Drama*, also turns his attention to the homoerotics of Shakespearean
comedy, and of *Twelfth Night* in particular. He suggests that in
Twelfth Night

> a man's desire for a woman may be the least 'natural' or most prob-
> lematic course of all. The objects of erotic desire in the play are men:
> Viola desires Orsino; Sebastian and Antonio desire each other.
> Cesario detects the shallowness of Orsino's 'will,' or sexual desire, for
> Olivia . . . Sebastian does not evince any erotic interest in Olivia; he
> marries her when swept away by a 'flood of fortune'. (p. 41)

He notes that, at the end,

> Instead of saying, as we might expect, that Cesario's change of attire
> will transform him into *Viola*, Orsino's mistress, Orsino's sustained
> address to 'Cesario' implies that he fancies seeing his page, 'a man,' in
> a woman's habit. That is, he imagines not *Viola* in her female clothes
> but a transvestite *Cesario*. (p. 42)

And finally he comments, 'Unlike Valerie Traub, who detects in
these closing lines Orsino's anxiety about desiring *Cesario*, I detect
in them his anxiety about desiring *Viola*' (p. 42).

As the analyses of Pequigney, Sinfield and DiGangi illustrate, most early uses of queer theory to read Shakespeare concentrated on men. As DiGangi's remarks suggest, though, one prominent exception was Valerie Traub, whose book *Desire and Anxiety: Circulations of Sexuality in Renaissance Drama* offers a theoretically sophisticated study which aims to unite materialist and psychoanalytic perspectives. Although Traub acknowledges that 'the erotic body is a material site for inscriptions of ideology and power' and that 'Many of the repressions which Freud argued were necessary to culture in *Civilization and its Discontents* are necessary only within the context of patriarchal and heterosexist ideologies' (p. 9), she nevertheless declares:

> many critics indict psychoanalysis as a mechanism of social control, a form of power-knowledge that creates, organizes, and subjugates subjects in the interests of white, Western, phallocentric, heterosexist ideologies. However, despite some sympathy with this perspective, I believe that the theory of the unconscious is crucial to an understanding of erotic fantasy, preferences, and practices. (pp. 10–11)

She therefore advocates a 'kind of critical *rapprochement* . . . feminist-historical-materialist-psycho-analysis' (p. 114). Above all, she suggests that 'even the most sophisticated feminist materialist analyses misrecognize gender as a signifier in such a way that eroticism is conveniently forgotten' (p. 114), and therefore reads cross-dressing as expressing female desire rather than male and takes issue with Jardine on this: for instance, Traub sees Phebe in *As You Like It* as attracted to Rosalind not just because she does not see through the male disguise but because she has strong homoerotic feelings, so that it is in fact the femaleness of Rosalind that Phebe is attracted to rather than the supposed maleness (pp. 107–8), and she also suggests that

> We might want to look, for instance, at the relationship between Rosalind and Celia in *As You Like It*, Helena and Hermia in *A Midsummer Night's Dream*, and Marina and Philoten in *Pericles*, and ask why we assume that the images of 'a double cherry' and of 'Juno's swans . . . coupled and inseparable' are qualitatively different, somehow less erotic, than the 'twin'd lambs' of Polixenes and Leontes in *The Winter's Tale*. To pose the question in this way is to highlight the fact that, whatever the actual erotic practice of women historically, in terms of critical discourse female homoeroticism must be thought into existence. (p. 107)

Recently, Theodora Jankowski has extended this approach still further in her article '. . . in the Lesbian Void: Woman–Woman Eroticism in Shakespeare's Plays'. She begins by considering the confusion often generated in students about what happens to Hermione in *The Winter's Tale*:

> While such student questioning of the 'facts' of Hermione's existence may seem either daft, perversely tangential – along the lines of 'how many children did Lady Macbeth have?' – or merely uncooperative, these kinds of resistance to an 'easy' answer do pressure our readings of plays, forcing us to consider interpretations we might not normally entertain. This is what I want to do as regards Hermione's disappearance. (p. 299)

Jankowski therefore ponders,

> where was Hermione kept so secretly for sixteen years that no hint of her presence was revealed? Did Paulina pay all of her servants to be silent? Are we to believe that no one noticed food or clothing going into – and waste products being removed from – some 'secret' place in Paulina's house? Did Hermione remain totally silent during this period? Did she not make any contact with Paulina? Was Paulina able, secretly, to take care of *all* of Hermione's needs? What did Giulio Romano do while he supposedly worked on a statue? And, for sixteen years, did Leontes, dense though we know him to be, never have *any* suspicion that his wife was living at Paulina's? (p. 300)

There is of course a simple way of dealing with all of these questions: pointing out that what we have in *The Winter's Tale* is not, by any stretch of the imagination, realism. In her opening paragraph Jankowski implied that this was an 'easy' answer, but it would be equally possible to argue that it is not only a sophisticated one but in fact represents the only possible way of getting to grips with *The Winter's Tale*.

For Jankowski, though, there is a very different solution to the problem:

> I suggest that part of the reason that we do not have any 'critical' answers to these questions, answers that have a history of scholarly debate, is because both questions and answers involve issues of various kinds of invisibility. My answers, therefore, will not be presented in a 'traditional' scholarly way. I have raised the above questions because I believe that *asking* them, as well as trying to figure out *how* to answer

them, allows me to challenge both modern and early modern assumptions regarding the position and extent of woman–woman eroticism in
early modern texts. (p. 300)

What she suggests is that Hermione and Paulina might in fact have
been lesbian lovers. She argues that

while there were quite literally no 'lesbians' in the early modern period
– the word 'lesbian' not achieving current usage until the nineteenth
century – there quite obviously *must* have been women who desired
other women and had erotic and/or sexual relations with them. But to
look specifically at literary texts of the early modern period, we might
suspect otherwise. (p. 300)

Since these women who '*must* have' existed must have been hidden,
we need to look hard for them. If we do, we will find that they
may include Titania and her vot'ress (p. 308); Portia and Nerissa
(p. 310); Cleopatra with Charmian and Iras; and Beatrice and Hero
(p. 311). Moreover, 'Accepting the erotic relationship between Beatrice and Hero – hidden though it may be in the "lesbian" void –
reveals a way of dealing with a persistent problem in *Much Ado
About Nothing* criticism: why has Margaret agreed to the plot to
condemn Hero?' (p. 313). Pausing only to affirm her commitment
to realism at any cost by observing that 'it is quite dark in Sicily
between midnight and 1 a.m.' (p. 313), Jankowski answers her own
question by suggesting that

Margaret's intimate encounters with Hero in their own private female
space could have become erotic or erotically charged. Or they could
not. Hero *could* have rebuffed Margaret's erotic overtures, preferring
those of her bedfellow. A rejected Margaret, a jealous Margaret, or
simply an unfulfilled Margaret could have 'gotten back' at Hero by
participating in Don John's plot. (p. 314)

In *The Year's Work in English Studies* for 2002, the reviewer of
Jankowski's book suggested that Hermione, so far from having an
affair with Paulina, might just as well 'have spent sixteen years playing ice hockey for Canada or packing fish fingers in a factory! This
is the kind of spurious fantasizing about literary characters which
compromises literary criticism' (p. 360).

In the case of feminism and gender studies, them, an astonishing
variety of readings can be produced. Postcolonial criticism, which is

the subject of the next chapter, may seem positively monolithic in comparison, but it too has an urgent claim to being of overriding political importance.

STOP and THINK

- What do you think feminist criticism can offer to the interpretation of Shakespeare's plays? Is it a legitimate approach or is it forcing Shakespeare's plays into an ideological framework of which he himself could not have known and might not have approved?

Further reading

Works discussed in this chapter

Armstrong, Philip. *Shakespeare in Psychoanalysis* (London: Routledge, 2001).

Barber, C. L. *Shakespeare's Festive Comedy* (Princeton: Princeton University Press, 1959).

Belsey, Catherine. 'Disrupting Sexual Difference: Meaning and Gender in the Comedies', in *Alternative Shakespeares*, edited by John Drakakis (London: Methuen, 1985), pp. 170–94.

Chedgzoy, Kate, ed. *Shakespeare, Feminism and Gender* (Basingstoke: Palgrave, 2001).

Cohen, Walter. 'Political Criticism of Shakespeare', in *Shakespeare Reproduced*, edited by Jean E. Howard and Marion F. O'Connor (London: Methuen, 1987), pp. 18–46.

DiGangi, Mario. *The Homoerotics of Early Modern Drama* (Cambridge: Cambridge University Press, 1997).

Greenblatt, Stephen. 'Fiction and Friction', in *Shakespearean Negotiations* (Oxford: The Clarendon Press, 1988).

Greene, Gayle. 'The Myth of Neutrality, Again?', in *Shakespeare Left and Right*, edited by Ivo Kamps (London: Routledge, 1991), pp. 23–9.

Jankowski, Theodora A. '. . . in the Lesbian Void: Woman–Woman Eroticism in Shakespeare's Plays', in *A Feminist Companion to Shakespeare*, edited by Dympna Callaghan (London: Blackwell, 2000), pp. 299–319.

Jardine, Lisa. *Still Harping on Daughters: Women and Drama in the Age of Shakespeare*. (London: Harvester, 1983).

——. 'Twins and travesties: Gender, Dependency and Sexual Availability in *Twelfth Night*', in *Erotic Politics: Desire on the Renaissance Stage*, edited by Susan Zimmerman (London: Routledge, 1992), pp. 27–38.

Leininger, Lorie Jerrell. 'The Miranda Trap: Sexism and Racism in Shakespeare's *Tempest*', in *The Woman's Part: Feminist Criticism of Shakespeare*,
edited by Carolyn Ruth Swift Lenz, Gayle Greene and Carol Thomas
Neely (Urbana: University of Illinois Press, 1980), pp. 285–94.

Levin, Richard. 'Feminist Thematics and Shakespearean Tragedy', *PMLA*
103 (1988): 125–38.

——. 'Ideological Criticism and Pluralism', in *Shakespeare Left and Right*,
edited by Ivo Kamps (London: Routledge, 1991), pp. 15–21.

McLuskie, Kathleen. 'The Patriarchal Bard: Feminist Criticism and Shakespeare: *King Lear* and *Measure for Measure*', in *Political Shakespeare:
Essays in Cultural materialism*, edited by Jonathan Dollimore and Alan
Sinfield, 2nd edition (Manchester: Manchester University Press, 1994),
pp. 88–108.

Pequigney, Joseph. 'The Two Antonios and Same-Sex Love in *Twelfth
Night* and *The Merchant of Venice*', *English Literary Renaissance* 22
(1992): 201–21; reprinted in *Shakespeare and Gender: A History*, edited
by Deborah Barker and Ivo Kamps (London: Verso, 1995), pp. 178–95.

Sinfield, Alan, 'How to Read *The Merchant of Venice* Without Being
Heterosexist', in *Shakespeare, Feminism and Gender*, edited by Kate
Chedgzoy (Basingstoke: Palgrave Macmillan, 2001), pp. 115–34.

Thompson, Ann. 'Feminist Theory and the Editing of Shakespeare: *The
Taming of the Shrew* Revisited', in *Shakespeare, Feminism and Gender*,
edited by Kate Chedgzoy (Basingstoke: Palgrave Macmillan, 2001),
pp. 49–69.

Traub, Valerie. *Desire and Anxiety: Circulations of Sexuality in Renaissance
Drama* (London: Routledge, 1992).

Other works which explore issues touched on in this chapter

Barker, Deborah, and Ivo Kamps, eds. *Shakespeare and Gender: A History*
(London: Verso, 1995). A useful and very focused collection of essays.

Callaghan, Dympna. *Woman and Gender in Renaissance Tragedy: A Study of
Othello, King Lear, The Duchess of Malfi and The White Devil* (Hemel
Hempstead: Harvester Wheatsheaf, 1989). Early but very acute analysis
of two tragedies by Shakespeare and two by John Webster.

Laqueur, Thomas. *Making Sex: Body and Gender from the Greeks to Freud*
(Cambridge, Mass.: Harvard University Press, 1990). The classic
account of the one-sex model.

Park, Katharine, and Robert A. Nye, review of Thomas Laqueur, *Making
Sex: Body and Gender from the Greeks to Freud, New Republic* 18: 2 (1991):
53–5. A sceptical review which calls Laqueur's arguments into question.

7
Postcolonial criticism

What is postcolonial criticism of Shakespeare? The simple answer to that is that it is criticism of Shakespeare produced from the perspective and informed by the awareness of the fact that we live in a world where some nations, including the United Kingdom, have historically colonised others, which may now have gained political independence but in many cases are still labouring under serious economic disadvantages and are also struggling to come to terms culturally with their new situation. It is, moreover, criticism which accepts as axiomatic that Shakespearean plays were implicated in the processes of colonialism, and is generally very interested in *how* they were. As Ania Loomba and Martin Orkin write in the introduction to their important collection of essays *Post-colonial Shakespeares*,

> new and exciting critiques ... have shown how Anglo-American literary scholarship of the last two centuries offered a Shakespeare who celebrated the superiority of the 'civilized races', and, further, that colonial educationists and administrators used this Shakespeare to reinforce cultural and racial hierarchies. Shakespeare was made to perform such ideological work both by interpreting his plays in highly conservative ways (so that they were seen as endorsing existing racial, gender and other hierarchies, never as questioning or destabilizing them) and by constructing him as one of the best, if not 'the best', writer in the whole world. He became, during the colonial period, the quintessence of Englishness and a measure of humanity itself. (p. 1)

To accept that this is so, moreover, may well imply not only that Shakespeare ought to be discussed in tandem with colonialism but

also that he *cannot* be discussed without it, as Loomba and Orkin go
on to suggest:

> Political criticism of Shakespeare as well as of early modern England
> has begun to show, with increasing detail and sophistication, that it
> is virtually impossible to seal off any meaningful analysis of English
> culture and literature from considerations of racial and cultural
> difference, and from the dynamics of emergent colonialisms. (p. 4)

Particularly important in the context of postcolonial criticism is
the concept of hybridity, which, broadly speaking, is what is produced by the encounter of the two cultures of coloniser and
colonised: 'Colonial masters imposed their value system through
Shakespeare, and in response colonized people often answered back
in Shakespearean accents. The study of Shakespeare made them
"hybrid" subjects' (Loomba and Orkin, p. 7). Since postcolonial
identities are dependent on an acute sense of the fact of having once
been colonised (or for that matter coloniser), and since we all live
in a postcolonial world, Loomba and Orkin declare that 'from the
perspective of this volume it could be argued that any act of reading
and performing Shakespeare in the later twentieth century generates
multiple levels of hybridity' (p. 8).

The task of discussing Shakespeare in this way is, not, however, a
simple one. There are a number of theoretical and, to some extent,
even practical difficulties besetting the enterprise. Perhaps most
crucial and troubling is the often-voiced worry about whether our
condition as *postcolonial* subjects in itself inherently precludes us
from ever understanding the position of *colonial* subjects. Put simply,
might it be the case that the more we understand what Shakespeare's
plays mean to us now, in the postcolonial world, the less we understand what they actually meant when he wrote them, in an emer-
gently colonial or (as some critics would have it) even precolonial
world? And how valid or meaningful a term is 'postcolonial' in the
first place? Is colonisation really over when the last governor leaves
the territory? And do the similarities in the experiences of former
colonies outweigh the differences? Certainly, as Loomba and Orkin
point out, 'Various critics have complained that not enough attention
is paid within post-colonial studies and theories to specific locations
and institutions. Thus "post-coloniality" verges on becoming a

rather vague condition of people anywhere and everywhere' (p. 11). Finally, what is or should be the relationship of postcolonialism to other critical perspectives? Loomba and Orkin note, for instance, that 'although each side usually tries to enlist feminists, considerations of gender are always sidelined if the battle is configured as one between post-modernism and Marxism, or between post-colonial intellectuals inside and outside the Western academy' (p. 16).

STOP and THINK

- Is there a danger of postcolonialism positioning itself as the only possible critical approach? Can you imagine ways of reconciling it with any others? Or does it not need to be combined with anything else?

Claiming a unique position is potentially a danger point with all theories, but, perhaps because it is still in its infancy, postcolonialism does seem to me to threaten sometimes to sound almost as totalising as psychoanalysis did in its early days. At the same time, though, the work of Philip Armstrong, which I discussed in Chapter 2, shows that psychoanalysis and postcolonialism can inform each other's approaches, and, as we shall see in the work of Ania Loomba, later in this chapter, there is also potential for some fruitful crossovers between postcolonialist and feminist analysis.

The Tempest

For reasons that are sufficiently obvious, many postcolonial accounts of Shakespeare have focused primarily on *The Tempest*. It is, after all, not hard to relate *The Tempest* to the history of colonialism. In the first place, there is a clear historical relationship between the play and some of the earliest English attempts to found colonies abroad. Serious attempts at colonisation, centred at Roanoke off the coast of North Carolina, had begun in 1584. The ensuing years had seen considerable interruption to the attempts to maintain the colony, but these resumed at the turn of the century, and in 1609 a ship called *The Sea Venture*, bound for Roanoke's successor colony at Jamestown, was wrecked on the coast of Bermuda. The crew survived and were eventually rescued, and on their return to London one of those aboard, William Strachey, published *True Repertory of the Wrack, and redemption of Sir Thomas Gates Knight, upon and from the ilands of the Bermudas, his coming to Virginia, and the estate of that colony* (1610). Unmistakable verbal echoes prove beyond doubt that Shakespeare used Strachey's account as a source for *The Tempest*. There is also another possible sign of interest in the New World on Shakespeare's part in the choice of the name Caliban, which could be an anagram of the word 'cannibal', or might relate to the term 'Carib' (though it is also possible that this may derive from the Romany word 'cauliban', meaning 'black').

Since its origins were so clearly traceable to this particular historical moment, it is both appropriate and unsurprising that *The Tempest* should in turn have become a key text in the subsequent history of colonialism. Few plays have been more frequently or extensively adapted than *The Tempest*, and very often the changes made have had the intention or at least the effect of pressing the text into the services of arguments for or against, or discussions about, colonialism. Aimé Césaire's *Une Tempête*, Marina Warner's *Indigo*, and numerous others have all constituted *The Tempest* as a key text for discussion of issues associated not only with the originary moment of colonialism but also with what it was subsequently to become. As Jonathan Hart observes,

> Between 1957 and 1973, most African and large Caribbean colonies won their independence. Dissenting intellectuals and writers from these regions decided to appropriate *The Tempest* as a means of supporting decolonization and creating an alternative literary tradition ... For forty years or more – in Spanish, French and English – African and Caribbean writers and critics have, directly and indirectly, appropriated or discussed the appropriation of Shakespeare's play. For instance, in 1969 Aimé Césaire's *Une Tempête: D'après "la Tempête" de Shakespeare – Adaptation pour un théâtre nègre* was published in Paris ... in "Calypso for Caliban", which is in *Highlife for Caliban*, Lemuel Johnson shows what Caliban has done with Prospero's language, life and history: 'papa prospero / jig me mama'. (*Columbus, Shakespeare, and the Interpretation of the New World*, p. 130)

Nor did the use of *The Tempest* stop there:

> Sustained encounters with *The Tempest* are recorded in a host of imaginative and theoretical texts of the postwar decades of national

emergence, beginning with Octave Mannoni's *Psychology of Coloniza-*
tion (1950) and Frantz Fanon's *Black Skin, White Masks* (1952),
and notably including George Lamming's *The Pleasures of Exile*
(1960) and *Water with Berries* (1971), Aimé Césaire's *A Tempest*
(1969), Roberto Fernández Retamar's *Caliban* (1971), and *A Grain of*
Wheat (1968), among other works, by the Kenyan Ngugi wa Thiong'o.
In most of these works, contemporaneous British and American
attempts to problematize the traditionally stereotyped critical esti-
mate of the relationship of Prospero and Caliban are resisted in favor
of recuperating the starkness of the master/slave configuration, thus
making it appear to function as a foundational paradigm in the history
of European colonialism. In this process, writers like Ngugi, Lamming, and Césaire regenerate out of their own firsthand experience of
colonization a conception of Shakespeare as a formative producer and
purveyor of a paternalistic ideology that is basic to the material aims
of Western imperialism. (Thomas Cartelli, *Repositioning Shakespeare:*
National Formations, Postcolonial Appropriations, p. 89)

It is little wonder, then, that so much recent criticism has approached
the play from this angle. In Peter Childs's *Post-colonial Theory and*
English Literature: A Reader, for instance, there are four pieces on *The*
Tempest (extracts from Trevor R. Griffiths, '"This Island's Mine":
Caliban and Colonialism', Rob Nixon, 'Caribbean and African
Appropriations of *The Tempest*', Meredith Anne Skura, 'Discourse
and the Individual: The Case of Colonialism in *The Tempest*' and
Sylvia Wynter, 'Beyond Miranda's Meanings: Un/silencing the
"Demonic Ground" of Caliban's "Woman"'). However, these essays,
like the numerous others on the play, are by no means monolithic in
their viewpoints, and indeed the struggles over the meaning of *The*
Tempest have sometimes been almost as fierce as those between
colonisers and colonised. In this section, I will look first at Paul
Brown's influential essay, '"This thing of darkness I acknowledge
mine"' (another piece which had its first appearance in the landmark
collection *Political Shakespeare*); secondly I will look at some of the
critics who have resisted Brown's account and others like it; and
finally I will consider some of the critics who have focused less on
what Shakespeare's plays tell us about their own time and more
on the cultural uses to which they have been put since.

Many of these essays will seem familiar in their approaches, and
we may indeed seem at times to be going over old ground again,

because there was a notable overlap between early postcolonial approaches and existing New Historicist and Cultural Materialist ones. In his essay '"This Tunis, sir, was Carthage": Contesting Colonialism in *The Tempest*', in *Post-colonial Shakespeares*, Jerry Brotton argues that 'It is significant that the subsequent perception of the play produced by both Brown and Barker and Hulme is very much in keeping with the critical concerns of materialist criticism of the early 1980s' (p. 26). Their approach to the play was, he suggests, fundamentally conditioned by their historical and geographical positioning in British universities of the 1980s, and the same, he says, applied also, albeit in different ways, to their counterparts on the other side of the Atlantic:

> While accounts of the play which emerged from a perspective of British cultural materialism tended to reproduce a reading of *The Tempest* inflected through the lens of nineteenth-century imperial history, the equally influential accounts of the play which emanated from the critical perspective of American new historicism since the 1980s also invested something of their own complex relation to nineteenth-century colonial history in their readings of *The Tempest*. (pp. 26–7)

This, he says, is because

> new historicists, eager to emphasize the 'American' contexts of *The Tempest*, while distancing themselves from the morally prescriptive nature of its supposed colonial politics, nevertheless reproduce a long-held preoccupation defining the play as part of America's own cultural heritage and abiding relationship with one of its colonial creators, early modern England. In claiming an exclusively American context for the play's production, American new historicist critics overinvest something of their own peculiarly post-colonial identities as American intellectuals within the one text that purports to establish a firm connection between America and the culture which these critics analyse with such intensity: early modern England. (p. 27)

It is perhaps a neat irony that early postcolonial criticism should thus have been doubly belated; in a sense, both British and American academics had, as Brotton sees it, already been 'colonised', or at least conditioned, by the dominant ideologies of their respective professional and national cultures.

In his influential essay '"This thing of darkness I acknowledge mine": *The Tempest* and the Discourse of Colonialism', published in the first edition of *Political Shakespeare*, Paul Brown argued that while *The Tempest* is indeed clearly and closely related to the issues and discourses of colonialism, the relationship is not a simple one:

> *The Tempest* is not simply a reflection of colonialist practices but an intervention in an ambivalent and even contradictory discourse. This intervention takes the form of a powerful and pleasurable narrative which seeks at once to harmonise disjunction, to transcend irreconcilable contradictions and to mystify the political conditions which demand colonialist discourse. Yet the narrative ultimately fails to deliver that containment and instead may be seen to foreground precisely those problems which it works to efface or overcome. The result is a radically ambivalent text which exemplifies not some *timeless* contradiction internal to the discourse by which it inexorably undermines or deconstructs its 'official' pronouncements, but a moment of *historical* crisis. This crisis is the struggle to produce a colonialist discourse adequate to the complex requirements of British colonialism in its initial phase. (p. 48)

To some extent, these are the attitudes and words that we might by now expect to find in *Political Shakespeare*. There is the characteristic emphasis on the mystification of political conditions, the objection to any idea of 'timelessness' and the call to historicise instead, and also, as in Kathleen McLuskie's essay on *King Lear* in the same volume, the acknowledgement that the reading being proposed is to a large extent one that goes against the grain, and robs the text of much of its pleasure. What is specific to Brown's argument, however, is his stress on a precise moment in the history of colonialism as the context most germane for *The Tempest*, and this departs from the frequent practice of Cultural Materialism of relating Shakespeare's plays not primarily to his time but to our own. For Brown, *The Tempest* is a play that attempts to tell a story about the English colonialist enterprise and to speak, indeed to create, a language which is appropriate to that particular moment, although ultimately it fails in that attempt because we are able to detect the signs of strain in its project.

As so often in New Historicist and Cultural Materialist accounts, the author has receded very much into the background here. There is no mention of Shakespeare in the passage from Brown which I quoted. Instead, it is the play itself which is seen as the active agent, and which governs the verbs in the passage: '*The Tempest* is . . . an intervention'; 'the narrative ultimately fails to deliver . . . containment'; the play is 'a radically ambivalent text which exemplifies . . . a moment of *historical* crisis'. Similarly, in New Historicist analysis it tends to be 'power' which speaks. Some critics object to this practice, but it seems to me quite reasonable. The novelist D. H. Lawrence famously advised readers to 'Never trust the teller, trust the tale', and I think a play such as *The Tempest* can be said to 'speak of' particular issues and cultural pressure points, regardless of whether its author intended it to do so or not. Perhaps Shakespeare will, as Ben Jonson foretold, be for all time, but he was certainly also of an age, and perhaps none of his plays talks more interestingly about that age than *The Tempest*.

Brown goes on to read *The Tempest* in the light of the English adventurer John Rolfe's 1614 letter seeking permission for his marriage to the native American Pocahontas, daughter of the chief Powhatan, which refers to her as 'an unbeleeving creature' (p. 48) who will be converted to Christianity by her marriage to Rolfe. Brown contends that 'Rolfe's . . . letter . . . may . . . be said to *produce* Pocahontas as an other in such a way that she will always affirm Rolfe's sense of godly duty and thus confirm him as a truly civil subject' (p. 49). As Brown acknowledges, such a view of the relationship between colonisers and indigenous inhabitants is clearly influenced by Edward Said's concept of Orientalism, which views colonialist discourse as always

> voic[ing] a demand for both order and disorder, producing a disruptive other in order to assert the superiority of the coloniser. Yet that production is itself evidence of a struggle to restrict the other's disruptiveness to that role. Colonialist discourse does not simply announce a triumph for civility, it must continually *produce* it, and this work involves struggle and risk. (p. 58)

In Brown's account, then, colonialist discourse works rather as power does for New Historicism. Power licenses a certain amount of apparent subversion in order to protect its own position; colonial discourse 'produces' a savage Other so that it can reaffirm its own status as civilised.

For Brown, however, there is a threat posed to this process by
the fact that 'The same discourse which allows for the transformation of the savage into the civil also raises the possibility of a reverse
transformation' (p. 57), and this means that there is an inherent
instability in all colonial transactions. Consequently, there are
distinct strains visible in the project of *The Tempest*:

> The second scene of the play is an extended demonstration of
> Prospero's powerful narration as it interpellates Miranda, Ariel and
> Caliban ... This reinvestiture in civil power through the medium
> of the non-civil is an essentially colonialist discourse. However, the
> narrative is fraught because it reveals internal contradictions which
> strain its ostensible project and because it produces the possibility of
> sites of resistance in the other precisely at the moment when it seeks
> to impose its captivating power. (p. 59)

'Interpellation', a term derived from the Marxist critic Louis
Althusser, refers to the rhetorical and ideological processes by which
people are constituted as 'subjects', who have the illusion of *subjec-
ti*vity (that is, of free individuality) but are in fact *subject*ed within
the ideological order. In Brown's account of *The Tempest*, Prospero
is attempting to constitute (or situate) Miranda, Ariel and Caliban
as subjects within his desired order, and the ways in which he
seeks to do this parallel the strategies used by colonisers when dealing with indigenous inhabitants. Prospero's project is disrupted,
though, by what the play reveals as cracks in the consistency and
capabilities of his enterprise – and therefore, by analogy, as cracks
in the consistency and capabilities of the English colonial enterprise
as a whole.

Brown detects a number of such fissures or faultlines in the play,
pointing out, for instance, that 'In the recitation to Miranda, for
example, Prospero is forced to remember his own past *forgetfulness*'
(p. 59), and he therefore concludes that

> *The Tempest*, then, declares no all-embracing triumph for colonialism.
> Rather it serves as a limit text in which the characteristic operations
> of colonialist discourse may be discerned – as an instrument of
> exploitation, a register of beleaguerment and a site of radical ambiva-
> lence. These operations produce strategies and stereotypes which
> seek to impose and efface colonialist power; in this text they are also
> driven into contradiction and disruption. The play's 'ending' in

renunciation and restoration is only the final ambivalence, being at once the apotheosis, mystification and potential erosion of the colonialist discourse. If this powerful discourse, thus mediated, is finally reduced to the stuff of dreams, then it is still dreamwork, the site of a struggle for meaning. My project has been to attempt a repunctuation of the play so that it may reveal its involvement in colonial practices, speak something of the ideological contradictions of its *political* unconscious. (pp. 68–9)

As we shall see, one of the major criticisms subsequently directed at Brown's work was that it was not sufficiently historical. A number of other later critics have declared that Brown's reading, and others like it, regard early modern England as a major colonial power when it was not really any such thing, although it is certainly true that the *idea* of colonisation was strongly in the air. Other critics, including Jerry Brotton, whom I will be discussing later in the chapter, have suggested that Brown had the right idea but was looking in the wrong place: Brotton argues that *The Tempest* is not about the new world but about the old, i.e. the Mediterranean, while other critics have read it as being primarily about Ireland. These other possible geographical contexts are omitted from Brown's account, and so are a number of other aspects of the play – but then it would be completely unreasonable to expect one article to engage with everything that could possibly be said about the play.

Brown's analysis was by no means without its critics. For instance, Deborah Willis, in 'Shakespeare's *Tempest* and the Discourse of Colonialism' (first published in the well-respected journal *Studies in English Literature 1500–1900*), objected to Brown's reading on a number of grounds. She cited several areas where she disagreed with Brown's interpretation or emphasis, but most of all she registered an overall aesthetic objection: 'Brown's account implies an author whose most powerful effects are those which have eluded his control' (p. 278). Willis, by contast, pleaded for the reinstatement of the figure of the author and for a reading of the play which focused essentially on what the authorial intent might have been:

By representing the play's 'ambivalences' as unintended by-products of an attempt to endorse colonialism unequivocally, Brown makes it difficult to see the more qualified endorsement the play is really making; he also makes it difficult to distinguish the play from other texts that *do* deliver such endorsements. His argument, it seems to me, reproduces an error that has haunted criticism of *The Tempest* – that is, the conflation of Prospero with Shakespeare. (p. 279)

In Willis's view, *The Tempest* is a play in which we are carefully and deliberately invited to look *at* Prospero, not *with* him. She argues that

> While Prospero clearly views Caliban as a threatening 'other,' the audience does not; the play invites us to sympathize with and to laugh at Caliban, but not to perceive him as a real threat. No necessity compels Shakespeare to give Caliban a speech giving him a persuasive claim to legitimate ownership of the island, or to undermine Prospero's claim that Caliban is ineducable by having Caliban state his intention to 'seek for grace' in the play's final scene. (p. 279)

For Willis, 'the play's true threatening "other" is not Caliban, but Antonio' (p. 280), though 'Oddly, Brown scarcely refers to Antonio or to Prospero's attitude toward him' (p. 281). Willis's reference to 'the audience' here, however, seems to me to threaten a collapse of both historical and geographical distances by implying that all audiences everywhere, at whatever time and whatever the nature and circumstances of the production, have a unified and predictable reaction to the play. Personally, I distrust that idea, not least because of the remarkable range of variety in Shakespearean production which the next chapter will explore. For me, one of the most interesting things about Shakespeare's representation of Caliban is how little we are actually told about him, and this leaves considerable scope for directors of the play to present a wide variety of Calibans.

Willis seems further to override the specifics of history when she observes that

> Brown's understanding of colonialism is shaped in part by categories he borrows from Immanuel Wallerstein. To Wallerstein, the colonial enterprise may be seen to operate in three domains, the 'core,' 'semi-periphery,' and 'periphery.' The colonialism of the core involves the reinforcement and expansion of royal hegemony within England itself; that of the semiperiphery involves its expansion into areas (such as Ireland) only partially under English control; that of the periphery, into the New World. The 'production of the other' takes place in all three domains, and Brown finds all three relevant to *The Tempest*. (p. 279)

Willis makes this point in order to argue that

> *The Tempest* celebrates what Wallerstein calls the 'colonialism of the
> core' while rendering the 'colonialism of the periphery' in more prob-
> lematic terms. Rather than a failed attempt to endorse a vaguely
> defined colonialism unequivocally, the play should be understood as an
> extremely successful endorsement of the core's political order. At the
> same time, the play registers anxiety about the legitimacy of peripheral
> colonial ventures and their ability to further core interests. (p. 280)

For Willis too, then, the play reveals anxieties about certain aspects
of the English colonial enterprise, but the difference between her
account and Brown's is that, in hers, Shakespeare knows that it does
and is creating the effect deliberately.

Another critic who disagreed with Brown and those who followed
his approach was Meredith Anne Skura, in 'Discourse and the
Individual: The Case of Colonialism in *The Tempest*', first published
in 1989 in the prestigious journal *Shakespeare Quarterly*. Skura
acknowledged that Brown's approach was not without its merits, but
argued that the time had come for a corrective:

> The revisionist impulse has been one of the most salutary in recent
> years in correcting New Critical 'blindness' to history and ideology
> . . . .But here, as critics have been suggesting about new historicism in
> general, it is now in danger of fostering blindness of its own. Granted
> that something was wrong with a commentary that focused on *The
> Tempest* as a self-contained project of a self-contained individual and
> that ignored the political situation in 1611. But something seems
> wrong now also, something more than the rhetorical excesses charac-
> teristic of any innovative critical movement. The recent criticism not
> only flattens the text into the mold of colonialist discourse and elimi-
> nates what is characteristically 'Shakespearean' in order to foreground
> what is 'colonialist,' but it is also – paradoxically – in danger of taking
> the play further from the particular historical situation in England in
> 1611 even as it brings it closer to what we mean by 'colonialism' today.
> (pp. 292–3)

Skura points to what she sees as three main areas of weakness or blindness in postcolonial accounts of the play. In the first place, as we have
seen, she objects that this approach is not in fact historicising at all:

> we have no *external* evidence that seventeenth-century audiences
> thought the play referred to the New World. In an age when real
> voyages were read allegorically, the status of allegorical voyages like

Prospero's can be doubly ambiguous, especially in a play like *The Tempest*, which provides an encyclopedic context for Prospero's experience, presenting it in terms of an extraordinary range of classical, biblical and romantic exiles, discoveries, and confrontations. (p. 294)

Instead,

When *The Tempest* was written, what the New World seems to have meant for the majority of Englishmen was a sense of possibility and a set of conflicting fantasies about the wonders to be found there; these were perhaps the preconditions for colonialism – as for much else – but not yet the thing itself. (p. 306)

However, Skura's argument that postcolonial readings are insufficiently historicised seems rather undermined by her contention that in these 'new' readings it is always assumed that

If Caliban is the center of the play, it is not because of his role in the play's self-contained structure, and not even because of what he reveals about man's timeless tendency to demonize 'strangers,' but because Europeans were at that time exploiting the real Calibans of the world, and *The Tempest* was part of the process. (p. 290)

It is hard to see how an allegedly historicising approach finds room for a phrase such as 'man's timeless tendency'.

As a related point, Skura further objects that because we are misguidedly concentrating on the early history of the English colonial enterprise, which, she maintains, is a red herring, we are no longer paying sufficient attention to the contexts that *were* relevant to an early seventeenth-century audience, most notably Shakespeare's other plays:

Long before writing *The Tempest*, Shakespeare had written another play about a ruler who preferred his books to government. Navarre's academy in *Love's Labor's Lost* was no island, but, like an island, it was supposed to be isolated from territorial negotiations. And Navarre, oblivious to colonial issues, though certainly not exempt from timeless aristocratic prejudice, brought his own version of Ariel and Caliban by inviting Armado and Costard to join him. (p. 309)

Skura also compares Prospero and Caliban to Hal and Falstaff in *Henry IV, Part One*, to Duke Senior and Jaques in *As You Like It* (p. 312), and to the Duke and Lucio in *Measure for Measure* (p. 313) – all plays which do not have a colonial setting or context of any kind.

Lastly, Skura raises another, more wide-ranging objection to Brown's reading and those which followed it: 'this shift in our attitude toward the object of interpretation entails a less explicit but extremely important move away from the psychological interpretation that had previously seemed appropriate for the play (even to its detractors) largely because of its central figure who, so like Shakespeare, runs the show' (pp. 290–1). Because of this, she complains, 'Even in less polemical examples the "political unconscious" often replaces, rather than supplements, any other unconscious; attention to culture and politics is associated with an implicit questioning of individuality and of subjective experience' (p. 291). Skura regrets this move away from the psychoanalytic, and thinks that we ought to notice, for instance, that Prospero appears to project his own darkest fears on to Caliban:

> If Prospero is to pass on his heritage to the next generation, he must at this moment repress his desire for power and for revenge at home, as well as any sexual desire he feels toward Miranda. Both desires are easily projected onto the fishily phallic Caliban, a walking version of Prospero's own 'thing' of darkness ... Caliban's function as a walking screen for projection may help explain why Caliban's sin does not consist in cannibalism, to which, one assumes, Prospero was never tempted, but rather in Prospero's own repressed fantasies of omnipotence and lust. (pp. 310–11)

For Skura, 'In a sense ... Caliban emerged from the rift between Prospero and Antonio, just as Ariel emerged from Sycorax's riven pine' (p. 318).

In a 2003 survey of the current state of *Tempest* criticism, Peter Hulme observes,

> Meredith Anne Skura's 'Discourse and the Individual: The Case of Colonialism in *The Tempest*' (1989) has rapidly become the standard reference point for those seeking to acknowledge something of the revisionary arguments, yet contain them in a higher synthesis through combining their insights with the best of the traditional criticism. Such an approach offers itself as scholarly and judicious, broad-minded and tolerant. Most of the time it just misses the point. ('Stormy Weather: Misreading the Postcolonial *Tempest*')

I agree with Hulme in so far as I am uncomfortable with the way Skura attempts to combine a plea for more careful historicising with a plea for the importance of a psychoanalytic reading of the play. As we have seen, there is a traditional, though perhaps not necessarily an irreconcilable, tension between these two approaches. I certainly think *The Tempest* would be a much less interesting play if it were really about the psyche of one man, even if that one man was to be seen as representing Shakespeare, which I think is in any case highly problematic. You may remember Deborah Willis describing the conflation of Prospero with Shakespeare as an error that has haunted criticism of *The Tempest*; it certainly seems to lie behind Skura's description of Prospero as a 'central figure who, so like Shakespeare, runs the show'.

Finally, Ben Ross Schneider, Jr, in '"Are We Being Historical Yet?": Colonialist Interpretations of Shakespeare's *Tempest*', first published in the important American journal *Shakespeare Studies*, surveyed eight recent analyses of *The Tempest*, including Brown's, and concluded:

> By choosing colonialism as a frame, and then 'reifying' it as if it were 'cotermin[o]us with the limits of discourse in general,' I find that the new historicists do indeed marginalize not only a large field of pertinent contemporary discourse, but also *The Tempest* itself. For as we are constantly reminded, we must explore, 'both the social presence to the world of the literary text and the social presence *of* the world in the literary text.' To carry out this project, we must answer the question, 'What difference did *The Tempest* make to which fields of discourse?' By too assiduously implementing the colonialist frame, the eight critics I study here effectively forestall any attempt to answer the question in terms of a full range of possibilities, despite the ostensible variety of approaches they take to the play. (p. 121)

Schneider complains that

> For some reason the great variety of theoretical underpinning in this set of essays does not produce a corresponding variety of interpretation. All critiques proceed in much the same fashion to dismantle a presumed 'authorized version' of the play that idealizes and romanticizes Prospero as a noble regenerator of fallen humanity. (p. 122)

As a counterweight to this alleged univocality, Schneider goes on to propose an alternative context which he sees as much more central to interpretation of the play:

All but one of these critics pick, as the opening fissure in the romantic surface of the play the 'refreshingly subversive' storm scene that
begins the play in which helpless, hapless nobles must endure the
insults of desperate mariners trying to save the ship. Immediately
power reveals itself in subversion. The nearly unanimous choice of
this scene is symptomatic of the whole critical approach. By framing
the scene as colonial discourse, these critics foreclose the possibility
that the storm (in nature and society) represents and dramatizes, as
in *Lear*, the social disorder that ensues when a state is irresponsibly
governed. What does the title signify? It seems more likely that
The Tempest is participating here in contemporary discourse on
government, about which I shall have more to say later. (pp. 122–3)

Like Skura, Schneider here denies that there is anything distinctive
about *The Tempest* which demands that it be read within a postcolonial framework; for him, *The Tempest* is like *King Lear*, and shares
with that play a major thematic concern with government.

Also, again like Skura, Schneider argues that adducing this new
context would represent a truer historicism than that practised by
the self-styled historicists:

The idea that Shakespeare is the universal man, tied to no time or
place, dies very hard, so hard that even the scholars most dedicated to
rehistoricizing him cannot seem to break themselves of the habit of
thinking of him as one of us, seeing his times through our eyes.
Between us and Shakespeare lie the development of capitalist society,
and the French, romantic, and industrial revolutions. But we read
Shakespeare almost as if nothing had happened. Should we not, in
order to understand him, his audience, and by virtue of the uncompromising law of believability, his characters, become familiar with
the "ethic" that preceded The Protestant Ethic and The Spirit of
Capitalism? What notions of good and bad governed early modern
decision-making? Social historians generally agree that they were quite
different from ours. (p. 127)

Paradoxically, however, the first thing we seem to have to do if we
adopt Schneider's approach is to collapse history entirely, for he
assures us that we will find that 'If we identify Prospero as an exem-
plar of the Senecan angry man, his behaviour is easier to explain. He
joins a sizable list of Shakespeare's angry madmen, whose fury
drives them down an irreversible course to certain disaster' (p. 133).
Here, we are invited to read *The Tempest* not in terms of anything

that was happening in its own time but in terms of the Roman philosopher and writer Seneca and his Stoic philosophy of proper behaviour.

For Schneider, however, the play is all about human ideas which have apparently not changed much over time. He declares that

> At the climax of the play, . . . Prospero wins freedom from the dark-ness that fills his mind. 'Freedom' is another of *The Tempest*'s power words, so important that Shakespeare uses his dramatic medium's points of strongest emphasis to call it to our attention. Three acts close on freedom, and the play ends with the word 'free'. (p. 134)

It seems implicit here that Schneider is happy to accept that 'free' meant to Shakespeare the same as it does to us. For Schneider, *The Tempest* is indeed virtually a meditation on freedom: he argues that 'voluntary servitude is the only freedom *The Tempest* offers' (p. 137) and that Caliban and Ferdinand represent contrasting attitudes to log-carrying, with Ferdinand emblematising voluntary servitude (p. 135).

Schneider concludes his analysis by declaring:

> *The Tempest* hears and contributes to many other fields of discourse: Arthurian legend, Jungian archetypes, Freudian psychoses, regenera-tion rituals, vegetation cults, Plato's three parts of the soul, good angels/bad angels, chess, Italy, drama theory, Shakespeare's life, magic, the ethics of magic, and who knows what else? And discourse of colonialism does of course participate. But if we open the window far enough to include Stoicism, Prospero's conquistadorial activities become a product of his anger, and his colonizing becomes a category of tyranny, which by definition governs by enslavement. Since both anger and tyranny are bad, and their consequences are bad, the play deplores colonization. But *The Tempest*'s relation to colonialism is more complex than the view from the colonialist critics' window. (p. 141)

I must say that bringing in 'Arthurian legends, Jungian archetypes, Freudian psychoses, regeneration rituals, vegetation cults' etc. seems to me to smack of desperation rather than discrimination, and, while it is certainly true that Seneca and his ideas continued to be very popular in early modern England, I wonder if they really constitute a more appropriate and immediate context than what was happening in Bermuda and America.

Schneider is not the only critic to have questioned whether post-colonial readings of *The Tempest* are properly historicised. In his essay "'This Tunis, sir, was Carthage": Contesting Colonialism in *The Tempest*', in *Post-colonial Shakespeares*, Jerry Brotton argues that

> in dismissing the significance of the Mediterranean, or Old World references in *The Tempest*, colonial readings have offered a historically anachronistic and geographically restrictive view of the play, which have overemphasized the scale and significance of English involvement in the colonization of the Americas in the early decades of the seventeenth century. The presence of a more definable Mediterranean geography which runs throughout the play, and which emanates outwards from the disputation over contemporary Tunis and classical Carthage, suggests that *The Tempest* is much more of a politically and geographically bifurcated play in the negotiation between its Mediterranean and Atlantic contexts than critics have recently been prepared to concede. (p. 24)

Brotton suggests that many accounts of the play have in fact 'ultimately reproduced the discursive logic of a colonialist discourse which they ostensibly sought to critique', complaining of Brown, for instance, that he 'explicitly relied upon the acceptance of a historically and geographically monolithic concept of "the" discourse of colonialism, as opposed to the possibilities of a more diverse range of historically and regionally distinct discourses and effects of cultural encounter and exchange' (p. 26). By contrast, Brotton himself argues that what *The Tempest* is actually about is

> a deep ambivalence regarding the nature of early English maritime encounters with territories over which it could exercise little or no political control. Even more problematically, these encounters placed the English crown in a position of political amity and diplomatic subservience to the publicly demonized 'infidel', the Ottoman Empire. In its occlusion of any traces of the controlling presence of the Ottomans, *The Tempest* offers a conveniently imprecise but sanitized version of the Mediterranean World, imbued with an aura of suitably familiar and assimilable myths of classical imperial travel and conquest, personified in its overdetermined [i.e. with multiple causes and hence meanings] references to Virgil's *Aeneid*. (p. 36)

For Brotton, therefore, as for Brown, *The Tempest* has a 'project', though here it is one that is directed not towards the New World but towards the Old. What is not clear here is what role Shakespeare himself is to be seen as having played in shaping this project. Was it in any sense his *intention* to '[offer] a conveniently imprecise but sanitized version of the Mediterranean World'? And to whom does the play make this 'offer'?

However, Brotton does not propose disregarding the New World context altogether:

> To interrogate the specificities of *The Tempest*'s complex negotiation of its Mediterranean contexts does not simply call for a rejection of its New World readings in favour of its Old World resonances. Such an argument would only reinstall the problematic binaries and exclusions which so much *Tempest* criticism has reproduced over recent years. Instead, I would argue that the play is precisely situated at the *geographical bifurcation* between the Old World and the New, at the point at which the English realized both the compromised and subordinated position within which they found themselves in the Mediterranean, and the possiblity of pursuing a significantly different commercial and maritime narrative in the Americas. (p. 37)

STOP and THINK

- Is Brotton's account more 'historical' than Brown's? How does his conception of the author compare with Brown's? Skura would probably regard Brotton's account as taking insufficient account of authorial intent. Would you agree with her?

Personally, I think that Brotton's reading of the play does take account of historical specifics, and also, importantly, does not present its own emphases as the only possible ones or as precluding or invalidating those of other readings. Rather it is a nuanced account that seeks to assimilate and incorporate other readings. Brotton too is more interested in the play than in its author, but I do not see why this should pose a problem.

Postcolonial *Tempests*

For many notable recent critics, the question of what the play did or did not mean in its own time is beside the point; what matters is not the relation of *The Tempest* to the originary moment of English colonialism but the role it has played since. Thus Ania Loomba declares in her book *Gender, Race, Renaissance Drama* that

> If 'cultural production occurs all the time and at every point where meaning is communicated' (Sinfield, 'Reproductions', p. 131), then these are not limited to the ideological and material conditions of the inception of the text but must include its subsequent deployments. (p. 2)

She notes that

> The export of English literature was a crucial component in establishing the ideological hegemony of the British Empire in Asia and Africa. English literature was strategically employed in the service of colonial education and had a role to play in what [the postcolonial critic Gayatri Chakravorty] Spivak has termed the worlding of the Third World. (p. 2)

From Loomba's perspective, moreover, this is no mere dry academic debate but a matter of urgency and real political importance:

> An overwhelming majority of those who choose to study English literature in India are women and the trend is sharpened by increasing devaluation of the subject. Fanon's [the French psychiatrist and political theorist Frantz Fanon, 1925–61] colonised subject is a male; for women, the split between black skin and white mask is intensified by their gendered alienation from white society, which is perhaps encapsulated in their relationship to the Western canonical text. It is somewhat ironical, then, that its understanding and knowledge is supposed to equip them for their roles as better wives and mothers. (p. 23)

Plays such as *The Tempest*, and more particularly *Othello*, thus become potent instruments of an imperial, colonising rule in which women are doubly disadvantaged:

> The much-vaunted theory of the spiritual chaos of Jacobean drama implicitly connected female disobedience with a degenerate social order, and thus contributed to silencing any notions of disobedience which actual women readers may harbour. In the Indian classroom, it commits another violence – that of imposing universalised models of human relationships upon subaltern readers [essentially those who belong to societies that are or have been colonised]; paradoxically, the points of intersection with our lives are carefully excluded. For

example, as undergraduates at Miranda House, Delhi . . . who were 'dissatisfied' with Desdemona's silence in the face of her husband's brutality, we were told that we did not 'understand' her because we had never been 'in love'. *Othello* thus became a sort of universal text of love, and love implied female passivity. (p. 39)

It is because of a history of appropriations such as this that Thomas Cartelli argues

The Tempest has long functioned in the service of ideologies that repress what they cannot accommodate and exploit what they can. One consequence of this subordination of text to ideological transaction is that it is still a generally uneducable, bestial Caliban who survives the adjustments that have been made in Western racial prejudices; mainly a blindly self-righteous, authoritarian Prospero who presides in Third World inversions of the same. Yet the text of *The Tempest* continues to allow Prospero the privilege of the grand closing gesture; continues to privilege that gesture's ambiguity at the expense of Caliban's dispossession; continues, in short, to support and substantiate the very reading of itself transacted by the ideologies in question. It is in this respect, among others, that *The Tempest* is not only complicit in the history of its successive misreadings, but responsible in some measure for the development of the ways in which it is read. (*Repositioning Shakespeare*, p. 104)

STOP and THINK

- Do you agree that *The Tempest* is essentially much like Shake-speare's other plays, or do you think its place in the history of colonialism sets it apart?
- Would it be possible to produce an analysis of this or any other Shakespearean play which was informed both by a postcolo-nial perspective and by formalist considerations?

This is of course perfectly legitimate, and moreover, as we shall see later in the chapter, *The Tempest* is not in fact unique in the Shake-spearean canon in its apparent concern with colonialism; *Othello* is another text that is of interest in this respect, and the impor-tance of the Indian boy in *A Midsummer Night's Dream* has meant that it too has been found susceptible to postcolonial analysis. However, *The Tempest* is clearly the play that resonates most strongly in the postcolonial world, and I do not think we should deny that. It seems to me to be a perfectly acceptable critical move to compare *The Tempest* with, say, *Love's Labour's Lost*, as long as this is not at the expense of acknowledging its place in the history of colonialism. Equally, however, we should not forget that other plays can also speak to the history of colonialism, and that is why I now turn to *Othello*.

Othello

Most of what has been said in this chapter has been about *The Tempest*, but, as Loomba's arguments indicate, *Othello* is relevant too. I want, therefore, to stop a moment to think about one of Shakespeare's most famous speeches, the account given by Othello of his courtship of Desdemona:

> Her father loved me, oft invited me,
> Still questioned me the story of my life
> From year to year – the battles, sieges, fortunes
> That I have passed.
> I ran it through, even from my boyish days
> To th'very moment that he bade me tell it,
> Wherein I spake of most disastrous chances,
> Of moving accidents by flood and field,
> Of hair-breadth scapes i'th'imminent deadly breach,
> Of being taken by the insolent foe
> And sold to slavery; of my redemption thence
> And portance in my travailous history;
> Wherein of antres vast and deserts idle,
> Rough quarries, rocks and hills whose heads touch heaven
>
> > *(antres: caves)*
>
> It was my hint to speak – such was my process –
> And of the cannibals that each other eat,
> The Anthropophagi, and men whose heads
> Do grow beneath their shoulders. This to hear
> Would Desdemona seriously incline,
> But still the house affairs would draw her thence,
> Which ever as she could with haste dispatch
> She'd come again, and with a greedy ear
> Devour up my discourse; which I, observing,
> Took once a pliant hour and found good means

To draw from her a prayer of earnest heart
That I would all my pilgrimage dilate,
Whereof by parcels she had something heard
But not intentively. I did consent,
And often did beguile her of her tears
When I did speak of some distressful stroke
That my youth suffered. My story being done
She gave me for my pains a world of sighs,
She swore in faith 'twas strange, 'twas passing strange,
'Twas pitiful, 'twas wondrous pitiful;
She wished she had not heard it, yet she wished
That heaven had made her such a man. She thanked me
And bade me, if I had a friend that loved her,
I should but teach him how to tell my story
And that would woo her. Upon this hint I spake:
She loved me for the dangers I had passed
And I loved her that she did pity them.
This only is the witchcraft I have used:

Enter DESDEMONA, IAGO, *Attendants.*

Here comes the lady, let her witness it.

Mark Thornton Burnett comments of this that 'Othello's story caters to assumptions about his status as a black man even as it seems to resist them: it closely resembles contemporary accounts of travels to newly discovered countries' ('"When you shall these unlucky deeds relate": *Othello* and Storytelling', p. 65). Jonathan Burton agrees, though he sees more catering than resistance. Burton draws an interesting distinction between the way Othello speaks here and the way the real-life African convert to Christianity Leo Africanus (1485–1554) described the culture from which he came. He argues that Africanus's '*Geographicall Historie* reproduces some of the fantastical and anti-Islamic tendencies of earlier works on Africa as a strategic form of textual mimicry. In other words, Africanus engages in a form of discursive negotiation that Mary Louise Pratt has identified as "autoethnography"' ('"A most wily bird": Leo Africanus, *Othello* and the Trafficking in Difference', in *Post-colonial Shakespeares*, p. 44).

Certainly the primary function of the narrative, to the fulfilment of which Othello ascribes its spectacular success in winning over Desdemona's affections, seems to be to depict the exoticism and dangers of his travels. But even in Shakespeare's day, when people had travelled much less and knew much less about the world, could this ever have been plausible? The Arden editor comments of the Anthropophagi and the 'men whose heads / Do grow beneath their shoulders' (I.iii.143–5) that 'such travellers' tales were current, and it seems as idle as the deserts to try to determine whether Shakespeare was primarily indebted to Mandeville or Raleigh or Holland's Pliny'. Patricia Parker, however, remarks that 'Othello's "dilated" traveller's tale recalls Africanus, Mandeville, Pliny, and the rest' ('Shakespeare and Rhetoric: "dilation" and "delation" in *Othello*', p. 98), whose veracity was much in doubt, and Jyotsna Singh characterises Othello's 'stories of slavery and adventure' as featuring him as 'a "character" in an imaginary landscape which viewers, then and now, recognize as a semi-fictional creation of colonialist travel narratives' ('Othello's Identity, Postcolonial Theory, and Contemporary African Rewritings of *Othello*', p. 288). Part of the attraction of 'travellers' tales' is surely their overt improbability, even in the Renaissance: an age with a growing interest in anatomy and medicine might well be sceptical of men with heads beneath their shoulders. In this case, the lack of immediacy of this narration of a narrative is further figured by Othello's tautological replacement of the word 'cannibal' with 'anthropophagi'. Cannibal, which (as already suggested) may in anagrammatised form have provided the origin of Caliban's name, perhaps functions as an isolated relic of the native speech of which we hear so little in *Othello*; its replacement by the classical term 'anthropophagi' thus symbolises not only Othello's learning but also the firmness with which he is inserted into pre-existing discourses of travel which must radically inform and structure his ostensibly experiential account. Even as Othello thinks he tells his story, it in fact tells him, but he is as blind to its constitutive structures as he is to the narrative constraints which make the telling of the story as much a part of the chronological history of his life as the experience of it.

Postcolonial criticism, then, requires that we never lose sight of both Shakespeare's and our own historical positioning. In marked contrast, the subject of my final chapter can indeed set Ariel free, even if Prospero could not – for in performance, the only limits are (or should be?) those of the imagination.

STOP AND THINK

• Have you found that the critics discussed in this chapter have offered useful insights into the plays? Are the meanings these critics have made of the texts meanings which would in any sense have been available to Shakespeare? Even if they are not, do you think it might still be true that this is a perspective which cannot be ignored?

Suggested further reading

Works discussed in this chapter

Brown, Paul '"This thing of darkness I acknowledge mine": *The Tempest* and the Discourse of Colonialism', in *Political Shakespeare*, 2nd edition, edited by Jonathan Dollimore and Alan Sinfield (Manchester: Manchester University Press, 1994), pp. 48–71.

Burnett, Mark Thornton. '"When you shall these unlucky deeds relate": *Othello* and Storytelling', in *Longman Critical Essays: Othello*, edited by Linda Cookson and Bryan Loughrey (Harlow: Longman, n.d.), pp. 61–71.

Cartelli, Thomas. *Repositioning Shakespeare: National Formations, Postcolonial Appropriations* (London: Routledge, 1999).

Childs, Peter. *Post-colonial Theory and English Literature: A Reader* (Edinburgh: Edinburgh University Press, 1999).

Hulme, Peter. 'Stormy Weather: Misreading the Postcolonial *Tempest*', *Early Modern Culture* 1.3. Online: http//eserver.org/emc/1-3/hulme.html.

Loomba, *Gender, Race, Renaissance Drama* (Manchester: Manchester University Press, 1989).

Loomba, Ania, and Martin Orkin, eds. *Post-colonial Shakespeares* (London: Routledge, 1998).

Schneider, Ben Ross, Jr, '"Are We Being Historical Yet?": Colonialist Interpretations of Shakespeare's *Tempest*', *Shakespeare Studies* 23 (1995): 120–45.

Skura, Meredith Anne. 'Discourse and the Individual: The Case of Colonialism in *The Tempest*', in *The Tempest: A Case Study in Critical Controversy*, edited by Gerald Graff and James Phelan (Basingstoke: Macmillan, 2000), pp. 286–322.

Willis, Deborah. 'Shakespeare's *Tempest* and the Discourse of Colonialism', *Studies in English Literature 1500–1900* 29 (1989): 277–89.

Other works which explore issues touched on in this chapter

Callaghan, Dympna. 'Othello Was a White Man: Racial Impersonation on the Renaissance Stage', in *Alternative Shakespeares II*, edited by Terence Hawkes (London: Routledge, 1996). Very intriguing essay about the way Othello would have been represented on Shakespeare's stage.

Newman, Karen. '"And wash the Ethiop white": Femininity and the Monstrous in *Othello*', in *Shakespeare Reproduced*, edited by Jean E. Howard and Marion F. O'Connor (London: Methuen, 1987), pp. 143–62.

Parker, Patricia. 'Shakespeare and Rhetoric: "dilation" and "delation" in *Othello*', in *Shakespeare and the Question of Theory*, edited by Patricia Parker and Geoffrey Hartman (London: Methuen, 1985), pp. 54–74. Interesting and theoretically informed analysis of *Othello*.

Singh, Jyotsna. 'Othello's Identity, Postcolonial Theory, and Contemporary African Rewritings of *Othello*', in *Women, 'Race' and Writing in the Early Modern Period*, edited by Margo Hendricks and Patricia Parker (London: Routledge, 1994), pp. 287–99. A look at some of the meanings that can be made of *Othello* from a postcolonial point of view.

8

Shakespeare in performance

In recent years, the study of Shakespeare in performance, whether in the theatre or on film, has assumed increasing importance, with a growing number of academic studies appearing in this area, most notably the Manchester University Press Shakespeare in Performance series, whose editors announce at the front of each volume that

> Recently, the study of Shakespeare's plays as scripts for performance in the theatre has grown to rival the reading of Shakespeare as literature among university, college and secondary-school teachers and their students. The aim of the present series is to assist this study by describing how certain of Shakespeare's texts have been realised in production.
>
> The series is not concerned to provide theatre history in the traditional sense. Rather, it employs the more contemporary discourses of performance criticism to explore how a multitude of factors work together to determine how a play achieves meaning for a particular audience.

They go on to add that the productions chosen

> illustrate how the convergence of various material conditions helps to shape a performance: the medium for which the text is adapted; stage-design and theatrical tradition; the acting company itself; the body and abilities of the individual actor; and the historical, political, and social contexts which condition audience reception of the play.

Along with this blossoming in performance studies has come a recognition that performances can in fact be interpretations in their own right. This was certainly true of Peter Brook's celebrated 1970 production of *A Midsummer Night's Dream*, which influenced a whole generation of critics. It is also true of, amongst others, films such as Peter Greenaway's *Prospero's Books* (1991) and Derek Jarman's *The Tempest* (1979), which both go well beyond mere productions or even adaptations of *The Tempest* to meditate and comment on its meaning. In return, there is two-way traffic, with academics often involved in productions as advisers or dramaturgs; and, just as the Arden editions of plays (the most comprehensive and prestigious scholarly editions) now include substantial sections on stage history, so theatre programmes often include comments by academics or extracts from criticism.

Jan Kott's 'Shakespeare Our Contemporary' approach was certainly influential on performance styles as well as critical approaches. His remark that 'When Shakespeare is dull and dead on the stage, it means that not only the theatre but also plays written in that particular period are dead' (p. 103) is directly echoed in Peter Brook's lament in *The Empty Space*:

> All through the world theatre audiences are dwindling. There are occasional new movements, good new writers and so on, but as a whole, the theatre not only fails to elevate or instruct, it hardly even entertains . . . Of course nowhere does the Deadly Theatre install itself so securely, so comfortably and so slyly as in the works of William Shakespeare. The Deadly Theatre takes easily to Shakespeare. We see his plays done by good actors in what seems like the proper way – they look lively and colourful, there is music and everyone is all dressed up, just as they are supposed to be in the best of classical theatres. Yet secretly we find it excruciatingly boring – and in our hearts we either blame Shakespeare, or theatre as such, or even ourselves. To make matters worse there is always a deadly spectator, who for special reasons enjoys a lack of intensity and even a lack of entertainment, such as the scholar who emerges from routine performances of the classics smiling because nothing has distracted him from trying over and confirming his pet theories to himself, whilst reciting his favourite lines under his breath. (p. 10)

Kott's refusal to be bound by the categories of genre, as when he declares part of *King Lear* to be essentially a pantomine, can also be seen underlying Brook's insistence that plays should be played moment by moment:

We could take *Measure for Measure* as a test case. As long as scholars
could not decide whether this play was a comedy or not, it never got
played. In fact, this ambiguity makes it one of the most revealing of
Shakespeare's works – and one that shows these two elements, Holy
and Rough [which Brook has identified as two crucial types of the-
atre], almost schematically, side by side. They are opposed and they
co-exist. In *Measure for Measure* we have a base world, a very real
world in which the action is firmly rooted. This is the disgusting,
stinking world of medieval Vienna. The darkness of this world is
absolutely necessary to the meaning of the play: Isabella's plea for
grace has far more meaning in this Dostoevskian setting than it would
in lyrical comedy's never-never land ... To execute Shakespeare's
intentions we must animate all this stretch of the play, not as fantasy,
but as the roughest comedy we can make ... at the same time we must
take great care, for all around the popular scenes are great areas of the
play that clumsiness could destroy. As we enter this holier land, we
will find that Shakespeare gives us a clear signal – the rough is in
prose, the rest in verse. (p. 88)

Here, Brook repays his debt to academia by pointing to a specific
formal feature of the play which we might otherwise not have
observed, and by offering, in effect, a reading of the play, which
accommodates its generic fluidity rather than, as so many purely
academic studies have been, being troubled by it.

As we can see in these passages from Brook, performance criticism has many strengths and attractions. In the first place, it takes
account of a fundamental aspect of Shakespearean plays which
many other approaches entirely disregard: it recognises that they
were written not to be read but to be watched. Strange as it may
seem to us now, Shakespeare appears to have been almost completely indifferent to the question of publication of his plays (though
he took a different attitude to his poetry). Not until seven years after
his death did his King's Men colleagues John Heminges and Henry
Condell gather his plays together in the First Folio of 1623. It is also
worth noting that on more than one occasion, but most notably in
Hamlet, Shakespeare lays considerable stress on the processes and
effect of watching a play and of being an audience member; it is hard
to imagine *The Mousetrap* having anything like the same effect if
Hamlet had sent Claudius off with a copy of the play to read on his
own in private, in the way that most people now read Shakespeare.

Moreover, there are many moments in Shakespeare which depend on either a purely visual effect or an effect which we are likely to observe only if we are watching the play. In Act V of *Measure for Measure*, for instance, Juliet, who is pregnant by Claudio, is on stage when Claudio is unexpectedly revealed to be still alive, but says nothing. Precisely because she says nothing, we are unlikely to register her presence when we are reading the play; but on stage much can be made of the presence of a heavily pregnant and pre-sumably overjoyed Juliet. Performance criticism recovers the importance of this crucial element of Shakespearean drama, and it also often makes for some of the most witty and entertaining writing about Shakespeare.

Performance criticism is not without its difficulties and caveats, however. Occasionally it can simply be vague and woolly, as when Peter Brook writes in *The Empty Space* of the last scene of *The Winter's Tale* that 'I discovered that the way to understand this scene is not to discuss it but to play it. In performance this action is strangely satisfying – and so it makes us wonder deeply' (p. 90). This is not analysis but a disabling of all possible categories of analysis. There is also the question of how much one needs to know. Discussing the Shakespearean films of Kenneth Branagh, for instance, Douglas Lanier writes,

> In his films Branagh has sought, often with great inventiveness, to accommodate Shakespeare to the apparatus of mass-market cinema, its visual and dramatic vocabulary, genres, star system, modes of produc-tion and marketing techniques. Indeed, I will argue that Branagh's Shakespeare films thematize the conditions of their own reception; they constitute an extended meditation on the ideal of Shakespeare (re)inte-grated into the cultural life of the common man, a meditation con-ducted from within the institutional imperatives of the contemporary stage and screen. Given those concerns, his 1996 *Hamlet* emerges as a pivotal work, for *Hamlet* and its cinematic paratexts *Swan Song* (1992) and *A Midwinter's Tale* (1995) turn from Branagh's early populist utopianism to a more conflicted account of the competing priorities involved in popularizing Shakespeare. ('Art thou base, common and popular?': The Cultural Politics of Kenneth Branagh's *Hamlet*', p. 149)

By 'the star system', Lanier means not only the obvious importance of certain individuals in Hollywood but the fact that, every time they appear in a film or a production, they bring with them echoes of other roles with which they have been associated and also of the composite persona which these roles have collectively built up. Thus when Charlton Heston appears as the Player King in Branagh's *Hamlet* (1996), we may remember, among other things, that he played Moses in *The Ten Commandments* and Ben Hur in the film of the same name, and so we are likely to perceive him as a figure of integrity and authority, as well as generally epitomising an older style of acting (which of course makes him a highly appropriate choice for the rôle of the Player King, since the players have just been complaining that they have been displaced and superseded by younger, more fashionable actors). Since there are, notoriously, numerous other 'stars' in Branagh's *Hamlet*, such moments and such effects are multiplied many times over, and this, especially for younger audiences, may well create a difficulty, since it may well seem impossible to discuss any particular production without knowledge of a potentially enormous number of other productions, films or TV shows, in which the actors have appeared and of which they may bring echoes or asssociations with them. Certainly it is notable that Lanier here directs us to two other films which he calls 'paratexts' for the Branagh *Hamlet*, without which, it seems, we cannot really appreciate what is going on in it (and the problem is compounded by the fact that what Lanier refers to as *A Midwinter's Tale* was released in Britain as *In the Bleak Midwinter*).

It is also important to distinguish between criticism of films, which is what Lanier is talking about, and criticism of stage performances. In the case of films (with the exception of a very few of the earliest), these are still available and you can thus see for yourself what the critic is describing. If you read a critical analysis of a Shakespearean film by, say, Kenneth Branagh, you may be hoping for a deeper insight into the film or a suggestion about what other films you might need to watch in order to detect when an actor is echoing an earlier role or the director is offering an *hommage* to an earlier shot or a technique, but you are not looking for a detailed description of what actually happens. Theatre productions, however, vanish for ever once the run has finished. It is true that you can consult prompt books, look at still photographs and reviews, and sometimes even watch a videotaped version, but all of these together offer only a pale shadow of the experience of actually seeing the production live in the theatre, with all the specifics of audience response, ambience, the location of your particular seat, and the rhythms and dynamics of individual performances, which can vary widely even within the same production. Therefore, critical accounts of such productions do have to provide a great deal of detailed description of what actually happened, supplemented whenever possible by photographs, and in this respect performance criticism often comes close to theatre history.

STOP and THINK

• How useful do you find it to see a performance of a play you are studying? Does it make any difference whether it is a live theatrical performance or a filmed version?

Apart from the sheer pleasure of going to the theatre or of watching a film, I have had some of my best ideas about plays while watching them. I enjoy both films and plays, and would happily go to see either a film or a production of any Shakespearean play – or for that matter any Renaissance play – but I do think that film and live theatre work in different ways, and should not be confused. Above all, I would say that, just because you may have seen one version of a Shakespearean play, you should not assume that you have seen the play. See as many different versions as you can, and then you will start to understand what some of the possibilities of that play are.

Henry V in performance

In this chapter, I will be looking at criticism of a number of different film and theatre versions of one play, *Henry V*. This may initially seem a surprising choice, but, as Martin White notes in his book *Renaissance Drama in Action*, '*Henry V* has been one of the most popular plays with twentieth-century audiences' (p. 44). There are two primary reasons for this. In the first place, White goes on to say that 'it is significant that it has often been staged at times of national conflict: productions starring Frank Benson and Lewis Waller coincided with the Boer War, and a production of the play was presented each year of the First World War' (p. 44). Branagh's film of *Henry V* was widely seen as a direct response to the Falklands War; Laurence Olivier's 1944 version was famously funded by the Ministry of Defence as part of the war effort. In times of national crisis, it is, it seems, to Shakespeare's wide-reaching examination of national identity that we are most likely to turn (think, for instance, of the four captains scene).

The second reason for the popularity of *Henry V* on the modern stage is that, as James N. Loehlin points out in his Shakespeare in Performance volume on the play, 'The modern performance history of *Henry V* may be summed up by the playwright John Arden's comment that Shakespeare seemed to have written a "secret play within the official one"' (p. 11). The 'official' play, in these terms, tells a glorious story about a heroic king who united his ethnically disparate people in a just war, defeated the devious and boastful French, and brought everything to a happy conclusion by marrying a beautiful princess. The 'secret' play, however, tells a very different story. It expresses considerable scepticism about all these events. It shows a king who is manipulated into war by a greedy churchman anxious to provide him with a distraction; it reveals that the English, the Scottish, the Irish and the Welsh are not a united nation at all but are riven by internal squabbles and prejudices; it shows that even some of the King's own nobles are not on his side, that he murders French prisoners and that the French princess Katherine had no choice but to marry him whether she wanted to or not. These sharply disparate views of the same play have been summed up by Norman Rabkin as a rabbit and a duck, along the lines of the old trick sketch which looks like a rabbit from one angle and a duck from the other, with the rabbit's ears becoming the duck's bill. What is important for my purposes is that the fact that the play can be inter- preted in such widely different ways means that it offers unusual opportunities for directorial intervention and leaves a lot of scope for the central actor, while the fact that it is often put on at times of war or unrest means that there is plenty of opportunity for pointed contemporary allusion: at one performance in 1804, for instance, 'the actor playing Henry in Manchester, one Mr Huddard, made a slight textual emendation to give the play extra patriotic force. According to the Manchester *Townsman*, Huddard's Henry rallied his troops before Harfleur with the cry, "God for Harry, England, and *King George!*'" (Loehlin, p. 18).

Productions of *Henry V* are, therefore, of particular interest to performance critics, as is shown in Loehlin's study of the play, in which he notes that

> The most obvious area in which modern productions have complicated the traditional *Henry V* is in their presentation of war. In eighteenth and nineteenth-century England, the battle scenes were occasions for patriotic spectacle and stirring rhetoric, sometimes involving literal calls to arms against the persistent French foe. By contrast, modern directors have tended to deglamorise war, shaping their depictions of it for a public familiar with television images of Vietnam. Many productions question Henry's motives and condemn the cynical self-interest of the bishops who encourage him. The unity of Henry's army and the justice of his cause may be undermined, especially by his argument with the soldier Michael Williams . . . The battle scenes, once displays of medieval pageantry, are often grim evocations of combat recalling twentieth-century wars. Many productions of *Henry V* emphasise elements of ruthlessness that were once suppressed, such as Henry's threats before the besieged Harfleur, or the executions of Bardolph and the French prisoners. Nevertheless, such productions often employ counter-strategies for valorising Henry and his victory. Kenneth Branagh's 1989 film is perhaps the clearest example: the savagery of battle is tempered by Branagh's penitent tears, while Henry's rape of France is negated by his charming wooing of Princess Katherine. The epithet 'anti-war', applied lightly to many modern productions, is generally inadequate to both the text's complexities and the conflicting sympathies engendered by even the most radically revisionist productions. (pp. 2–3)

In an understated but I think impressive way, what Loehlin is doing here is briefly but cogently surveying the whole recent performance history of the play, comparing it with earlier performance history, registering an important feature of the composite critical response to it (i.e. the general assumption that many modern productions are anti-war) and outlining an argument, which consists of contesting the accuracy of this label. The clarity and accessibility of Loehlin's prose and the lightness with which he wears his learning here may make performance history look like an easy option, but that would be a very mistaken impression, because a lot of work has gone into this.

Loehlin goes on to add that

> Other important ways modern productions have complicated the text
> involve the performance of the lead role, the relation of the play to
> Shakespeare's other histories and the self-conscious exploration and
> exploitation of the performance medium. Many of the 'secrets' dis-
> covered in the character of Henry have resulted not so much from
> changes in political attitudes as from changes in acting style. In the
> Stanislavskian tradition of acting that dominates Western theatre,
> actors require internal as well as external conflicts. (p. 3)

And he also observes that 'Henry's moments of crisis often involve
the personal and political inheritance from the *Henry IV* plays and
Richard II, which have weighed heavily on *Henry V* in this century'
(p. 4).

This means that, for Loehlin, there are a number of factors
which need to be considered in the analysis of any one production.
These include, but are not limited to, the major public events
that are happening or have just happened at the time of the play's
production; the presentation of key events and characters; the presence or abence of any elements of the iconography of twentieth-
century combat; cuts to the text; the training and acting philosophy
of the lead actor (and perhaps of other actors too); and whether
or not any other parts of the second tetralogy (i.e. *Richard II*
and *Henry IV, Parts One and Two*) are being performed by the
same company at the same time, or have been recently performed
elsewhere.

STOP and THINK

- Do any of these factors strike you as more important than the
  others? Are there any other factors which you consider relevant
  to analysis of a particular production?

This is entirely a matter of personal opinion, but I would attach
particular importance to the historical moment of a production. I
think, for instance, that it would be both fruitless and misleading
to give an account of Olivier's *Henry V* that failed to mention that
there was a war on when it was made. Another factor that I would
personally consider important, at least in the case of a live

production, is *where* it takes place, and what the likely composition of the audience is.

The Olivier version

One of the productions which Loehlin picks out for special consideration is, inevitably, the famous Laurence Olivier film of 1944, something of a benchmark for all subsequent productions, and certainly all films, of the play. He begins with some comments about the opening sequence of the film:

> The holiday occasion, pristine weather and toy-kingdom quality of the model prepare us for the idealised version of Elizabethan London that the Globe scenes give us. The elegiac quality of the shot would have been all the more poignant to a London film audience of 1944, who had seen many such aerial city views in newsreels of bomb devastation. (pp. 29–30)

Here, Loehlin focuses specifically on what this section of the film would have meant to its original audience, looking particularly at the iconography of the shot. He then moves on to unpack the ideological significance of these images:

> The Globe, revealed in a long mobile shot that descends into and pans round its interior, is a detailed evocation of the ordered yet vigorous society idealised in Tillyard's notion of 'The Elizabethan World Picture'. All the levels of this harmonious commonwealth are present, from the buxom orange-seller to the haughty nobleman who declines her wares and goes to take his seat on the stage. (p. 30)

These are details which occupy so short a space of time that we might well fail to register their significance unless it was thus pointed out to us. The same is probably even more true of Loehlin's comment that

> with the line 'On your imaginary forces work' . . . William Walton's symphonic score is heard for the first time, in contrast to the period fanfares we have heard (and seen) played by the Globe's musicians . . . The moment passes quickly, but it establishes a distance between the cinematic style used later in the film and the overblown acting of the Globe. (p. 30)

Film scores are certainly a powerful means of stimulating or even controlling the emotional response of the audience, but they are more likely to affect us subliminally than to be consciously noticed.

STOP AND THINK

• Would you agree that audiences are unlikely fully to register such details as the way the full social spectrum is represented at the Globe of Olivier's film? If so, do you think that such details still contribute to the film's 'meaning'? Have we moved away from literature to film studies here?

I certainly never noticed any of these details until Loehlin pointed them out. On the other hand, I certainly *will* notice them next time I watch the film, and they have thus now become a part of its meaning for me. Loehlin's methodology does have something in common with that of film studies, but it also offers insights which relate directly to literary study, particularly when he relates what he observes to the influence of Tillyard.

Stratford-upon-Avon

As arguably the most prestigious venue for Shakespearean productions, Stratford-upon-Avon inevitably forms another substantial part of Loehlin's book, especially since, as Martin White points out, 'the size of cast demanded by the play has meant that in recent years it has been seen most often in productions by the RSC' (p. 44). In particular, Loehlin looks at Terry Hands's 1975 production of *Henry V*, which, he says,

> was, for several reasons, the most important British production of the play since Olivier's film . . . It was the opening play of the RSC's centenary season, at a time of crisis for both the country and the company. As such, it provides a vivid example of the ways a production's meaning is generated in a complex negotiation between text, interpretation, audience expectations and the social, political and economic circumstances of the production. (p. 49)

Specifically, while the RSC's previous production had

> expressed Vietnam-style cynicism, Hands's needed a more positive

approach to regain widespread support for the RSC in an era of
budget cuts. Put simply, the goal of the production was to condemn
war while keeping the play's celebratory, even patriotic aspect. Hands
solved this problem by representing the war not as conflict with an
enemy, but as an occasion for spiritual struggle and growth, both
within Henry and within the whole English army. The principal
metaphor Hands used for the interdependence achieved by Henry and
his men was not combat but theatre itself. Hands explored a non-illu-
sionistic performance style the company had been developing since
1970, focusing on the theatrical event rather than the grim campaign
it represented, and Alan Howard's bravura performance of spiritual
agonies and final self-awareness embodied the decade's general shift
from the political to the personal. (p. 50)

According to Loehlin, 'Hands saw *Henry V* as a metaphor for the
company's own condition' (p. 50). Here, then, the kinds of information that Loehlin considers it relevant to adduce before proceeding
to analyse the production include the economic situation of the
company producing the play (which certainly often does have a
major impact on particular productions), the recent history of the
company and the director's vision of the play. What is perhaps not
helpful is that Loehlin does not really tell us how he obtained this
information. Much of it – for instance the RSC's financial situation
and history – is in the public domain, but how does he know how
Hands saw the play?

Obviously he could have asked him, or he could equally have
asked other people who were involved either with the production or
with the Royal Shakespeare Company at the time. Maybe Hands
gave interviews to newspapers or has written in some other forum of
what he intended. However, we are simply not told, and I do think
that the nature of the source might well make a difference, because
it might have conditioned the kind of information that is likely to be
offered. It would also be useful to know, say, whether this was
Hands's perception of his own motives at the time, or how he came
to see them when he looked back from some later date. To this
extent, the magisterial control and fluency of Loehlin's account
seems to me to offer rather too smooth a surface. Everything is
presented as if it were fact, but some of this might well be closer to
opinion, or even to anecdote. I don't say that it *is*, but there is no
proof offered that it is *not*.

Loehlin goes on to describe what actually happened in the Hands
production:

> the entire stage of the Royal Shakespeare Theatre was redesigned
> to focus attention on the actor. All the masking was stripped away,
> leaving the plain brick of the back wall and proscenium arch visible to
> the audience. The stage was made of bare black boards running
> towards the house, with a deep thrust and a steep one-in-twelve rake.
> 'It was a stage designed to launch the actors into the audience', said
> Farrah. 'The comment that pleased me most was that it was like the
> great deck of an aircraft carrier.' The actors were nakedly exposed,
> forced to create a convincing sense of place and action through
> performance alone (p. 54)

The comment made by Farrah (the designer) reveals an interesting
difference between Loehlin's approach to the Olivier film and his
approach to this production. In his opening comments on the Olivier
film, Loehlin focused on what it might have meant *to the audience*.
Here, he is more interested firstly in what the director (and to a lesser
extent the designer) *wanted* it to to mean – as when he declares that
'The principal metaphor Hands used for the interdependence
achieved by Henry and his men was not combat but theatre itself' –
and secondly in the fact that the director cannot always control
what meanings the audience will make of his vision. For instance,
'The actors were on-stage warming up in rehearsal clothes when the
audience entered the theatre' (p. 54), and Loehlin observes that

> Some saw it as a reference to the company's financial desperation, a
> snide joke at the expense of the Arts Council: 'Evidently the RSC are
> about to show us, yah boo sucks, that cut-price Shakespeare simply
> doesn't work, and that if the Arts Council doesn't come up with a
> better cheque this is how we'll be getting our bard in the future'
> (Morley, *Punch*, 16 April 1975). This reading – diametrically opposed
> to Hands's intention – was frequent among the critics. (pp. 54–5)

Loehlin also points to other ways in which what the director meant
was not always what the audience saw:

> Hands saw Henry's decision to go to war as part of his programme to
> reform his kingdom. He tried to communicate this by making Henry
> stand apart and unconvinced during the Archbishop's bee speech . . .
>   Gary Taylor points out the illogic of this . . . Even if the audience
> had noticed Henry's distancing of himself from the bee speech, it

could hardly find its way to the reading 'that Henry, appalled by the content of Canterbury's speech, decides that the system it glorifies must be dismantled, *by war with France*, just what the Archbishop and the nobles (= the system) want. This is simply an incommunicable interpretation'. (p. 59)

Similarly,

Henry's killing of the prisoners in a war he initiated is interpreted as an *anti-war* gesture. The absurdity of this notion demonstrates the lengths to which directors can go to rationalise their choices, and to square intractable textual material with the production's interpretive slant. (p. 66)

We are back here with the old intentional fallacy – with the difference that we can actually know what directors' intentions are, since they are likely either to have articulated them in interviews and programmes or to be still alive to tell us. Ironically, however, establishing the director's intention may well serve only to show us how far removed it was from the eventual effect.

There certainly seems to be an illustration of this in Martin White's book *Renaissance Drama in Action*, which also includes a chapter on an RSC production of *Henry V*, though this time it is the 1994 one. White begins by giving us some brief facts about the production:

The director of the 1994 RSC production was Matthew Warchus. It opened at Stratford on 2 May 1994, with set designs by Neil Warmington, costumes by Kandis Cook, lighting by Alan Burrett, sound by Paul Slocombe and music by Mark Vibrans. The setting was a disused theatre, brought alive by the Chorus, who began the play by throwing a lever to light the stage. The production explored 'the overlays of history, the historicising of Henry and the Agincourt campaign into a peculiarly national myth'. The upstage area often held tableau images of a heroicised version of what the audience witnessed and, as the play progressed, a front section of the stage floor lifted and opened and a tomb, engraved with the dates of Henry's life, pushed its way to the surface. (p. 45)

It is interesting to see what White regards as salient information here: the date; the names of the director, designers, and those responsible for sound, lighting, and music; a brief description of the set; a statement (presumably from the programme) of the production's philosophy; and a brief description of what was presumably the production's most striking visual effect. Much of this information is in fact standard in academic reviews of productions such as those in *Shakespeare Bulletin*, where reviewers are advised that

A headnote, modeled on the following, should begin the review.

Romeo and Juliet

Presented by **The Stratford Festival** at the **Festival Theatre**, Stratford, Ontario. June 6–November 9, 1997. Directed by Diana Leblanc. Set by Douglas Paraschuk. Costumes by Dany Lyne. Lighting by Louise Guinand. Sound by Jim Neil. Music by Andre Gagnon. Choreography by Claudia Moore. Fights by John Stead and James Binkley. With Matthew Armstrong (Balthasar), Stephen Bogaert (Tybalt), Xuan Fraser (Benvolio), Roy Lewis (Capulet), Chick Reid (Lady Capulet), Michael Mawson (Montague), Conrad Coates (Chorus, Escalus), Jonathan Crombie (Romeo), Graham Abbey (Paris), Robert Perischini (Peter), Diane 0' Aquila (Nurse), Marion Day (Juliet), Geordie Johnson (Mercutio), Benedict Campbell (Friar Laurence), and others.

Name of author

For production credits, follow order indicated above ('Directed by . . .,' 'Set by . . .,' etc); if set and costumes are by the same artist, use the rubric 'Designed by . . .' In listing members of the cast, follow the order in the program; do not alphabetize or prioritize.

The more familiar we are with the Shakespearean performance scene, of course, the more there is to be gleaned from such details: one might, for instance, have an idea of what music by Mark Vibrans is likely to sound like, or what kind of visual style a combination of Neil Warmington and Kandis Cook might be likely to produce. To some extent, then, this is a little like the workings of the 'star system' of which Douglas Lanier spoke in connection with the Shakespeare films of Kenneth Branagh.

White then goes on to interview the director of the production, Matthew Warchus, who observes that 'before going into rehearsal I did a lot of background reading, looked at the Folio and Quartos, watched Olivier's and Branagh's films and chose a specific text [Gary Taylor's Oxford edition]' (p. 45). Again, it is interesting to see what information White thinks it necessary to supply. As it happens,

Gary Taylor's Oxford edition of *Henry V* is particularly controversial, since as Taylor writes in the introduction, 'In accepting Q's version of Agincourt, this edition departs from the practice of all editors since 1623' (p. 25). It is not clear whether Warchus knows this (though White certainly does), so again we are faced with the question of how far the director's grasp of the production dictates its ultimate effect and meaning.

White then goes on to put it to Warchus that

> *It seems to me that in the midst of all the things a director does in preparation – background research, textual study, looking at past productions, and so on – there is often a key image that fires his or her imagination for the production and, in a sense, draws all that disparate thinking together. Was there such an image for you?* (pp. 46–7)

To this Warchus answers:

> Yes. The main stimulus for me was the beginning of *Henry VI* Part 1. I became very interested in the order that the history plays had been written in because I was trying to understand why a writer would write his final statement of history in the way that Shakespeare had written *Henry V*. I looked at the first part of *Henry VI* and I started to think about the order in which the history plays had been written . . . you begin with Henry's funeral and end with his marriage. In other words, you begin with a dark time of English history and end with a golden moment . . . But because you know exactly what follows – i.e., Henry VI follows Henry V – then the structure operates more like Pinter's play *Betrayal*, or Sondheim's musical *Merrily We Roll Along*, in that you head towards something climactic and glorious but always with the knowledge that it's going to be followed by a disaster. And that's the only way that I could ever show this glory onstage as a final event. Then I could commit to the idea of optimism – a new tomorrow with the prospect of Anglo–French union in peace – without feeling cheap. (pp. 46–7)

There is of couse a difficulty here: the meanings of Warchus's production of *Henry V* depend on another play which we may or may not have seen or know. (There is an interesting contrast here with Kenneth Branagh, whose 'working assumption is that his audiences have never seen a particular Shakespeare play before, and thus will not be engaged in assessing a production's place in performance history' (Lanier, p. 150).) White picks Warchus up on this:

So on the assumption that most of your audiences won't have seen or read
Henry VI *(even though Katie Mitchell's production of* Henry VI *ran*
concurrently at The Other Place *in Stratford) what was your solution to*
mediate the play's climax of triumph? (p. 47)

The Other Place (now purely a rehearsal rather than a performance
space) was at the time arguably the best-rated but certainly by far the
smallest of the Stratford venues; it would have been a physical impossibility for all those who saw *Henry V* to fit into The Other Place to
see *Henry VI* too, even if they had wanted to, so White's question is
certainly justified. Warchus's answer is that

> It lay partly in the way we played the Chorus and partly through the
> ever-present image of Henry's tombstone. The reason we came up
> with the idea of the tombstone is that *Henry VI* Part I starts off with
> a fantastic opening scene. Black everywhere, and you get the impres-
> sion that there's thunder. (p. 47)

I must admit that, though I know the *Henry VI* plays well, I am not
at all sure that I would have realised that I was meant to be thinking
about them here (though other audience members might of course
have been more acute). Nevertheless, White does not challenge
Warchus about this, and, though it would of course have been socially
difficult for him to do so, this section of the interview does seem
to me to raise what might what might well be seen as a weakness
of performance criticism: unlike feminist or Cultural Materialist
approaches, performance criticism tends purely to comment on what
has been done rather than to set an agenda for what should be done.
It is also notable that Warchus's list of his background reading does
not include any performance criticism, further suggesting that it has
limited or no influence. (Though the final section of this chapter will
look at some performance criticism which does aim at political or
other intervention.)

Warchus goes on to elaborate on his concept for the opening
scene of the play:

> I also had this idea of this court scene being rather like a self-contained
> historical event in a museum, so we put museum-type cordons around
> the stage, and other people, the rest of England, come and look at
> it, almost like an exhibit that they can't get to, but can see being acted
> out. And during that scene all those mothers and husbands and

children, like those that Henry says will be 'mocked' out of their lives by the Dauphin's tennis-ball joke, were there onstage watching this happen. And that idea of the rest of England being there waiting and watching started very early, about the third time I read the play. I imagined a huge plinth, a sort of very high platform, the court taking place on it, very high up, and the citizens and peasants with farming implements and old clothes [1940s period], just standing looking up, waiting, standing round the base while this event that was going to affect their destiny was played out above. In terms of design that just became too extravagant to do in practice, but we tried to keep that feeling. (pp. 48–9)

Here we seem to me to have wandered into the realms of the absurd: not only does this production need to be interpreted in the light of the *Henry VI* plays, which we may not have read or seen, it also needs to be interpreted in the light of a directorial concept which couldn't in the end be brought to the stage. Again, though, White does not challenge this.

White's reluctance to criticise does however have considerable benefits, in that it clearly encouraged the director to open up and to go on to provide real insights into specific moments of the production which it would have been very hard to obtain by any other means. Firstly, Warchus describes how for him,

What Canterbury says is a fantastic shedding of light on something, and a revolutionary discovery, and it really does mean that it would be a just war, because the French have been lying all this time, and the English are in the right. The list of names in his Salic law speech *is* extensive, but the fact is that there are so many examples of the lies that the French have told – not only did this happen but also this person only inherited because of his grandmother, and then this person because of his wife, and so on. But what I really wanted to put over is all the references to women in that speech, so I asked the actor to stress daughter, grandmother, mother, rather than King Pepin, Louis IX, and so on. (p. 49)

This must have made for an interesting and unusual effect. Even more unconventional was the delivery of the St Crispin's Day speech in Warchus's production:

For the last four days of rehearsals we had a mock-up of the ramps so we could do the fighting, and I suddenly realised that by having the ramp Henry could speak to people in front of him downstage and still be seen by the audience – he could even sit down for the Crispin's Day speech and the sightlines would still be OK. After one rehearsal we were all sitting on the ramp while I was giving the company notes. Everybody was listening, and I thought, hang on, so I said to Iain [Glen], 'just come here, sit here', and I went and sat with the other actors, and I said to him 'just talk to us about Crispin's Day'. At first he was still quite 'big', because we'd been doing it that way, but gradually he changed it, made it more intimate, and everybody was listening intently, and he finished, and I remember a wonderful silence. I was very moved – almost tearful; I think we all were. (p. 55)

Here, I think we get a real sense not only of the staging of the production but also of the mood it is likely to have created, as well as an insight into how a production takes shape.

STOP and THINK

- Do you find it helpful to know how the director envisaged this particular production? Does examining a particular production in this way give you new insight into the play itself?

Personally I find it useful and interesting to read this kind of insight into how a director's mind works. I am particularly interested to see that Warchus is able to take Canterbury's speech entirely seriously. I have grown so used to being cynical about this that I had rather lost sight of the possibility of anyone reading it any other way, so it serves as a useful reminder to me of how profoundly ambiguous the effect of the play is; it really can be both a rabbit and a duck.

Political performance criticism?

Not all performance critics aim simply to comment. In his article 'A Tale of Two Branaghs: *Henry V*, Ideology, and the Mekong Agincourt', Chris Fitter declares of Branagh's film version of *Henry V* that

Reviewers have often defined [it] through contrast with Olivier's 1944 version, with its clowning (rather than conspiratorial) clerics in the opening scene, its excision of scenes that morally undercut Henry (Scroop and the conspirators, the Harfleur speech, Williams's challenge

to the king over his responsibility for the war, the reference to Richard
II and Henry's dubious title), and the pretty chivalry of its battle scene
. . . Branagh's Henry, we are told, restores the cuts and thus the honesty,
gives us a credible, pained, demotic Henry, and an Agincourt that will
not hide from us that war is hell.

This perspective, I will argue, is unsupportable. It is credible – initially – only due to the film's contrast with two commanding legacies:
the overtly (and dazzlingly successful) propagandist character of
Olivier's film, which was structured to boost patriotic morale in the
months prior to the D-Day offensive; and the deadening influence of
the Victorian and Tillyardian tradition of Shakespeare as committed
upholder of monarchical ideology. (p. 259)

Here, Fitter seems initially to contest the classic performance criticism tactic of reading one film or production in the light of another.
In fact, though, he does proceed to do that; it is just that he does not
think that the Olivier film of *Henry V* is the right comparator for the
Branagh film.

Fitter points out that

There are . . . two Branagh versions of *Henry V*, and we shall see that
they are politically polar. Knowledge of the first – directed by Adrian
Noble at Stratford in 1984 – casts transforming light on the supposed
toughness and honesty of the second, directed by Branagh himself.
This paper seeks to scrutinize the two productions, assessing each
in the light of a close reading (my own) of the text the seventeenth
century has left us. (p. 260)

Again, then, we are dealing with extraneous knowledge that needs
to be invoked: the Branagh film, Fitter says, cannot be analysed
only in terms of itself, but must also be related to the Royal Shakespeare Company production – also starring Branagh – which preceded it. It is also notable that Fitter adduces another piece of
information, telling us that he will be assessing both film and
production 'in the light of a close reading (my own) of the text
the seventeenth century has left us'. If this were a conventional
analysis rather than a performance one, the presence of that brack-
eted phrase would be inconceivable, since we would of course
assume that any close reading offered would be the critic's own; but
Fitter seems to assume that performance criticism does not necessarily entail personal engagement with the actual text. Presumably

the implication is that it need involve only observation of the production or film.

Fitter, however, not only engages with the play in performance but does so in order to offer a reading of the text itself. Firstly, he looks at a number of specific moments and aspects of Branagh's film in order to press his case that it is not nearly as radical as has been supposed: he argues, for instance, that 'We have only *honorific* blood in this film: virtually always a facial ornament, a red badge of courage . . . In Henry's triumphal march at the close, all the corpses he passes are unbloodied, with calmly closed eyes and sleeping faces . . . Contrast of the overall effect with Polansk[i]'s *Macbeth* will make my point very clearly' (p. 270). He even complains that 'the film won the Oscar for Best Costume', which he terms 'Testimony to its atmospheric seductions' (p. 273). His point, however, is not merely the Cultural Materialist one that this is an unfortunate meaning for the play to be made to bear in the twentieth century; rather he goes beyond that to say that this is not what the play *actually does* mean:

> Compelled to provide panegyric and chauvinst surfaces to the play (the Chorus's encomia of Henry, the occasional moments of French-baiting) in order to please the royal censor and to secure the play commercial success, Shakespeare systematically proceeded, as we have seen, structurally to undercut such jingoism and hymning of royal authority through the *action* of the play. Monarchical interests, Shakespeare repeatedly shows, are inimical to those of the common people, whose support must thus be ideologically reinforced through oratorical inductions of false consciousness. (p. 274)

Fitter, then, thinks that he knows not only what Branagh's film of the play means but what the play itself meant, and indeed even what the author's intentions were.

Fitter's account, then, takes us back to perhaps the fundamental question of this book: is Shakespearean criticism a way of imposing meaning *on* Shakespeare, or is it a way of accessing meaning(s) already *in* Shakespeare? There is of course no answer to this question, but it is one that seems likely to continue to be contested, as Shakespeare criticism grows ever more vibrant and complex.

STOP and THINK

• Now that we have reached the end of this survey of currently popular modes of Shakespearean criticism, can you imagine any ways in which Shakespeare studies might develop in the future?

Further reading

Works discussed in this chapter

Brook, Peter. *The Empty Space* (London: MacGibbon and Kee, 1968).

Fitter, Chris. 'A Tale of Two Branaghs: *Henry V*, Ideology, and the Mekong Agincourt', in *Shakespeare Left and Right*, edited by Ivo Kamps (London: Routledge, 1991), pp. 259–75.

Lanier, Douglas. '"Art thou base, common and popular?": The Cultural Politics of Kenneth Branagh's *Hamlet*', in *Spectacular Shakespeare*, edited by Courtney Lehmann and Lisa S. Starks (London: Associated University Presses, 2002), pp. 149–71.

Loehlin, James N. *Henry V* (Manchester: Manchester University Press, 1996).

Rabkin, Norman. 'Rabbits, Ducks, and *Henry V*', *Shakespeare Quarterly* 28.1 (Summer 1977): 279–96.

White, Martin. *Renaissance Drama in Action: An Introduction to Aspects of Theatre Practice and Performance* (London: Routledge, 1998).

Other works which explore issues touched on in this chapter

Jackson, Russell. *The Cambridge Companion to Shakespeare on Film* (Cambridge: Cambridge University Press, 2000). An excellent selection of essays on a range of subjects, directors, and films.

The Manchester University Press Shakespeare in Performance series offers comprehensive accounts of the stage histories of many of the plays. More recent volumes include *Macbeth*, *A Midsummer Night's Dream*, *Othello*, *Richard II*, and *Hamlet*, as well as the *Henry V* volume discussed here.

Index